Early French Reform

To our respective parents

Henry and Cathy Zuidema

Clarence and Ryma Van Raalte

Early French Reform

The Theology and Spirituality of Guillaume Farel

JASON ZUIDEMA
Concordia University, Canada

THEODORE VAN RAALTE
Calvin Theological Seminary, USA

ASHGATE

Published by
Ashgate Publishing Limited
Wey Court East
Union Road
Farnham
Surrey, GU9 7PT
England

Ashgate Publishing Company
Suite 420
101 Cherry Street
Burlington
VT 05401-4405
USA

www.ashgate.com

British Library Cataloguing in Publication Data
Early French Reform: The Theology and Spirituality of Guillaume Farel. --
(St Andrews Studies in Reformation History)
1. Farel, Guillaume, 1489–1565. 2. Theology, Doctrinal – History –
16th century. 3. Theology, Doctrinal. I. Series II. Zuidema, Jason.
III. Raalte, Theodore van.
230.4'2'092–dc22

Library of Congress Cataloging-in-Publication Data
Zuidema, Jason.
Early French Reform: The Theology and Spirituality of Guillaume Farel /
Jason Zuidema and Theodore Van Raalte.
    p.   cm. – (St. Andrews Studies in Reformation History)
Includes bibliographical references (p.   ) and index.
1. Farel, Guillaume, 1489–1565. 2. Reformation – Switzerland – Sources.
3. Reformed Church – Doctrines – History – 16th century – Sources.
I. Van Raalte, Theodore. II. Farel, Guillaume, 1489–1565. Selections.
English. 2010. III. Title.
BR350.F3Z85 2010
230'.42092–dc22   2010043832

ISBN 9781409418849 (hbk)
ISBN 9781409418856 (ebk)

MIX
Paper from
responsible sources
FSC
www.fsc.org   FSC® C018575

Printed and bound in Great Britain by the
MPG Books Group, UK

Contents

Preface

Guillaume Farel (1489–1565) forms an intriguing figure for study because of his leading role in the culture of persuasion that was the Reformation. Farel's persistence and passion at the outset of Reform among the French-speaking Swiss established most of the basic theological commitments and much of the spiritual tone for the developing Reformed churches in that area. Since he expressed himself not only orally but also in popular writing – and did so at a very early stage in the Reform movement – we would argue that his writings deserve closer scrutiny. The last three decades have been rich in findings regarding the era of Reform before Calvin, especially as regards the role of book publishing among early French Evangelicals. Study of Farel has continued since the last major English publication on Farel appeared in 1980, thanks to the *Colloque Guillaume Farel*. Thus we considered the time right to bring together some of the results and to invite readers to get to know Farel better by reading some of his early works in translation.

We thank the many people and organizations who helped in the production of this work on Guillaume Farel. The following libraries and individuals were vital in this process: the Johannes a Lasco Bibliothek, Emden, Germany; the H. Henry Meeter Center for Calvin Studies in the Hekman Library of Calvin College and Calvin Theological Seminary, Grand Rapids, Michigan; the Bibliothèque de Genève and the Institut d'histoire de la Réformation in Geneva; the encouragement, comments and corrections of Reinhard Bodenmann (who is presently re-editing all the printed works of Farel), Jean-François Gilmont, Richard Muller, Albert Gootjes, Daniel Timmer, John McCormack, Daniel Shute, W.J. Torrance Kirby, Diane Desrosiers-Bonin, William Kemp, Karin Maag, Howard Slenk, Paul Fields, Terrance Tiessen and Joel Beeke.

Some of Chapter 2 was first presented at a conference in the summer of 2006 organized by Diane Desrosiers-Bonin and William Kemp of McGill University on the printer Pierre de Vingle, and printed in the journal *Littératures* Vol. 24, No. 1 (2007), pp. 103–25. Other sections of Chapter 2 were published in the *Revue Farel* Vol. 4, pp. 27–35. Some of Chapter 3 appeared in an earlier form in the *Westminster Theological Journal* Vol. 70 (2008), pp. 277–301. We thank the publishers of these journals for permission to utilize this material.

To Andrew Pettegree and the St. Andrews Studies in Reformation History we express our gratitude for seeing merit in this monograph and accepting it into the series. The improvements offered have truly benefited us.

Both of us have also benefited from the great patience and encouragement of our present and former academic and ecclesiastical colleagues. More, each of us has been accompanied and encouraged by a wonderful wife and children. They are the *sine qua non* of our research and writing.

For their many years of love, patience and prayer we dedicate this volume to our respective parents. *Soli Deo Gloria*!

JASON ZUIDEMA
Concordia University

THEODORE VAN RAALTE,
Calvin Theological Seminary

PART I
Guillaume Farel's Theology and Spirituality

CHAPTER 1

Guillaume Farel in Early French Reform

Jason Zuidema

The need for a reappraisal

In recent years there has been a change in the perception of the influence of particular figures in early French Reformed theology. Far from simply an arcane historical dispute over a date here or an attribution there, this new round of research has brought about a serious reappraisal of the rise and development of French Reformed Protestantism. For several centuries, John Calvin has been viewed as the pre-eminent force in the establishment and development of Reformed thought. On a larger scale, this thesis has been debunked as numerous studies on the so-called 'Reformers in the Wings' – Heinrich Bullinger, Wolfgang Musculus, Martin Bucer and Peter Martyr Vermigli, to name only a few – show that Reformed theology is neither totally original to Calvin, nor entirely defined by Calvin's works.[1] On a smaller scale, within the confines of the French Reformation, this also holds true. Calvin's thinking must be understood alongside that of the other French Reformers. Although several centuries of history – especially the late nineteenth and the twentieth – have lionized Calvin, he was one among several important French Reformers. This is most clearly the case in the early period of the French speaking Reform movement.

One of the French Reformers who is in the process of 'rehabilitation' is Guillaume Farel. Popular perceptions have envisioned a fiery-tempered and long-winded reforming preacher handing over the reins of his disorganized Genevan Reformation to the mighty Calvin for codification and solidification.[2] Histories that treated Farel as a mere lackey of Calvin did not

---

[1]   See David Steinmetz, *Reformers in the Wings: From Geiler von Kaysersberg to Theodore Beza*, 2nd ed. (Oxford: Oxford University Press, 2001); Richard A. Muller, 'Reformed Confessions and Catechisms', *The Dictionary of Historical Theology*, Trevor A. Hart (Grand Rapids: Eerdmans, 2000), p. 466; Muller, *Post-Reformation Reformed Dogmatics: Vol. I Prolegomena to Theology*, 2nd ed. (Grand Rapids: Baker, 2003), p. 45 *et passim*; Philip Benedict, *Christ's Churches Purely Reformed: A Social History of Calvinism* (New Haven: Yale, 2002), p. 49.

[2]   For example, 'So sah Farel überall neue, große, schwere Aufgaben vor sich. Es galt, die Kirche neu zu organisieren, Kirchenzucht einzuführen, der Bevölkerung eine christlich-sittliche Lebensordnung zu geben, Dinge, die wenig in Farel's Natur lagen'. Alfred

help.[3] Various excesses in Barthian historiography drew on these popular perceptions to portray Farel as Calvin's foil – Calvin the man far ahead of his times, made in the image of Karl Barth, and Farel the simplistic, vitriolic, violent and subversive trouble-maker.[4] These are at best one-sided caricatures, at worst, self-serving inventions.

As for Farel's long-windedness, it is true that one can observe this together with a somewhat wandering style in some of his writings (one need only read the 488 pages of the 1550 *Glaive de la Parolle veritable*)[5], but one must keep in mind that in French the sentence as we know it was only coming into vogue in Farel's day. Farel's sentences which string along one clause after another represent a style found in other writers of the period. Calvin's writings played an important role in developing the crisper French sentence.[6] In addition, crisp sentences or not, there is a great deal more to say about Farel's theological importance in early Reformed

---

Stucki, *Guillaume Farel: Evangelist, Kämpfer, Reformator* (St. Gallen: Buchhandlung der Evangelischen Gesellschaft, 1942), p. 96.

[3]　For example, Justo L. Gonzàlez, *The Story of Christianity* (San Francisco: Harper Collins, 1985), Vol. 2, p. 65.

[4]　For example, in 1922 Karl Barth wrote, 'Farelism, that is pastoral daring and rashness to the glory of God . . . is not really Calvinism'. Karl Barth, *The Theology of John Calvin*, trans. G. W. Bromiley (Grand Rapids: Eerdmans, 1995), p. 245. Basil Hall parrots Barth: 'Farel, a storm-trooper of the evangel rather than a theologian, found that breaking altars, pictured windows and statues of the saints, was not a very effective reformation and that he needed the help of a man with a gift for organization and a sound theological training to help him in Geneva'. Basil Hall, *John Calvin: Humanist and Theologian* (London: The Historical Association, 1956), p. 17. Philip Holtrop generalized from a January 11 1552 letter of Farel to Calvin regarding Jerome Bolsec that it 'expressed the vitriol and simplism that we have come to expect from the "firebrand"'. Philip Holtrop, 'The Bolsec controversy from 1551 to 1555: Theological currents, the setting and mood, and the trial itself' (Ph. D. diss., Harvard University, 1988), Bk 2, Pt 1: p. 901.

[5]　See J.F. Gilmont's comments on the *Glaive de la Parolle veritable*: 'L'ouvrage était achevé en été 1549. Viret donnait un avis amical, avis réservé, le 20 juillet 1549; Calvin exprimait aussi quelques réserves dans une lettre du 1er septembre 1549. Il faut ajouter que la critique ultérieure considère le traité, le plus volumineux de ceux de Farel, comme fort confus et prolixe'. Gilmont, 'l'Oeuvre imprimé...', in: *Actes du Colloque Guillaume Farel*, Vol. 2 (1983), p. 131; also Reinhard Bodenmann says of Farel: 'Cet homme de parole confesse lui-même qu'il n'aimait pas prendre la plume, mais qu'une fois lancé, il ne savait plus comment s'arrêter. Cela transparaît évidemment dans son *style*. Les idées se pressent avec une impétuosité qui ne lui permet pas d'élaborer un texte progressant de façon méthodique – ce dont il se plaint d'ailleurs lui-même. Le résultat n'en est pas pour autant désagréable. Car, même si son texte est quelque peu décousu, il est rarement ennuyeux. Les comparaisons insolites et inattendues dont il le parsème et l'écriture spontanée qui est la sienne lui confèrent une saveur indéniable'. Bodenmann, 'Farel et le livre réformé français', in *Le Livre evangélique en français avant Calvin*, eds. Jean-François Gilmont and William Kemp (Turnhout: Brepols, 2004), p. 26.

[6]　Francis Higman, *Lire et Découvrir* (Geneva: Droz, 1998), pp. 344–8.

theology, especially his theological relationship to Calvin.[7] A fair amount of recent research shows that Farel was still very active in Geneva after the coming of Calvin. Much of this research points out that Farel was not simply eclipsed by the coming of Calvin. Farel certainly wanted the young Calvin to help organize the Reformed cause, but he continued to exert an important influence and to produce influential writings.[8] According to Reinhard Bodenmann, editor of the new critical edition of Farel's works, it is in part because of the lionizing of Calvin that we are only now seeing the publication of this critical edition.[9]

Several important monographs and essays have highlighted the formation and continuing importance of Farel's thought on Reformed Theology. Elfriede Jacobs has clearly shown that Bucer and Oecolampadius were more important than Zwingli with regard to the early influences on Farel's doctrine of the Eucharist. She notes that Farel did not simply swing from being Zwinglian to being Calvinist, but was able to defend his own thinking.[10] Too much theological authority and originality are accredited to others when speaking of Farel's thinking. In fact, much more ought to be said about the influences of French speaking Reformers like Farel *on Calvin*.

Three short examples on the case of Farel in recent scholarship should suffice. First, in his excellent book on the ties between French Eucharistic and political theology Christopher Elwood remarked that the ancient liturgical concept of *sursum corda* or 'lifting one's heart to God' idea was introduced into French Protestant Eucharistic thought by Farel in the 1533 *Maniere et Fasson*.[11] Second, the recent attribution of the 1536 Geneva

---

[7]   Perhaps Wendel overstates the case: 'Ses [Farel's] défauts l'ont empêché d'accomplir lui-même ce que Calvin réussira avec tant d'éclat, mais non sans peine. Du moins sut – il discerner, dès sa rencontre avec celui – ci, l'homme qui, mieux que lui – même, pouvait réaliser les desseins qu'il avait conçus. Et, faisant violence à son caractère entier et autoritaire, il eut la sagesse de s'effacer devant le nouveau venu'. Wendel, *Calvin: Sources et evolution de sa pensée religieuse* (Paris: Presses Universitaires de France, 1950), p. 30.

[8]   See Charles Partee, 'L'Influence de Farel sur Calvin', in: *Actes du Colloque Guillaume Farel*, Vol. 1 (1983), pp. 173–86.

[9]   Reinhard Bodenmann, 'Farel et le livre réformé français', *Le Livre évangélique en français avant Calvin*, eds J.F. Gilmont and W. Kemp (Turnhout: Brepols, 2004), pp. 37–8. The first volume of this critical edition appeared late in 2009: Guillaume Farel, *Œuvres imprimées*, Vol. I: *Traités messins*, eds. Reinhard Bodenmann and Françoise Breigel with Olivier Labarthe (Geneva: Droz, 2009).

[10]   Elfriede Jacobs, *Die Sakramentslehre Wilhelm Farels* (Zurich: Theologischer Verlag, 1978), pp. 353–6; *ibid.*, 'Die Abendmahlslehre Wilhelm Farels', in: *Actes du Colloque Guillaume Farel*, Vol. 1 pp. 161–171. See also Todd J. Billings, *Calvin, Participation, and the Gift* (Oxford: Oxford University Press, 2007), pp. 72–4.

[11]   Elwood writes that the introduction of the *sursum corda* by Farel into the French liturgy of 1533 is Farel's 'unique and most enduring contribution to the Reformed liturgy

Confession in scholarship principally to Farel shows that whatever the influence of Strasbourg or Zurich on Calvin's thought, it was evidenced in this first period in his upholding of this *Farellian* confession.[12] Finally, Frans Pieter Van Stam has shown convincingly that Farel was the principal author of the 1537 Geneva articles.[13] This was proven in two articles and in a more detailed way in the recent and enormously detailed first volume of Calvin's correspondence.[14] What has been taken at face value as Calvin's thinking in a great deal of secondary literature now seems to have flowed originally from the pen of Farel.[15] For example, François Wendel remarks concerning these 1537 articles, which he attributed to Calvin, that we already find a number of the *'idées maîtresses qui caractériseront l'oeuvre calvinienne'*.[16] A frequent communion is often cited as Calvin's

---

and eucharistic thought'. *The Body Broken: The Calvinist Doctrine of the Eucharist and the Symbolization of Power in Sixteenth-Century France* (Oxford: Oxford University Press, 1999), p. 43.

[12]   On Farel's relationship to this confession see Olivier Labarthe, 'La relation entre le premier catéchisme de Calvin et la première confession de foi de Genève: Recherche historique à partir d'une comparaison de textes catéchétiques et de particularités typographiques', Thesis for Licencie en théologie (University of Geneva, 1967). See also 'Confession de la Foy…' in *La Vraie Piété: divers traités de Jean Calvin et confession de foi de Guillaume Farel*, eds. Irena Backus and Claire Chimelli (Geneva: Labor et Fides, 1986), p. 49.

[13]   The text has been newly transcribed and edited by Cornelis Augustijn and Franz Pieter Van Stam, *Ioannis Calvini Epistolae* Vol. I (1530–September 1538), (Geneva: Droz, 2005), Ep. 31; See also *Registres du Conseil de Genève à l'epoque de Calvin, Tome. II*, Vol. 1, eds Paule Hochuli Dubuis and Sandra Coram-Mekkey (Geneva: Droz, 2004), pp. 21 and 23. In these passages Farel is the official spokesman for the pastors and seems to be presenting articles that he has written: '*Audito magistro Guilliermo Farello, arrestatur que demain apres disner soit assemblé le Conseil de Deux Centz pour veoir les articles qu'il a l'aultre jour baillé*', Registres, 21.

[14]   Frans P. van Stam, 'Die Genfer Artikel vom Januar 1537 : Aus Calvin's oder Farel's Feder?' *Zwingliana* 27 (2000), pp. 87–101; *ibid., et al.* 'Calvin in the Light of the Early Letters' in: *Calvinus Praeceptor Ecclesiae*, ed. Herman J. Selderhuis (Geneva: Droz, 2004), pp. 139–58; *Calvini Epistolae Vol. I*, pp. 153–4 and notes for pp. 157–70.

[15]   Two examples out of a host of literature: Herminjard (*'La netteté de conception, la clarté et la fermeté de style qui le distinguent nous autorisent à croire qu'il a été rédigé par Calvin. Mais ce n'est pas assez de dire que la forme lui appartient; le fond même des idées est à lui'. Correspondance IV*, p. 154), and the 1870 Calvini Opera (*'La rédaction, autant qu'il est permis d'en juger d'après le style, n'appartient pas directement à Calvin, mais on ne saurait méconnaître qu'il en est l'auteur réel'*. CO X/1, p. 5); Also *Guillaume Farel: Biographie Nouvelle*, p. 352; T.H.L. Parker, *Calvin: A Biography* (Philadelphia: Westminster Press, 1975), p. 62; Bernard Cottret, *Calvin: A Biography*, trans. M. Wallace McDonald (Grand Rapids: Eerdmans, 2000), p. 138; Eberhard Busch *et al.* eds, *Calvin-Studienausgabe*, Vol. 1 (Neukirchen-Vluyn: Neukirchener, 1994), p. 110; Jeannine Olson, 'Calvin as pastor-administrator during the Reformation in Geneva', *Pacific Theological Review* 14 (1981), p. 10; Benedict, *Christ's Churches Purely Reformed*, pp. 87 and 94.

[16]   Wendel, *Calvin*, p. 30.

idea, but here we can see that it was equally Farel's idea if not more so.[17] The place of Farel should continue to be studied in light of these important developments of interpretation.[18]

Farel before Calvin

More attention, then, should be given to the actual thinking of Farel before the coming of Calvin. There is no doubt that Farel recognized in Calvin one who was better equipped to organize Genevan Reform, but Farel was nonetheless capable of propounding and defending Reformed doctrine on his own. He was, after all, a major reformer in several significant cities including Neuchâtel, Lausanne and Geneva. Several of Farel's early works have come down to us, most notably the *Summaire et Brève Déclaration* – the *Summary and Brief Exposition*. Farel was not new to the faith when he wrote the *Summaire*. His thinking, at times difficult for the reader to understand, was clearly and firmly held. Although his *Summaire* would not become a great classic of the Reformation, it was nonetheless published at least six times.[19]

Born in 1489 near Gap, in Dauphiné, France, Guillaume Farel was an important first generation French speaking Reformer and one of the most influential early leaders of the Reform movement in what is now French speaking Switzerland.[20] Educated in Paris, he was influenced by the piety and thought of the important humanist Jacques Lefèvre d'Etaples. It was through Lefèvre d'Etaples's influence that Farel took up a teaching post at

---

[17] Take, for example, this oft-cited material: '*Il seroyt bien à desirer, que la communication de la saincte cene de Jesucrist fust tous les dimenches pour le moins en usage quant l'esglise est assemblee en multitude, veu la grand consolation que les fideles en reçoipvent et le fruict qui en procede en toute maniere tant pour les promesses qui sont là presentees en nostre foy – c'est que vrayment nous sommes faicts participans du corps et du sang de Jesus, de sa mort, de sa vie, de son Esprit et de tous ses biens — que pour les exortations qui nous y sont faictes à recognoestre et magniffier par confession de louanges les merveilleuses choses, graces de Dieu sur nous, finablement à vivre crestiennement, estans conjoincts ensemble en bonne payx et unité fraternelle comme membre d'ung mesme corps*'. *Calvini Epistolae*, Vol. 1, p. 160. Compare this with the later letter of Calvin and Farel to the meeting at Zurich (Between 2 May and 10 June 1538), '*12. Prius est, ut frequentior coenae usus instituatur, si non secundum veteris ecclesiae consuetudinem, at saltem singulis quibusque mensibus semel*'. *Calvini Epistolae*, Vol. 1, p. 472.

[18] Machiel van den Berg's short study of Farel may be commended. See his *Friends of Calvin*, trans. Reinder Bruinsma (Grand Rapids, MI: Eerdmans, 2009), pp. 78–88.

[19] On the dating and text history, see below.

[20] The most comprehensive biography of Farel is the multiple authored *Guillaume Farel, 1489–1565: Biographie Nouvelle* (Neuchâtel, 1930). Many articles (listed in the bibliography at the end of the present work), have modified a number of details in this biography, but the work is still substantially useful.

Collège du Cardinal Lemoine after receiving his Master of Arts in 1517.[21] Over the next several years Farel had an intense spiritual struggle and began to criticize current Roman Catholic piety.[22]

To gain a perspective on his conversion we need to look at Farel's writings later in life. Although very negative in their perception of his former Catholicism, these short accounts are nonetheless extremely helpful in reconstructing his conversion experience. In his treatise on the *Vray Usage de la Croix de Iesus-Christ,* Farel reminisces of the 'first notable idolatry' of which he partook.[23] It was a pilgrimage to the holy cross on a mountain near Tallard in the diocese of Gap. This cross was believed to give sight to the blind. What strikes Farel as ironic (and blasphemous) is that upon seeing the relic of the Cross in the *Sainte Chapelle* in Paris and other places in Europe, he noticed they were all made of different kinds of wood.[24] This evident trickery served as ammunition for his treatment of the 'true use' of the Cross in that later treatise, but, as in the *Summaire,* here it lies behind much of his critique of Catholic piety and doctrine.

The growing mistrust in this outward piety moved Farel towards conversion. Years after the fact, Farel speaks about his conversion in an open letter to all those who helped him.[25] For a time he believed in the Pope as much as in God; he had great faith in pilgrimages, images, vows and the like.[26] But upon reading scripture, he was shocked at the difference between its teaching and what he was being taught at the University of Paris.[27] Farel writes that the more he thought about the stark contrast the more he hated papal teaching as 'diabolical' and the 'Holy Word of God began to have first place in [his] heart'.[28] Farel notes that the purging of his heart did not happen all at one time, but, he writes, 'little by little the papacy fell from my heart'.[29]

---

[21] *Guillaume Farel: Biographie Nouvelle,* pp. 99ff.; Farel continued his relationship with Lefèvre even after leaving Paris. See Herminjard, Vol. 1, Letters 85, 98 and 103.

[22] On his conversion see Henri Meylan, 'Les étapes de la conversion de Farel', in *L'humanisme français au début de la Renaissance* (Paris: Librarie Philosophique J. Vrin, 1973), pp. 253–9.

[23] Guillaume Farel, *Du Vray usage de la croix de Iesus-Christ suivi de divers écrits du même auteur* (Geneva: Fick, 1865), p. 146.

[24] Farel, *Du Vray usage,* p. 147.

[25] 'Epistre a tous Seigneurs, et peuples et pasteurs...qui m'ont aidé et assisté en l'œuvre de nostre Seigneur Iesus', in Guillaume Farel, *Du Vray usage,* pp. 164–75.

[26] 'Epistre a tous Seigneurs', in *Du Vray usage,* p. 165.

[27] 'Epistre a tous Seigneurs', in *Du Vray usage,* p. 168.

[28] 'Epistre a tous Seigneurs', in *Du Vray usage,* p. 173.

[29] 'Epistre a tous Seigneurs', in *Du Vray usage,* p. 175. Interestingly, Farel's long conversion contrasts quite starkly with Calvin's '*subita*' or 'sudden' conversion. For the account in English see John Calvin, 'Author's Preface', *Commentary on the Book of Psalms,*

As with other French evangelicals of his time, he became a preacher in Meaux under Bishop Guillaume Briçonnet in 1521.[30] The Reform in Meaux would not last for long. The political history of France at this time is important to contextualizing the short duration of the evangelical preaching in Meaux.[31] Upon the disastrous defeat of the French forces by the Emperor Charles V at Pavia in February 1525, the King of France was captured and imprisoned in Madrid. In his absence (and that of his sister, Marguerite of Navarre, a protector of the Protestants) the *Parlement* of Paris, backed by the Faculty of Theology, tried to stop the spread of evangelical preaching in France, most notably in the diocese of Meaux. Although there is some dispute about the relationship of *Parlement* and Faculty in this censorship, the group of Meaux was successfully disrupted.[32] Yet, Farel would not be stopped in his preaching of a more thoroughgoing reform and chose to leave that city. After a voyage to Aquitaine and Gap, Farel ended up in Basel.[33]

In the city of Basel he hoped to refine some of his theological ideas by interacting with important reforming humanists like Johannes Oecolampadius. With its famous university, Basel attracted many international humanists, theologians and ideas.[34] In order to engage these intellectuals Farel proposed 13 articles for debate there in 1524.[35] Although initially refused by the university, his request for a dispute was upheld by the local town council and he posted his placard publicly on 23 February

---

Part 1, trans. James Anderson, *Calvin's Commentaries*, Vol. IV (Grand Rapids: Baker, 1979), p. xl.

[30] See Michel Veissière, *L'évêque Guillaume Briconnet (1470–1534): contribution à la croissance de la Réforme catholique à la veille du Concile de Trente* (Provins: Société d'histoire de d'archéologie, 1986); René-Jacques Lovy, *Les Origines de la réforme française: Meaux, 1518–1546*, 2nd ed. (Paris: Concordia/Les Presses du Village, 1983), Ch. 3.

[31] A short general history of the Reform movement in France is provided in Jonathan A. Reid, 'France', in *The Reformation World*, ed. Andrew Pettegree (London: Routledge, 2000), pp. 211–24.

[32] See James K. Farge, *Orthodoxy and Reform in Early Reformation France: The Faculty of Theology of Paris, 1500–1543* (Leiden: Brill, 1985), and Francis Higman, *Censorship and the Sorbonne: A Bibliographical Study of Books in French Censured by the Faculty of Theology of the University of Paris, 1520–1551* (Geneva: Droz, 1979), pp. 24–30.

[33] For Farel's later feelings about the group of Meaux see Franz P. Van Stam, 'The Group of Meaux as First Target of Farel and Calvin's Anti-Nicodemism', *Bibliothèque d'humanisme et renaissance*, Vol. 68, No. 2 (2006), pp. 253–75.

[34] On Farel in Basel see Peter G. Bietenholtz, *Basle and France in the Sixteenth Century* (Toronto: University of Toronto Press, 1971), pp. 88ff. and 181ff.

[35] Letter 91 'Guillaume Farel aux Lecteurs chrétiens', Herminjard, Vol. 1, p. 193.

1524.[36] Such overt defence of the Reform did not sit well with the famous humanist Erasmus who resided in the city at the time. Most particularly, he resented the fact that Farel had called him a 'Balaam'.[37] Farel was soon seen to be a foe of the humanist cause. One of Farel's friends tried to temper Farel's invective to save the situation, but to no avail.[38] Owing in part to Erasmus' enormous influence, Farel was forced to leave Basel.[39]

It was in this situation that the first known French publication of Farel appeared. In 1524 he compiled a brief commentary on the Lord's Prayer and the Creed in French intended to fill a void in French Evangelical vernacular literature and had it printed in Basel.[40] Further, Farel is credited by some scholars as the author of the small Reform-minded pamphlet, *Epistre Chretienne Tresutile,* published around 1524.[41] But these modest publications were not enough to respond to the increasing demand for French Evangelical literature. Because a single preacher could only preach in one place at a time, a preacher's influence, although considerable, was limited.[42] Even more persuasive was preaching combined with the printed text. These early printed texts in French were very similar in content and style to that which was preached.[43]

---

[36]   Letter 92 'Le Conseil de Bâle à tous ecclésiastiques et laïques', Herminjard, Vol. 1, pp. 195–8. On the strategic importance of religious disputations in the Pays de Vaud, see Michael Bruening, *Calvinism's First Battleground: Conflict and Reform in the Pays de Vaud, 1528–1559* (Dordrecht: Springer, 2005), pp. 137–41.

[37]   Herminjard, Vol. 1, p. 290. Erasmus's term for Farel was 'Phallicus'.

[38]   Letter 99 'Hilaire [Bertolph] à Guillaume Farel', Herminjard, Vol. 1, pp. 210–3.

[39]   Cornelis Augustijn, 'Erasmus und Farel in Konflikt', in *Actes du Colloque Guillaume Farel*, pp. 1–9; J. P. Massaut, 'Erasme et Farel', in: *Actes du Colloque Guillaume Farel*, pp. 11–30.

[40]   Guillaume Farel, *Le Pater Noster, et le Credo en Françoys* (Bâle: Andreas Cratander, 1524). A modern edition: Guillaume Farel, *Le Pater Noster et le Credo en Françoys*, ed. Francis Higman (Geneva: Droz, 1982). See also Herminjard, Vol. 1, pp. 246–8 and Theodore G. Van Raalte, 'Guillaume Farel's Spirituality: Leading in Prayer', *Westminster Theological Journal* Vol. 70, No. 2 (Fall 2008), pp. 277–301.

[41]   [Guillaume Farel] 'L'Epistre Chrestienne Tresutile', eds. Isabelle C. Denommé and William Kemp, in: *Le Livre evangélique en français avant Calvin*, eds. Jean-François Gilmont and William Kemp (Turnhout: Brepols, 2004), pp. 54–70.

[42]   See Andrew Pettegree, *Reformation and the Culture of Persuasion* (Cambridge University Press, 2005); David J. Nicholls, 'The Nature of Popular Heresy in France, 1520–1542', *The Historical Journal* Vol. 26, No. 2 (1983), pp. 261–75.

[43]   Writing about Calvin and the other early French Reformers, Andrew Pettegree states: 'For all the scholarly authority of the *Institutes* and his biblical commentaries, in his early years Calvin had shown an unexpected talent for prose invective, a tradition in which his principal collaborators Farel and Viret also excelled'. Pettegree, *Reformation and the Culture of Persuasion*, p. 67. Note, however, that in the period 1524–34 the content of the polemics underwent development. See Chapter 4 of this work for more on this.

It was crucial for the advancement of Farel's reforming agenda to find reliable printers. Higman notes 'Farel was acutely conscious of the importance of printing to the Reformation movement, and in particular of the need to install presses in localities firmly won over to the Reformation'.[44] Hence, new centres of printing were established to respond to this important need.[45]

Although departed from Basel, Farel was encouraged by Oecolampadius to continue his reforming work in the area of Montbéliard. Occolampadius urged him not to be concerned with making learned disciples, but making good ones.[46] After visiting Strasbourg and Metz, Farel, using the pseudonym 'Ursinus', found a teaching position in the small town of Aigle in November 1526 upon the recommendation of the authorities of Bern.[47] Indeed, much of Farel's reforming activity was at the behest of the Bernese authorities. Michael Bruening has recently highlighted this Bernese influence: 'The most decisive factor in bringing Protestantism to the *Suisse romande* was Bern's decision to accept the Reformation. Without the influence of Bern, it is highly unlikely that any of the lands of French speaking Switzerland, including Geneva, would ever have become Protestant'.[48] Although Bernese political desires and Farel's missionary goals sometimes came into conflict, most often they could work together.[49]

From this beginning in Aigle, Farel, protected by the Bernese authorities, began to preach in other Bernese controlled and influenced cities as well. The Bernese commissioned him to translate their baptismal liturgy which probably remained in manuscript form until published by Pierre de Vingle in 1533.[50] It was also in Aigle that Farel wrote the first

---

[44]   Francis Higman, 'French-speaking regions, 1520–62', in: *The Reformation and the Book*, ed. Jean-François Gilmont, English ed. and trans. Karin Maag (Aldershot: Ashgate, 1998), p. 111.

[45]   Tracing the history of book printing and distribution in the French Reformation has become an extremely valuable aid for understanding the Reformation more generally. See Francis Higman, *La Diffusion de la réforme en France, 1520–1565* (Geneva: Labor et Fides, 1992), p. 33; Higman, *Piety and the People: Religious Printing in French, 1511–1551* (Aldershot: Scolar Press, 1996); Jean-François Gilmont, *Le livre réformé au XVIᵉ siècle* (Paris: Bibliothèque nationale de France, 2005), pp. 28ff.

[46]   '*Dabis operam non ut doctos, sed ut bonos, hoc est, vere doctos et Theodidaktous multos gignas. Facile enim est aliquot dogmata auditorum instillare et inculcare auribus; animum autem immutare, divinum opus est*'. 'Oecolampade à Farel', Letter 110, Herminjard, Vol. 1, p. 254.

[47]   For a far more detailed account of the journeys of Farel during these years see *Guillaume Farel: Biographie Nouvelle*, pp. 91–118.

[48]   Bruening, *Calvinism's First Battleground*, p. 31.

[49]   Ls-Ed. Roulet, 'Farel, agent bernois? (1528–1536)', in: *Actes du Colloque Guillaume Farel*, pp. 99–106; Higman, *Lire et Découvrir*, p. 605.

[50]   Bruening, *Calvinism's First Battleground*, pp. 106ff.

edition of the *Summaire*. Starting in 1529, Farel began itinerant mission work in other French speaking cities: Lausanne, Orbe, Grandson, Yverdon and Neuchâtel.[51] With Pierre Viret, Antoine Marcourt, Antoine Saulnier and others, he vigorously preached for and organized the Reform of these various cities. His fiery preaching and call for thoroughgoing reform drew the wrath of many Catholic leaders upon him (it had already drawn the critique of other more cautious colleagues[52]) but in the end several cities opted for Farel's reforming agenda. Further, Farel's work was being supported by many of the Waldensians in France. His message of Bible-based reform sounded refreshingly familiar to them.[53]

Characteristic of Farel's reform was a push for public disputation based on the authority of Scripture alone and, subsequently, a push for the abolition of the mass. For Farel, as for Marcourt, the mass was one of the major problems of the Roman Catholic Church.[54] For them, it was characteristic of everything that was wrong and perverted in the Roman Church. Farel and the other sacramentarians used all the means at their disposal, especially preaching, printing and iconoclasm, to go 'straight for the jugular of the medieval church'.[55]

Most radical in this push for the abolition of the mass were the placards printed by Pierre de Vingle and posted in Paris and in several provincial cities of France on the night of 17 October 1534, and again on 12 January 1535.[56] The author, Antoine Marcourt, an associate of Farel, chose to publish these placards anonymously.[57] The placards spoke of the one, perfect sacrifice of Christ, the idolatry of the bodily presence of Christ, the sophistry of transubstantiation, and the spiritual fruitlessness of the mass. Marcourt and Farel are of the same persuasion on the need to abolish the mass:

---

[51]   See Bruce Gordon, *The Swiss Reformation* (Manchester: Manchester University Press, 2002), Ch. 5.

[52]   See Oecolampadius' critique of Farel in Herminjard, Vol. 1, letters 111 and 115.

[53]   Reinhard Bodenmann, 'Les Vaudois et la production du livre évangélique français (1525–1550)', in *Libri, biblioteche e cultura nelle valli valdesi in età moderna*, ed. Marco Fratini (Turin: Claudiana, 2006), pp. 21–59. See also Gabriel Audisio, *Preachers by Night: The Waldensian Barbes (15th–16th Centuries)*, trans. Claire Davison (Leiden: Brill, 2007), esp. Chs. 9–10.

[54]   Farel, *Summaire* (1534), Ch. 19.

[55]   Bruening, *Calvinism's First Battleground*, p. 112; Audisio, *The Waldensian Barbes*, esp. chs. 9-10; and Euan Cameron, *Waldenses: Rejections of Holy Church in Medieval Europe* (Oxford: Blackwell, 2000), Ch. 9.

[56]   [Antoine Marcourt], *Articles veritables sur les horribles, grandz et importables abuz de la Messe papalle, inventee directement contre la saincte Cene de Jesus Christ* [Neuchâtel: Pierre de Vingle, 1534]. For an English translation see Appendix I of John Calvin, *Institutes of the Christian Religion, 1536 Edition* (Grand Rapids: Eerdmans, 1975), pp. 339–42.

[57]   Elwood, *The Body Broken*, pp. 28–9.

But the fruit of the mass is very different, as our experience tells us, for by it all knowledge of Jesus Christ is erased, preaching of the Gospel rejected and hindered, and time occupied by bell-ringing, cries, chanting, ceremonies, candles, incense, disguises, and all such manner of monkeying around. By these the simple folk are as sheep or lambs miserably deceived, and by these ravaging wolves eaten, chewed, and devoured.[58]

This overt repudiation of the Mass characterized much of the message of this circle of French speaking Reformers. The work of the printer of the placards, Pierre de Vingle, would be integral for them in this vigorous polemic against the Catholic Church.[59] Indeed, while he was still in Lyon, Pierre de Vingle published Farel's *Summaire* in 1529 and 1531.

The Catholic authorities and Church did not appreciate such radical critique. In fact, the placards were in some ways counter-productive. Not only did they not lead to the abolition of the mass or more freedom of religion, they actually led to a stricter treatment of the Reform in France. The King became so incensed by the posting of these placards that he published a decree forbidding, not just the radical books, but *all* books until further notice![60] The King saw this not simply as an affair of the theologians, but a major disturbance of the social order and an affront to his royal power.[61] Other partisans for the Reform cause were also not happy with this blunt confrontation with royal power by Marcourt and de Vingle, but nonetheless, the deed was done.[62]

The Reformers needed some sort of political protection. This protection came in the Bernese conquest of the territory of Vaud in December 1535 and January 1536. The campaign gave Bern political control over the territories of Vaud and Gex, and the western half of Chablais.[63] Although Bern did not have complete control over Geneva, its influence considerably increased. What were once scattered Reform movements became allied into a single state-organized Reformed Church.[64]

It was in Geneva that Farel came to have the greatest influence. Having already preached the Reform in Geneva, he was finally called to lead the cause of reforming the city which had chosen to abolish the mass

---

[58]   [Antoine Marcourt], *Articles veritables*.

[59]   Gilmont, *Le Livre réformé*, pp. 30–38.

[60]   Gilmont, *Le Livre réformé*, p. 32.

[61]   For the reaction of the King see Christopher Elwood's account in *The Body Broken*, pp. 27–9.

[62]   Gilmont, *Le Livre réformé*, p. 32.

[63]   Bruening, *Calvinism's First Battleground*, p. 39; Gordon, *The Swiss Reformation*, pp. 150ff.

[64]   Bruening, *Calvinism's First Battleground*, p. 40.

in August 1535.[65] More importantly, it was here in July 1536 that he persuaded the young theologian John Calvin, promising Calvin the wrath of God should he refuse, to join the cause of the Reformation in Geneva. Proposing *Ecclesiastical Ordinances* and a *Confession of Faith* in 1537, Farel continued to lead the reformed cause in Geneva with Calvin until Easter 1538.[66] In this year, following the election of new *Syndics* (principal magistrates) opposed to the strict ecclesiastical discipline upheld by Farel and Calvin, both preachers were banished from the city.[67] Following his banishment from Geneva, Farel took up the post of minister in Neuchâtel – a post he held until his death in 1565. From the safety of Geneva and Neuchâtel the French speaking Reform movement was protected and would have an influence on France and the rest of Europe.

The history of the *Summaire*

In tracing the history of the *Summaire* it is clear that Farel's influence on French Reform before and after 1536 should not be forgotten. Indeed, many of the central concerns and ideas raised by Farel would actually be taken up and developed by Calvin in his subsequent writings. Interestingly, Farel did not slow down his production of texts after the coming of Calvin, but, in fact, produced even more. Some of his most ambitious works were published post-1536.[68] Clearly, many of the themes that are seen as central to Calvin's thought are shared by Farel. Although Farel would admit that Calvin was a clearer and more capable thinker, this takes nothing away from their sharing of foundational ideas and their collaborative effort in the French Reform movement.

Farel himself gives us the reasons for which he wanted to publish a more extended summary of Reformed doctrine. In the 1534 text of the *Summaire* his reasons for writing are largely theological. His goal was

---

[65]   For a contemporary Catholic perspective on Farel's reforming work see Jeanne de Jussie, *The Short Chronicle: A Poor Clare's Account of the Reformation of Geneva*, ed. and trans. by Carrie F. Klaus (Chicago: University of Chicago Press, 2006). For Farel's role in the Genevan Reformation more generally see Henri Naef, *Les Origines de la Réforme à Genève*. Vol. 2 (Geneva: Droz, 1968), pp. 214–21, 315–82 and Pt. 5; E. William Monter, *Calvin's Geneva* (New York: John Wiley & Sons, 1967), Ch. 2.

[66]   See *Registres du Conseil de Genève à l'epoque de Calvin*, ed. Paule Hochuli Dubuis and Sandra Coram-Mekkey, Vol. 2, Pt 1 (Geneva: Droz, 2003), pp. 21ff.

[67]   Among other activities during the following years, Farel celebrated the marriage of John Calvin and Idelette de Bure in Strasbourg in August 1540.

[68]   See Farel bibliography by Jean-François Gilmont, *Actes du Colloque Guillaume Farel*, Vol. 2, eds Pierre Barthel, Rémy Scheurer, and Richard Stauffer (Geneva: Droz, 1983).

twofold: to give a defence of the biblical theology of the Reformation and to attack what he considered to be the man-made theology of the Roman Catholic Church. This twofold goal accounts for the structure behind the entire *Summaire* – and nearly all his writings! In this 1534 edition, however, Farel does not tell us much more than these explicitly theological reasons for writing the work. Indeed, even in the rest of the document he gives precious few references to his specific situation or to the names of those with whom he was in conflict.

To gain more specific information, we must look to the 1542 and 1552 editions of the *Summaire* published by Jean Girard, to which Farel appended an extremely helpful *Raison pour quoy ceste oeuvre a esté faite.*[69] There Farel is more explicit about the reasons that prompted the *Summaire*. He indicates that he wrote at the request of Johannes Oecolampadius of Basel. Although he felt insufficient to the task, he opened his mouth to preach and took up his pen to write after Oecolampadius invoked the name of God upon his work.

Although self-deprecatory, Farel nonetheless agreed to the republication of his *Summaire* twice following the appearance of Calvin on the scene. One gets an idea of the reason that he felt this republication important based on the continued clear distinction Farel makes between the work of the Devil and the work of the Spirit. He believed that both the Devil and the Spirit were still at work and any work suppressing the Devil, no matter how meagre, was helpful. Hence, even 13 years on, Farel's message was largely the same.[70]

---

[69] See Chapter 7 of this volume for the full translated text.

[70] *Summaire* (1542), pp. 220–1.

CHAPTER 2

Farel's *Summaire*: Theology in Early French Reform

Jason Zuidema

Introduction

There has been a modest revival of interest in the ideas of Farel in recent years. Until the advent of the recent first volume of the critical edition of Farel's writings,[1] the most notable essays were several works dealing with Farel's Eucharistic thought[2] and a collection of essays from the 1980 conference devoted to Farel's life and theology.[3] Until the full critical edition of Farel's writings appears in the coming decades many of Farel's major works can be found on IDC Microfilm.[4] In this chapter we correlate the recurring themes in Farel's letters and printed sources with the central ideas of his *Summaire*.[5] This helps us understand the doctrinal position of the Reformed churches in the Pays de Vaud prior to Calvin, and thus provides vital material for answering the question why so many people were convinced to make the radical break with Rome.

---

[1]   Guillaume Farel, *Œuvres imprimées Vol. 1: Traités messins*, eds. Reinhard Bodenmann and Françoise Breigel with Olivier Labarthe (Geneva: Droz, 2009).

[2]   See Elfriede Jacobs, *Die Sakramentslehre Wilhelm Farels* (Zurich: Theologischer Verlag, 1978); Christopher Elwood, *The Body Broken: The Calvinist Doctrine of the Eucharist and the Symbolization of Power in Sixteenth-Century France* (Oxford: Oxford University Press, 1999).

[3]   Pierre Barthel, Rémy Scheurer, and Richard Stauffer, eds. *Actes du Colloque Guillaume Farel*, Cahiers de la Revue de Théologie et de Philosophie 9 (Geneva: Droz, 1983).

[4]   Outside of the IDC microfilm some of the most accessible of Farel's works are: *Du Vray usage de la croix de Iesus-Christ suivi de divers écrits du même auteur*, (Geneva: Fick, 1865); *Le Pater Noster et le Credo en Françoys*, ed. Francis Higman (Geneva: Droz, 1982); *Sommaire et brève déclaration: 1525*, ed. Arthur L. Hofer (Neuchâtel: Belle Rivière, 1980); 'Confession de la foy' in *La Vraie piété: divers traités de Jean Calvin et Confession de foi de Guillaume Farel*, eds I. Backus et C. Chimelli (Geneva: Labor et Fides, 1986), pp. 39–53. Many of Farel's letters can be found in A. J. Herminjard ed., *Correspondance des reformateurs dans les pays de langue française* (Geneva and Paris, 1866).

[5]   A recent and helpful introduction to Farel's thought in the Summaire is Robert White's article 'An Early Doctrinal Handbook: Farel's *Summaire et Briefve Declaration*', *Westminster Theological Journal* 69 (2007), pp. 21–38.

Themes in *Summaire*

The two wills

Ironically, it would perhaps be easier to label the unsystematic Farel as a thinker with a 'central dogma' than it would the much more organized Calvin.[6] To be sure, Farel was not looking for a single 'central dogma' but attempted, as did all the Reformers, to preach scripture. What we can observe are his persistent contrasts. Farel, on the one hand, held to the utter purity of God's will and the clear revelation of the same in scripture. On the other hand, he bemoaned the filth of human will and the utter inability to understand or follow God's clearly revealed will. For this, as Farel often quoted scripture, we need Jesus Christ 'who died for our sins and was raised for our justification'.[7] Being justified by grace Christians can, indeed must, now willingly follow that clearly revealed will of God.[8] This clash of the divine and human (*viz.* diabolical) wills, in a nutshell, is one of Farel's recurring messages. Certainly, Farel mentions frequently the will (*volonté*), and statute (*ordonnance*) of God in his writings.

It is fundamental to recognize the importance of the clarity of scripture in Farel's thinking. Perhaps in part owing to his contacts with Lefèvre d'Etaples and other like-minded humanists, Farel developed a dislike for the multiple senses of scripture.[9] Although clearly differing from Lefèvre or Erasmus, Farel still shared their humanist desire for correct understanding of the text of scripture.[10] Unfortunately, we have very little in the way of exegesis or Bible commentary in Farel's writings to illuminate his approach to hermeneutics. What we do have, however, is his constant reference to the purity and clarity of the message of scripture.[11] Scripture's message is twofold: it reveals the right way and the wrong way. In the 1541 *Tressaincte*

---

[6]   Such would still be erroneous, but nonetheless nearer to the truth than if applied to Calvin. See Muller, *Post-Reformation Reformed Dogmatics Vol. 1*, 2nd ed. (Grand Rapids: Baker, 2003), pp. 123ff.; Muller, *Christ and the Decree: Christology and Predestination in Reformed Theology from Calvin to Perkins* (Grand Rapids: Baker, 1988), pp. 1–13; Partee, 'L'Influence de Farel sur Calvin', p. 184; Wendel, *Calvin*, pp. 273–5.

[7]   Guillaume Farel, *Oraison tresdevote*, A iii r.; Farel, *Epistre Envoyee aux Reliques*, 7r.

[8]   Farel, 'Confession', p. 48.

[9]   Farel, *Glaive de la Parolle*, pp. 39, 321.

[10]   Farel wrote of his foe Le Moyne '*Et puis que ce poure seduit est en l'erreur Libertine de cœur et esprit double, se donnant licence de tourner l'Escriture à son plaisir, et qu'il veut par tout faire allegories et rien prendre au naif et propre sens, et ne se tenir à la simplicité que mesme Iesus et ses Apostres ont gardée, c'est de prendre les motz en leur propre signification: là il faut*'. *Glaive de la Parolle*, p. 74.

[11]   [Guillaume Farel], 'L'Epistre Chrestienne tresutile', p. 68; Farel, *Summaire* (1534), Fol. C iii v.

oraison,[12] Farel makes his case for scripture clear: the writers of scripture 'wrote nothing but the pure truth, proposing for us the holy will of God, that is, what God wants us to keep and what he wants us to avoid, and this by showing us examples of what happened to those who walked according to the will of God and of those who did the contrary'.[13] Indeed, all of scripture is unified and subsumed under this twofold focus.[14]

Farel was above all concerned with denouncing what he considered the errors of the 'papal church'. Even when speaking of other groups like the 'libertines', he always talks of their fundamental similarity in promoting their will over God's.[15] This radical opposition of Farel's thinking to all other 'human' thought reinforces our claim regarding his emphasis on the binary nature of the two wills. Indeed, for him, the Catholic Church is the absolute example of a perverse, even Satanic will.[16] Not one to mince words, Farel calls the Pope the 'first born of the Devil'.[17] For him, the Pope and all his followers are diametrically opposed to the clear and pure will of God. They are the very archetype of heresy in that they willingly chose to usurp the place of God in worship.[18] Indeed, for Farel, the Papal Church is just as bad, if not worse, than 'Machomet' and his 'Alcoran'.[19]

The *Summaire* is perhaps the best example of the dialogical relationship in Farel. The first 16 chapters have what Francis Higman calls a 'clear, though not entirely rigid, pendulum movement between pairs of chapters'.[20] One chapter has positive doctrine and the other negative. One

---

[12] This small treatise was known to exist, but no copy had been found until recently. A single copy was found in the Universitäts- und Landesbibliothek in Halle, Germany. See *Actes du Colloque Guillaume Farel*, Vol. 2, pp. 126–7.

[13] '...*n'ont escript que la pure verité, nous proposans la saincte volonté de Dieu, c'est a dire, ce qu'il veult que nous gardions, que nous evitons, en nous monstrant pour exemple ce qui est advenu à ceux qui ont cheminé selon la volonté de Dieu, et à ceux qui ont fait au contraire*'. Farel, *Tressaincte oraison*, 1541, p. a4r.

[14] Guillaume Farel, *Summaire* (1534), Ch. 15 'De La Saincte Escripture', Fol. C iii verso ff.

[15] Guillaume Farel, *Glaive de la Parolle*, pp. 218, 431. On the *libertins* and Farel and Calvin's reaction see Mirjam Van Veen's introduction in *Contre les libertins spirituelz, epistre contre un Cordelier, response a un certain holandois*, Series IV, *Scripta didactica et polemica*, ed. Mirjam Van Veen (Geneva : Droz, 2005), pp. 9–41.

[16] '*les ordonnances du pape sont plutôt synagogues du diable qu'Eglises chrétiennes*'. Farel, 'Confession', p. 51; Farel, *De la Saincte Cene*, 121; Farel, 'A tous cueurs affamez...' in: Fick ed., p. 247; Farel, 'Epistre a tous Seigneurs...' in: Fick, ed., pp. 169, 173.

[17] Farel, *Glaive de la Parolle*, p. 197.

[18] Farel, *Glaive de la Parolle*, p. 431.

[19] That is, Mohammed and his *Koran*. Farel, *Oraison tresdevote*, B ii v/r; Farel, *Tressaincte oraison*, Fol. a7v.

[20] Francis Higman, 'Farel's Summaire: The Interplay of Theology and Polemics', in *Le Livre Evangélique en français avant Calvin*, eds. Jean-François Gilmont and William Kemp

chapter speaks of the pure divine will and the next of the corrupt human will. However, after these initial chapters the *Summaire* turns mainly into a bitter, polemical attack on Catholic theology and practice. Robert White helpfully notes that 'Chapters 16 through 36 constitute a much larger amalgam of material whose theme may be loosely defined as the church, its nature, powers and practices. This section of the work is noticeably more prolix in style and diffuse in content, the author's initial concern to *explain* being in part overtaken by the need to *defend* evangelical doctrine and to *discredit* where possible contrary positions'.[21] In the last several chapters (37–42) Farel returns to more positive instruction of scriptural doctrine.

One very important chapter setting the stage for the bulk of the *Summaire* is Chapter 14 – on human doctrine and traditions. Farel makes a critical judgement about human traditions which would be shared by Calvin and the other French Reformers:

> Human doctrine wants to meddle in the things of God which relate to the salvation of the soul and to the adoration and service of God. Such meddling is nothing else than an abomination before God, vanity, a lie; it is diabolical doctrine, error, and vain trickery. By this God is served in vain and his wrath is provoked upon those who serve him in this way. These are given over to a disordered conscience. They are servants of creatures and not of the Creator.[22]

This view of human traditions as not being neutral or indifferent is a particular theme of French Reformation writings in general.[23] As such, all the externals in worship were strictly limited to that which could be proved from scripture.[24] Indeed, Farel notes, 'the more human doctrine presents the appearance and the shape of holiness, the more it is dangerous'.[25] Even the elect can be drawn in by this error, which may seem to be made in the name of Christ. The only sure test of the proper use of externals in worship is to examine scripture: one can only know the tree when one looks at the root.[26]

(Turnhout: Brepols, 2004), p. 74.

[21]   White, 'An Early Doctrinal Handbook', p. 23.

[22]   Farel, *Summaire* (1534), Fol. c ii verso.

[23]   See Carlos M. N. Eire, *War Against the Idols: The Reformation of Worship from Erasmus to Calvin* (Cambridge: Cambridge University Press, 1986), pp. 3, 231–3, 308.

[24]   Farel, *Du Vray usage de la Croix*, p. 85.

[25]   Farel, *Summaire* (1534), Fol. c iii recto.

[26]   *'qui ne regarde la loy de nostre Seigneur, en prouvant toutes leurs ordonnances, regardont quelz fruictz font telles constitutions et coustumes quilz ont introduictes; et ainsi lon congnoistra l'arbre'.* Farel, *Summaire* (1534), Fol. C iii recto; See Farel, *Summaire* (1534), Fol. B iv recto ff.; Farel, *Summaire* (1542), p. 9.

Justification and predestination

In Farel's thought the human will and heart are radically sinful; sin affects all aspects of human life. In Chapter 2 of the *Summaire* Farel writes: 'Man is wicked, incapable, foolish, headstrong, ambitious, full of error and hypocrisy, inconsistent, and changeable. He only thinks of evil and sin – that in which he was born and conceived'. Farel clearly links the original disobedience of Adam with the continuing disobedience and corruption of the subsequent human race.[27] As such, humans are incapable of gaining the grace of God – they continually make their situation before God even worse. For this reason, Jesus Christ, he who could submit his will to that of his Father, bore the sin of humanity to reconcile the world with his Father.[28] Interestingly, Farel notes on several occasions that God did not save the world out of his love for us, but out of his 'love of himself'.[29] Understandably, then, Farel rejects any notion that human good works can merit the grace of God.[30] Farel writes that humans can only live before God by faith.[31]

For Farel, God's free justifying will is related to God's free predestining will. Farel can be seen to hold a position which is clearly double predestinarian, even though he does not provide an extended discussion on the subject. Chapter 42 of the *Summaire* gives several clear indications of his position. Farel writes that nothing in this creation can 'block the election of God and his unchanging purpose'.[32] Farel writes:

> The decree of God is firm. For the election and grace of God and his Spirit, by whom he sanctifies his own in Jesus, are not bound by any time, place, persons,

---

[27]   Farel, *Summaire* (1534), Fol. A vii verso.

[28]   Farel, *Summaire* (1534), Fol. A viii verso.

[29]   Farel, *Summaire* (1534), Fols A viii verso; B vii verso; C i verso; G i recto; K iv verso; L ii recto.

[30]   See David N. Wiley, 'The Dispute of Lausanne and the Theology of William Farel: The Doctrine of Justification and its Sources', in: *La Dispute de Lausanne (1536), La théologie réformée après Zwingli et avant Calvin*, ed. Eric Junod (Lausanne: Presses Centrales Lausanne, 1988), pp. 142–8.

[31]   Ozment writes that in Farel 'the key to this new Protestant way of life is the new concept of faith with its almost brash security and certitude'. Steven E. Ozment, *The Reformation in the Cities: The Appeal of Protestantism to Sixteenth-Century Germany and Switzerland* (New Haven: Yale, 1975), p. 70.

[32]   Farel, *Summaire* (1534), Fol. K vii verso.

or ways of doing things. God gives freely, without regard to parents, peoples, places, or the life of the person to whom it is given.[33]

On the other hand, the reprobate can also do nothing to change their situation. No matter how much they try to imitate holiness, they will never succeed at being holy – they will simply make their situation worse.[34] Farel's doctrine of predestination in the *Summaire* becomes even clearer in his recurring discussion of the predestining will of God in his *Glaive de la Parolle Véritable*. Farel, explaining the Apostle Paul, states, 'the holy Apostle wants to show that God can rightly by his counsel ordain certain of his creatures to life and others to death: like a potter has the power to make certain vessels for honour and others for dishonour'.[35] It is God who takes whom he wishes, as he has ordained, and rejects and leaves those whom he has not chosen.[36] Such a decree, however, should not be peered into too closely[37] and certainly does not give the right to live as an antinomian – as, apparently, the libertines were arguing.[38] Even though God has chosen, he has also revealed his will in his word. Knowing this decree, then, should give the elect confidence to follow the clear ordinances of God.[39] We do not know exactly what God's secret or predestining will is, writes Farel, but we do know his revealed will, that is, his commandments, very well.[40] Hence, he argues that we cannot live as if such commandments were simply figments of the imagination.[41]

The doctrine of God

The 1534 edition of the *Summaire* does not go into great lengths to defend the doctrines of the Trinity or of the two natures in Christ. In between this

---

[33]   Farel, *Summaire* (1534), Fol. K viii recto.

[34]   Farel, *Summaire* (1534), Fol. K viii recto.

[35]   'Or le sainct Apostre veut monstrer, que Dieu peut à bon droit en son conseil ordonner de ses creatures, les unes à la vie, et les autres à la mort : comme un potier de terre a puissance d'une masse faire un vaisseau en honneur, et l'autre en deshonneur'. Farel, *Glaive de la Parolle*, p. 254.

[36]   'A cecy secourt ce conseil et ordonnance de Dieu eternelle, que Dieu prend ceux qu'il luy plaist, comme il a ordonné, et qu'il reiette et laisse ceux qu'il n'a point choisiz'. Farel, *Glaive de la Parolle*, p. 186.

[37]   Farel, *Glaive de la Parolle*, pp. 187–8

[38]   Farel, *Glaive de la Parolle*, p. 189.

[39]   Farel, *Glaive de la Parolle*, pp. 187, 255ff.

[40]   Farel, *Glaive de la Parolle*, p. 264.

[41]   Compare Farel's comments against the libertines with Calvin's: Jean Calvin, *Contre les libertins spirituelz, epistre contre un Cordelier, response a un certain holandois, Series IV: Scripta didacta et polemica*, ed. Mirjam Van Veen (Geneva: Droz, 2005).

edition and the 1542 edition Farel was criticized for this. Most notably he was criticized by Pierre Caroli, a Catholic priest who preached the Reform for several years, but reverted back to Catholicism after having locked horns in debate with Farel and Calvin.

In 1536 Caroli was named minister in Lausanne by the Council of Bern, but in only a few months came into conflict with his younger, yet experienced colleague Pierre Viret. Caroli's theological direction for the Lausanne Church differed from Viret's. The matter came to a debate before the council of Bern. As Calvin and Farel became involved and Caroli started to lose influence, he charged the two preachers of Geneva with heterodoxy on the doctrine of the Trinity.[42] He demanded that they prove their loyalty to the creeds by signing them in the presence of other delegates. Calvin refused – he did not want the creeds to usurp the place of scriptural language. He was quick to show that his *Institutes* clearly upheld the creeds, but did not want to be bullied by Caroli into making tradition more important than scripture. Although Caroli fled, questions of Trinitarian theology lingered on in Geneva. Actually, Pierre Caroli would attack again in 1545 with his *Refutatio blasphemiae Farellistarum in sacrosanctam trinitatem*.[43] Both Calvin and Farel would reply, but nonetheless it is interesting that Caroli aimed at the heretical 'Farelists'.

The reasoning of Calvin in this matter is well documented, but Farel had a stake in this controversy as well.[44] We see it most clearly in his extended Chapter 1 and appendix on 'why this work was written' in the 1542 edition of the *Summaire*.[45] Farel adds a lengthy paragraph clearly setting out an orthodox Trinitarian logic. Although, Farel says, we cannot know God in himself, we can know him in his word. Scripture testifies to a Trinitarian God who is three persons in one essence. Interestingly, Farel adds a half-phrase to the beginning of the former opening of Chapter 1:

---

[42]   Franz Pieter Van Stam, 'Le Livre de Pierre Caroli de 1545 et son conflit avec Calvin', in *Calvin et ses contemporains*, ed. Olivier Millet (Geneva: Droz, 1998), pp. 21–41; Cornelis Augustijn, 'Farel und Calvin in Bern 1537–1538', in *Calvin im Kontext der Schweizer Reformation*, ed. Peter Opitz (Zurich: Theologischer Verlag, 2003), pp. 9–23.

[43]   Van Stam, 'Le livre de Pierre Caroli', p. 21.

[44]   See Muller, *Post-Reformation Reformed Dogmatics*, Vol. 4, pp. 65–9. In note 17 on page 66 Muller writes that certain historians of Unitarianism like Earl Morse Wilbur use Farel as an example of a Reformer who made 'not the slightest reference to the Trinity or the dual nature of Christ'. Muller notes quite rightly that these historians only made reference to the early editions of Farel's *Summaire*, thus not taking into account any of Farel's later writings or other motives.

[45]   See Chapter 6, Note 2 and Chapter 7 of this volume.

> But considering him in what he has done, by which he manifests himself, we
> know him to be goodness, power and infinite wisdom....[46]

Here he continues with the former paragraph. This half-phrase is interesting
because Farel is underlining the fact that his former definition focused on
the work or manifestation of the persons of the Trinity.

Farel further treats the doctrine of God in the appendix to the 1542
edition. He points out that his little book was not meant as an exhaustive
treatment of doctrine, but a summary of the important points.[47] His
opponents did not appreciate this important detail and expected more of
his work than what was intended. In any case, Farel here clearly fends off
those he would consider to be modern 'Arians' and all those who would
question his orthodoxy. Interestingly, he notes that Saint John was most
clear in writing about who Jesus Christ was.[48] He underlines the biblical
origins of Christology. Further, he notes that these new Arians are wrong
because they do not even understand the logic of Trinitarian theology.[49]
His opponents understand neither orthodox Trinitarian theology, nor
scripture.

When speaking of the Trinity Farel writes that above all he wanted to
speak in the simplest way possible without leading his readers 'to consider
God in his naked being, which is by all incomprehensible'.[50] Rather than
burdening the spirit of the simple folk with these incomprehensible things,
Farel admits that he 'stuck to speaking of God and presenting him as
he declared himself in the things that he did'.[51] His reason for not fully
describing orthodox Trinitarian theology in the earlier editions of his
Summaire, hence, was not a 'latent antitrinitarianism'[52] but pedagogical
prudence. If the simple folk were 'little by little' accustomed to Trinitarian
language, they would 'proceed further ahead' than they would if they were
exposed immediately to everything that Farel knew on the subject.[53]

---

[46]   See Chapter 6 (*Summaire*, Ch. 1), below.

[47]   Farel, *Summaire* (1542), p. 227.

[48]   Farel, *Summaire* (1542), p. 223.

[49]   Farel, *Summaire* (1542), p. 224.

[50]   Farel, *Summaire* (1542), p. 228.

[51]   Farel, *Summaire* (1542), p. 228

[52]   Cited in Muller, *Post-Reformation Reformed Dogmatics*, Vol 4, p. 67, n. 22.

[53]   Farel, *Summaire* (1542), p. 228. Heyer writes: 'It is regrettable that Farel had not
been compelled to study this dogma more thoroughly. Undoubtedly, with his great dedication
and desire to sound the depth of things, he would have arrived at some interesting views on
the subject'. Henri Heyer, *Guillaume Farel: An Introduction to His Theology*, trans. Blair
Reynolds (Lewiston: Edwin Mellen Press, 1990), p. 88. It is doubtful that Farel would ever
have written 'interesting views' on the Trinity or Christology. In the statements of the 1542
Summaire he was stating orthodox dogma.

Community

Farel's ecclesiology is based on the clash of wills: a false Church serves the human perverted will and a true Church serves God's pure will. This divergence of wills has several important implications for Farel's conception of the Church. This conception is most clearly seen in Chapter 16 of the *Summaire*.

The distinction of wills shows itself in all the activities of the Church. A false Church is full of people who serve themselves and their own advancement; a true Church is full of members who serve each other. Indeed, this communal interconnectedness is seen throughout the early works of Farel.[54] The Lord brings together the faithful not just for a relationship with himself, but also with each other – a Church is no Church, thinks Farel, without mutual service. Farel says, 'the faithful members of Jesus do not serve themselves, but others'.[55]

Practically, this communal interconnectedness meant several things for Farel. First, that the true Church was willing publicly to preach the gospel. Not only was the Church to serve those who were physically in need, but especially those who were spiritually in need. The burden of preaching was especially laid on those who were 'strong' in the faith. Those with more knowledge of the Bible, argues Farel, have an obligation to impart that knowledge to the weak and simple.[56] Actually, Farel wrote his *Summaire* just for this purpose – to teach the will of God to those who did not know it.

Yet, secondly, this interconnectedness also underlined the need for strong church discipline. Both Farel, and subsequently Calvin, argued that for the good of the flock the pastors of the Church needed to be able to pick up those who had fallen. The major point of the 1537 January Articles of the Genevan preachers sent to the Council of Geneva was the ability of the pastors to discipline members who showed by their lives that they did not live in conformity to their confession. Although the Council agreed for a time, it was this point which got Farel and Calvin kicked out of the city in 1538.[57]

---

[54] Van Stam and Augustijn note that in the 1537 Geneva Articles: 'Farel considered the assembly of believers to be the essence of the church with an obligation for mutual care as a consequence', in *Calvini Epistolae*, Vol. 1, p. 160, n. 30.

[55] Farel, *Summaire* (1534), Fol. C v.

[56] Farel, *Summaire* (1534), Fol. C vi.

[57] Lambert writes that Farel and Calvin had 'spent their political capital' in trying to push a strict discipline and confession of faith in these early years of the Reformation. Thomas Lambert, 'Preaching, Praying, and Policing the Reform in Sixteenth–Century Geneva' (Ph. D. diss., University of Wisconsin–Madison, 1980), p. 175. See also Frans Pieter

Finally, this interconnectedness showed itself practically in the Reformed liturgy. The human, papal will had robbed the congregation of the benefit of a communal celebration by the individual and unintelligible 'mumbling' of the Latin mass.[58] To combat the excessive coldness of the church services, Farel recommended congregational psalm singing which could 'incite the congregation to lift their hearts to God and marvel at his name'.[59] Congregational psalm singing flowed naturally out of the communal nature of the Church. Although Farel and Calvin were banished from Geneva before they could implement the suggestions of congregational singing in 1537, several years later Calvin returned and the Genevan psalm tradition was born.[60]

The model pastor

A major concern of the *Summaire* is the recognition (since he is writing to lay folk and not pastors) of a good pastor. This concern is greatly accentuated in the 1542 edition of the *Summaire*. Farel moves up Chapters 32–36 to put them after Chapter 17 concerning the keys to the kingdom and before the material on the sacraments. These chapters look at excommunication (a major responsibility of the pastor), and the characteristics of a good and bad pastor. Each chapter is significantly increased in size with fuller explanations of the various subjects already treated in 1534.

The divine will and human will are modeled in the pastor. Either he will follow God's word or pervert it for his own profit. In some ways Farel is here making a defence of his own ministry. Although Farel had a certain theological education, he was never ordained officially as a pastor by any church. Rather, he was encouraged by Oecolampadius and installed by the authorities of Bern to be preacher in their territories.[61] Obviously he felt an internal divine call for his work as pastor, but the most important external requirements were not having been ordained by a member of the Church hierarchy, but being able faithfully to live and preach scripture, to perform the sacraments, and to administer discipline in the Church.[62]

---

van Stam, 'Farel's und Calvin's Ausweisung aus Genf am 23. April 1538', *Zeitschrift für Kirchengeschichte* 110 (1999), pp. 209–28.

[58]   *Calvini Epistolae*, Vol. 1, p. 169.

[59]   'Les pseaulmes nous porront inciter à eslever noz cueurs à Dieu et nous esmovoyr de son nom'. *Calvini Epistolae*, Vol. 1, p. 169.

[60]   See the various articles in Eckhard Grunewald, Henning P. Jürgens and Jan R. Luth, *Der Genfer Psalter und Seine Rezeption in Deutchland, der Schweiz und den Niederlanden* (Tübingen: Max Niemeyer Verlag, 2004).

[61]   Jean-Daniel Burger, 'Le Pasteur Guillaume Farel', *Theologische Zeitschrift* 21 (1965), p. 412.

[62]   See Farel, *Summaire* (1542), Chs. 18–22.

The Lord's Supper

It is important to note that this binary logic of wills in Farel is not an expression of the 'material' over the spiritual, but rather of the 'sinful' against the spiritual. Others in the Swiss Reformation would tout the phrase 'the flesh profits nothing' from John's gospel as the victory chant over the crass realism of the mass.[63] Farel, however, does not interpret 'the flesh' as being simply the material world, but as the sinfulness of humanity – especially the sinful human will. The central problem for Farel, as for Calvin, is not the inherent material nature of the world, but the fact that the human heart is so good at making idols out of all that is material.[64] Salvation is not from this body, but of the whole body.[65] As such, Farel's use of the *sursum corda* concept becomes critical. In the Lord's Supper, the Christian's heart must be lifted by the Spirit not because she needs to forget about the physical world, but because she might be tempted to make the physical world into a god.[66]

Many have pointed out that Farel's Eucharistic thought changed over time owing to various influences.[67] Apparently, later in his career Farel puts more emphasis on the presence of Christ at the sacrament and the power of the Spirit. Yet, interestingly, Farel never seems to have admitted such a change or that scripture was any less clear. Throughout his career, Farel would consistently write that his understanding of the Lord's Supper was according to the will of scripture. Numerous examples are found in Farel's writings where he encourages the use of the Reformed Lord's Supper by using such 'wills' language.[68] Farel argues continually that scripture denies the sacrifice of the mass and supports the Reformed Lord's Supper. According to Farel, the mass is man's will; the Lord's Supper is God's.[69]

---

[63]   Huldrych Zwingli, 'Rechenschaft über den Glauben 1530', in *Huldrych Zwingli Schriften IV*, ed. H. U. Bächtold (Zurich: Theologischer Verlag, 1995), p. 121.

[64]   Guillaume Farel, *Summaire* (1534), Fols B i recto; B iii recto; B v verso; Farel, *Du Vray Usage de la Croix*, 85; Farel, *Epistre exhortaire*, 19–20; Farel, *Glaive de la Parolle*, p. 116.

[65]   Farel, *Glaive de la Parolle*, p. 229.

[66]   Farel, *Maniere et fasson*, 17; Farel, *Du Vray usage de la Croix*, 1865, pp. 69–70, 262; Farel, *Summaire* (1534), Fol. B iii verso; Farel, *Epistre exhortaire*, p. 14; Farel, *Epistre envoyee au Duc de Lorraine*, pp. 36, 59; Farel, *De la Saincte Cene*, pp. 5, 16, 83.

[67]   See Jacobs, *Sakramentslehre*, pp. 317ff.; Elwood, *Body Broken*, Ch. 4.

[68]   Farel, *Summaire* (1534), Fol. C viii recto; Farel, *Maniere et fasson*, pp. 15ff.; Farel, 'Confession', p. 50; Farel, *Tressaincte oraison*, C 2v; Farel, *Epistre envoyee au Duc de Lorraine*, p. 23; Farel, *Oraison tresdevote*, Aviii v/r; Farel, *Epistre exhortaire*, pp. 21, 39; Farel, *Glaive de la Parolle*, pp. 2, 198; Farel, *De la Saincte Cene*, passim; Farel, *Du vray usage de la Croix*, pp. 156–7.

[69]   Michael Bruening, *Calvinism's First Battleground: Conflict and Reform in the Pays de Vaud, 1528–1559* (Dordrecht: Springer, 2005), pp. 93–4 and 111.

Farel is in accord with his Reformed colleagues on this point. Although Farel presented the issue in his peculiarly stark and verbose manner, his argumentation about the conflict of wills would become standard place in French Reformed theology.[70]

The text of the *Summaire*

Owing to the substantial influence of Calvin's work in Geneva and on the later Reformation, Farel's thinking and writings have gone largely unnoticed by subsequent historiography. Calvin's prose is much easier to read and has more clarity in the presentation of Reformed ideas; yet Farel's importance in early French speaking Reform should make the study of his ideas a higher priority in early French Reformation studies. Critical editions of all of Farel's major publications are presently underway. He is certainly not a systematic theologian (the great majority of his work is occasional – written for specific situations), but throughout his work one can find evidence of interaction with most of the major theological ideas of the times.

Francis Higman has noted the great difference between France and Germany in the early years of the Reformation with respect to printers of Protestant theology. In Germany in 1519, Luther was already being published in 11 cities by 22 different printers.[71] This high print volume was partly the result of the independent nature of the cities in Germany. No such explosion of printing was seen in the more centralized France. In France there were two centres of Protestant printing: Paris with Simon de Colines printing from 1523–4 and Simon Du Bois printing from 1525–9 (and from 1529–34 in Alençon), and Lyon with Pierre de Vingle. Outside the French kingdom French texts were printed in Basel, Geneva, Neuchâtel, Strasbourg and Antwerp.[72] Among the writings published were Olivétan's Bible, explanations of the creed or liturgical texts, and several translations of German or Latin writings from elsewhere in Europe. The need, however, became more noticeable for a larger exposition of Protestant doctrine.

Due to the often clandestine nature of the printing and distribution of Reformed theology throughout the life of Farel, the exact dating of the editions is often quite difficult. The dating of the *Summaire* is no exception.

---

[70]   See Jean Calvin, *Institutes*, II.8.17 and IV.10.8; Carlos Eire, *War Against the Idols: The Reformation of Worship from Erasmus to Calvin* (Cambridge: Cambridge University Press, 1986), pp. 172, 232ff.

[71]   Francis Higman, *La Diffusion de la réforme en France, 1520–1565* (Geneva: Labor et Fides, 1992), p. 34.

[72]   Higman, *Diffusion*, pp. 34–6; Higman, 'French-speaking regions', pp. 104ff.

In a recent article Francis Higman notes the now common assumption that the edition signed '*Venise, par Pierre du Pont, à l'enseigne du Pigeon Blanc, le 12e de novembre 1529*', was by Pierre de Vingle in Lyon. The provenance of this first edition is known only by a condemnation by the Parliament of Dôle which transcribed the colophon.[73] A second is likewise only known through archival records as printed in 'Anvers, par Pierre Du Pont' in 1531 almost certainly by Vingle again. More controversial is the edition described as coming from Turin in 1525. Found in the British museum, this edition was made known to the public in a detailed way in 1929[74] and subsequently in editions of Arthur Piaget in 1935 and Arthur L. Hofer in 1980.[75] Upon closer inspection, however, this low-quality edition seems to have been printed by Simon du Bois between 1530 and 1534 in Alençon.[76] A fourth edition, the most reliable early edition available of the *Summaire*, was published in Neuchâtel by Pierre de Vingle in December 1534. Indeed, Pierre de Vingle was the publisher of the two earliest editions noted above.[77] In 1542 an edition of the *Summaire* probably by Jean Michel in Geneva came out without Farel's approval.[78] To counter these poorly printed and unauthorized versions, he published a new, updated edition of the *Summaire* in 1542, reprinted in 1552.

The translation in the second half of this volume has been made from the 1534 de Vingle edition of the *Summaire*.[79] The foliation of the original

[73] Higman, 'Farel's Summaire', p. 72, n. 1.

[74] J. Meyhoffer, 'Une édition du Sommaire de Farel 78 (1525)', *Bulletin de la Société de l'histoire du protestantisme français* (1929), pp. 361–70.

[75] Guillaume Farel, *Sommaire et briefve declaration*, fac-similé de l'edition originale publié sous le patronage de la Société des textes français modernes, ed. Arthur Piaget (Paris: Droz, 1935); Farel, *Sommaire et brève déclaration. 1525*, ed. Arthur L. Hofer (Neuchâtel: Editions 'Belle Rivière', 1980).

[76] Higman, 'Farel's Summaire', p. 72, n. 1; Hans Helmut Esser, 'Die Stellung des 'Summaire' von Guillaume Farel innerhalb der frühen reformierten Bekenntnisschriften', in: *Reformiertes Erbe: Festschrift für Gottfried W. Locher zu seinem 80. Geburtstag*, Vol. 1, eds Heiko A. Oberman, Ernst Saxer, Alfred Schindler, and Heinzpeter Stucki, [Zwingliana 19/1 (1992)] (Zurich: Theologischer Verlag Zurich, 1992), pp. 93–106; Jacobs, *Sakramentslehre*, pp. 29–44. In his recent article, Robert White still bases his comments on the less reliable du Bois edition: White, 'An Early Doctrinal Handbook', p. 22.

[77] Higman, 'Farel's Summaire', p. 72, n. 1.

[78] See *Actes du Colloque Guillaume Farel*, Vol. 2, p. 121.

[79] In 1985 Blair Reynolds translated the 1533 *Maniere et fasson* and the so-called 1525 edition of the *Summaire* into English. His translation is difficult to find and has no introduction or footnotes. Although the translation of Reynolds should be lauded for being the first substantial work of Farel published in English, it is frequently awkward or erroneous in its choice of words. Guillame Farel, *Manner and Method: First Liturgy of the Reformed Churches of France*, 1533 and *Summary and Brief Declaration: Promises Very Necessary for Each Christian to Trust in God and to Aid the Neighbor* ('1525 Turin Edition'), trans. Blair Reynolds (Bristol, IN: Wyndam Hall Press, 1985). A reliable translation with a very brief

edition is represented in this edition in square brackets in the text – for example: [B iii]. These printers' marks are only on the recto pages of the original. However, because the Arthur Hofer edition of the so-called 1525 text is the most readily available in modern libraries (and has very helpful notes), I have also added that pagination – for example: [60]. Lettered foliation with a Roman numeral refers to the 1534 De Vingle edition and an Arabic numeral refers to the pagination of the Hofer 1980 reprinting of the du Bois edition.

A note on the translation itself. Clearly, Farel intended this work as a popular defence of the budding French speaking Reformation movement and pointedly did not address himself to Latin speaking academics. As such, the original style and rhetoric are close to that of an oral delivery.[80] In the present translation, the often obtuse sentences of the original have been smoothed out for clarity and readability. Farel's written French is less carefully structured than that of Calvin. In the originals Calvin's is much more accessible and readable than Farel's.[81] Any necessary clarification of Farel's French usage is made in the notes.

Biblical references in the original edition are reproduced in the notes – I have not added more references to biblical passages that might be referred to. I have, however, added several annotations to persons, terms or events which would have been clear to the reader in 1534, but are not so clear to the modern reader. A full list of works written by Farel or by his contemporaries and employed for this translation can be found in the bibliography at the end of this work.

For comparison I have made reference to significant additions to the text in the 1542 edition. The 1542 edition has a great deal more material than this earlier edition, but much is further explanation of theological principles found already in the 1534 edition. Yet, on several occasions, Farel has added a significant discussion of theology not treated in that earlier edition – these are referred to in the notes.

---

introduction has more recently been published in: *Reformed Confessions of the 16th and 17th Centuries in English Translation*, Vol. 1, trans. and ed. James T. Dennison, Jr. (Grand Rapids: Reformation Heritage Books, 2008), pp. 51–111.

[80]   See notes by Mary McKinley on her edition and translation of Marie Dentière, *Epistle to Marguerite de Navarre and Preface to a Sermon by John Calvin* (Chicago: University of Chicago Press, 2004), pp. 37ff.

[81]   See Francis Higman, *The Style of John Calvin in his French Polemical Treatises* (Oxford: Oxford University Press, 1967), esp. pp. 171–2; Higman, *Lire et Découvrir*, pp. 337–51.

CHAPTER 3

Farel's Upward Spirituality: Leading in Prayer (1524)

Theodore Van Raalte

Introduction

'Prayer was the element in which [Farel] lived'. Such was the observation of the nineteenth century German historian of the Reformation, Melchior Kirchhofer.[1] If this is true – and this author thinks it is – the reappraisal of Guillaume Farel's role in early French Reform must study his pastoral spirituality, in terms both of what he advocated and practised. The next two chapters will examine some key early writings of Farel to argue that he makes spirituality an essential component of the reform, even front and centre (especially in its upward movement where the believer lives toward and communes with God). Mainly because of the nature of the sources, this study concerns itself more with intellectual than social history; thus our focus will fall more on what Farel advocated than what he practised. However, given the nature of sources on prayer – especially published prayers – it is unlikely that there was any great discrepancy between norm and practice, since the advocated action was being carried out in the very act of advocating it.

A word about terms is in order. Using *spirituality* for Farel might seem anachronistic, given that in his time *spiritualité* still largely referred to ecclesiastical jurisdiction (the goods under control of the Church) in contrast to the temporal realm. The semantic domain of our term *spirituality* was probably closer to their *piété*, which had come into use via Gerson and then Calvin, together with *coeur* and *intérieur*.[2] *Dévotion* also had an important place, for instance, with the *devotio moderna*, and certainly

---

[1] Melchior Kirchhofer, *Life of William Farel: The Swiss Reformer* (London: Religious Tract Society, 1837), p. 281. See also Melchior Kirchhofer, *Das Leben Wilhelm Farels*, 2 vols (Zurich: Drell, 1831–33), Vol. 2, p. 169.

[2] See, for example, Jean-François Cottier, '*Cum Deo colloqui*: les *Precationes novae* d'Érasme et le latin de la dévotion privée', in *La prière en latin, de l'Antiquité au XVIᵉ siècle: formes, évolutions, significations*, ed. Jean-François Cottier (Turnhout: Brepols, 2006), pp. 473–4. He states that their *pietas* is what we today would call spirituality.

occurs in Farel's writings.[3] Thus, while 'devotion' or 'piety' might seem to
fit Farel best, the semantic domain of the former has narrowed while the
latter has suffered pejorative connotations since late nineteenth century
historiography. This may be why spirituality has become ensconced in the
literature as a broad descriptive term for personal and corporate religious
practices, and teachings about these practices. Spirituality may be thought
of as one's attachment to the things of the spirit – although for Farel this
would first of all be of the Spirit – in contrast to one's attachment to
material and corporeal things. Few if any people in the sixteenth century
would have recognized the spirituality of surfing, knitting, eating, or aging
– not because everyone thought such activities had nothing to do with
faith (see 1 Cor. 10:31), but because spirituality or piety was specifically
religious in the personal and corporate senses. It was that realm of life which
was especially open to the Holy Spirit and was understood particularly
to proceed from the Spirit's regenerating work. At times we will employ
the term 'piety' for Farel, but usually stick to the wider umbrella term
'spirituality'.

The following sections of this chapter will first justify this study of
Farel's spirituality, then sketch the late medieval background, and then
move through some three writings of Farel from 1524 which all address
the topic of prayer, either by teaching about prayer or by modelling it.

State of the question

The argument for the present study of Farel's spirituality appeals first of
all to the need to get the story right. Various one-sided generalizations
of Farel's character have left us with the caricatures noted at the outset
of this book, all of which ignore the pastoral, sensitive, empathic, deeply
religious side of Farel. In the case of Farel's contemporary Theodore
Beza, Scott Manetsch defends his study of Beza's *Household Prayers* by
pointing out, 'the need to reassess the common portrayal of the reformer's
theology and theological method as unduly speculative and rationalistic'.
Manetsch adds:

> At least in these prayers, we discover a profoundly experiential and pastoral
> side to his theology, a concern to bring the truth of God's word to people
> beginning a new day, eating at table, suffering illness, preparing to die. Here
> we find theology that is intended not only to instruct, but also to comfort
> and edify. The practical devotional quality of the *Household Prayers* should

---

[3]   In addition to period dictionaries, see Sister Lucy Tinsley, *The French Expressions for
Spirituality and Devotion: A Semantic Study* (Washington, D.C.: The Catholic University of
America Press, 1953), pp. 58–71, 136–9, 151–3, 289–90.

cause scholars to pause before they dismiss Theodore Beza's theology as being merely 'metaphysical' or 'scholastic'.[4]

Something similar may be said of Farel, although the caricature in question is different than Beza's. In order to aim for the requisite level of detail in our historical knowledge of the period, Farel's spirituality deserves much more attention.

In line with this, most of the following study examines works of Farel that predate Calvin's appearance. In this respect, especially in terms of the historiography of the Geneva Reformation, this study takes its place among those which seek to put Calvin back into his own historical context as a second-generation Reformer, and one among many. French Protestant piety may owe as much to Farel as to Calvin, if we heed Francis Higman's words about Farel's *Le Pater Noster*, which he stated, 'represent[s] well the profound spirituality and burning conviction of Guillaume Farel, traits which, thanks to this large dissemination [of *Le Pater Noster*], have strongly marked the piety and the language of the church in the French language'.[5] It is my contention that Farel's piety warrants a place alongside studies of the spirituality of Gerson, Luther and Calvin, as well as Anabaptist and *Devotio Moderna* spirituality.[6]

Questions of spirituality loom large when Reformation historians ask just *why* people adopted evangelical views. What were the decisive factors? Both Andrew Pettegree and Philip Benedict have devoted extensive attention to this question in the French context. Pettegree masterfully outlined the role of preaching, singing, printing and even drama, particularly by noting the sheer volume of printed works, the pervasive practice of Psalm-singing and the frequent preaching.[7] The French Vernacular Book Project, which Pettegree spearheaded, has collated the resources needed

---

[4]   Scott M. Manetsch, 'A Mystery Solved? Maister Beza's Household Prayers', *Bibliothèque d'Humanisme et Renaissance* Vol. 65, No. 2 (2003), pp. 287–8.

[5]   Guillaume Farel, *Le Pater Noster et le Credo en françoys (publié d'après l'exemplaire unique nouvellement retrouvé par Francis Higman)*, (Geneva: Librairie Droz, 1982), p. 26. All translations are my own, unless otherwise specified.

[6]   See the approximately 150 volumes in the *Classics of Western Spirituality* series by Paulist Press. Brian Patrick McGuire, ed. and trans., *Jean Gerson's Early Works* (New York: Paulist Press, 1998); Philip D. W. and Peter D. S. Krey, eds. and trans. *Luther's Spirituality* (New York: Paulist Press, 2007); John Calvin, *Writings on Pastoral Piety*, ed. and trans. Elsie Anne McKee (New York: Paulist Press, 2001); Daniel Liechty, ed. and trans. *Early Anabaptist Spirituality: Selected Writings* (New York: Paulist Press, 1998); John van Engen, ed., *Devotio Moderna: Basic Writings* (New York: Paulist Press, 1988).

[7]   Andrew Pettegree, *Reformation and the Culture of Persuasion* (Cambridge: Cambridge University Press, 2005).

for a major advance in answering this question.[8] Gilmont and Higman have also devoted extensive study to the history of the book in French Protestantism.[9] Benedict underlines the need for all this fine bibliographic study to generate renewed attention to the actual doctrines that were being printed, preached, and prayed especially during the most explosive periods of evangelical growth.[10] In his view, the following six areas of evangelical teaching which historians have already highlighted seem to be the most promising for further study of questions of persuasion and conversion:

1. Relief from guilt and fear was available in Reformed teachings, especially via predestination (Crouzet).
2. There was a freshness to worship 'in spirit and in truth' which avoided holy materiality (Eire).
3. The Reformed doctrine of the Lord's Supper must have appealed to many (Elwood).
4. The Reform movement worked in the conquest of poverty by redirecting Church benefices to the poor (Heller).
5. Late medieval cities desired a more demanding moral code, yet wanted to be liberated from the confessional (Ozment).
6. Anticlericalism was rampant (Goertz).[11]

---

[8]   Andrew Pettegree, Malcolm Walsby and Alexander Wilkinson, eds., *French Vernacular Books: Books Published in The French Language Before 1601* (Leiden: Brill, 2007); See also Andrew Pettegree, *The French Book and the European Book World* (Leiden: Brill, 2007).

[9]   Jean-François Gilmont, *John Calvin and the Printed Book*, trans. Karin Maag (Kirksville, MO: Truman State University Press, 2005); Jean-François Gilmont, *Le livre réformé au XVIe siècle* ([Paris]: Bibliothèque nationale de France, 2005); Jean-François Gilmont, *The Reformation and the Book*, trans. Karin Maag (Aldershot: Ashgate, 1998); Jean-François Gilmont and William Kemp, eds, *Le Livre évangélique en français avant Calvin* (Turnhout: Brepols, 2004); Francis M. Higman, *Piety and the People: Religious Printing in French, 1511–1551* (Aldershot: Scolar Press, 1996).

[10]   Sustained academic study on the role of prayer in the Reformation is hard to find. Even studies of liturgy say little about it. For example, Mark Greengrass's fine essay in the *Cambridge History of Christianity* discusses fasting, feast days, pilgrimages, images, iconoclasm, the cult of saints and music, but says nothing about prayer. Mark Greengrass, 'The Theology and Liturgy of Reformed Christianity', *The Cambridge History of Christianity*, Vol. 6, *Reformation and Expansion 1500–1600*, ed. R. Po–Chia Hsia, (Cambridge: Cambridge University Press, 2007), pp. 104–24, 623–7.

[11]   Philip Benedict, 'Propaganda, Print, and Persuasion in the French Reformation: A Review Article', *Bibliothèque d'humanisme et renaissance* 69, No. 2 (2007), pp. 462–5. Benedict writes, '[M]ore work needs to be done on the contents of songs and sermons to get away from the excessive focus on printed books as vectors of the French Reformation' (p. 471).

Interestingly, these six pointers for future study all speak to the topic of spirituality – both upward and outward – suggesting that a study of prayer and other aspects of spirituality is precisely the kind of thing that will advance the state of the question around conversion and persuasion. Not only will this topic add to the several topics that Pettegree studied in *Reformation and the Culture of Persuasion* (he did not write about prayer or prayer books), but it will also provide material towards answering the questions Benedict has raised. We argue that there are few better figures to advance the state of this question than Farel.

Studying Farel also pays heed to Amy Nelson Burnett's remarks about the parish clergy having been largely neglected in the spate of recent sociological studies of the Reformation which have focused on ritual and popular religious practice. She points to the vital role these men played in both theology and spirituality, calling the parish pastors, 'the crucial link in teaching the Reformation'.[12]

Presently, no monograph studies of Farel's spirituality exist. One dissertation examined Farel's advocacy of prayer, but unfortunately the author had no access to Farel's most important work on prayer, *Le Pater Noster et le Credo*.[13] Another looked at his liturgical forms, but based its most important conclusions about Farel's contribution to early Reformed liturgy on dating since proved faulty.[14] Other articles and essays have examined one or another aspect of Farel's spirituality, such as his rhetoric in preaching and praying,[15] his published prayers for persecuted evangelicals,[16] his missionary zeal,[17] his desire for preaching and printing

---

[12]   Amy Nelson Burnett, *Teaching the Reformation: Ministers and Their Message in Basel, 1529–1629* (Oxford: Oxford University Press, 2006), p. 5.

[13]   Robert G. Hower, 'William Farel: Theologian of the Common Man, and the Genesis of Protestant Prayer' (Westminster Theological Seminary, Ph.D. thesis, 1983). Besides lacking study of Higman's 1982 critical edition of *Le Pater Noster* (which was announced as discovered at the 1980 *Colloque Guillaume Farel*). Hower's elucidation of the continuities and discontinuities from the late medieval era to Farel also lacks detail.

[14]   Andre Emile Kaltenrieder, 'The Liturgies of Guillaume Farel, Their Meaning and Relevance' (Ph.D. diss., Rhodes University, 1981). Kaltenrieder unfortunately accepted the dating of the copy of *Summaire* alleged to be printed in Turin in 1525 and on this basis dated Farel's French liturgies earlier than the German liturgies of Berne, suggesting a reverse influence. However, his study of the contents of the forms and his alertness for Farel's late medieval antecedents is commendable.

[15]   Michel Peronnet, 'Images de Guillaume Farel pendant la Dispute de Lausanne', *La Dispute de Lausanne 1536: La theologie réformée après Zwingli et avant Calvin* (Lausanne: Presses Centrales Lausanne S.A., 1988), pp. 133–41.

[16]   Christoph Burger, 'Farels Frömmigkeit', *Actes du Colloque Guillaume Farel* (Geneva: Revue de theologie et de philosophie, 1983), Vol. 1, pp. 149–60.

[17]   Louis-Ed. Roulet, 'Farel, agent bernois? (1528–1536)', *Actes du Colloque Guillaume Farel* (Geneva: Revue de theologie et de philosophie, 1983), pp. 99–106.

in the vernacular,[18] and, of course, his paraphrase of the Lord's Prayer and the Apostles' Creed in the form of a prayer.[19] Given that several of Farel's works were dedicated to prayer – indeed, were published prayers as such – and given that he was known by his contemporaries for his lofty praying, no one can question that this aspect of Farel and his reforming work rates further careful study.[20] Although this chapter and the next study several important prayers Farel published, it would no doubt be profitable to further this study in another publication by a close reading of his *Tressaincte oraison* which he published later in his career, in 1541, of which only one copy exists today.[21]

Late-medieval spirituality

Although making the case for attention to Farel's spirituality is not difficult, assessing continuities and discontinuities in Farel's conversation with late-medieval spirituality raises challenging questions for research. We need to determine, for instance, whether paraphrasing prayer books similar to his own preceded him. How original was he? Similarly, did the practice of late-medieval prayer regularly include freely composed prayers on the part of the laity? In connection with this, was Farel actually advocating free prayers? Do we encounter a development in this regard? How important

---

[18]   Francis M. Higman, 'Farel, Calvin, et Olivétan, sources de la spiritualité gallicane', *Actes du Colloque Guillaume Farel* (Geneva: Revue de theologie et de philosophie, 1983), pp. 45–61.

[19]   Francis M. Higman, 'Theology for the Layman in the French Reformation 1520–1550', *The Library* Sixth series, Volume IX, No. 2 (June 1987), pp. 105–27.

[20]   Already in the sixteenth century his contemporary Beza spoke of Farel's 'most fervent prayers' which could not be heard 'without feeling almost as though [one] was being carried up to heaven'. Theodore Beza, *The Life of John Calvin*, trans. Henry Beveridge (Carlisle, PA: Banner of Truth Trust, 1982), p. 23. Sayous quotes another Beza edition, *et ses prières étaient si ardentes*. André Sayous, *Études littéraires sur les écrivains français de la Reformation* (Paris: Gratiot, 1854), p. 38. For biographies of Calvin – there were variations of Beza's account already in the sixteenth century – see Irena D. Backus, *Life Writing in Reformation Europe: Lives of Reformers by Friends, Disciples and Foes* (Aldershot: Ashgate, 2008), pp. 125–227.

[21]   In 1541 Farel published a new prayer based on the Lord's Prayer and designed to teach true Christians how to pray, 'made in a manner to stimulate the understanding of the believers to pray with great affection'. Its title was, '*La très saincte oraison que Nostre Seigneur a baillée à ses Apôtres, les enseignant comment ils et tous vrais Chrétiens doibent prier, avec un Recüeil d'aucuns passages de l'Ecriture, fait en manière pour éveiller l'entendement des Fideles à prier de plus grande affection, avec les Prieres et Oraisons dont on use à present en l'Eglise de Genève*'. The Universitäts Landesbibliothek in Halle possesses a copy. A second printing occurred in 1543. Both were by Jean Girard of Geneva. *Actes du Colloque Guillaume Farel*, Vol. 2, pp. 126–7.

to him was the precise wording of the Lord's Prayer? It will be obvious enough that Farel did not advocate prayers to saints, but how much does he emphasize intercessory prayer among the living, or perhaps the intercessory role of Christ as heavenly high priest? Also, if late-medieval spirituality was well-ordered, with regular prayers made at the tolling of the city bells, how did Farel envision the evangelical practice of prayer when the bells no longer tolled? Again, what was the relation of the new clergy to the people in terms of prayer? If all believers had the office of prayer, and if their prayers were just as efficacious as their pastors' prayers, what was the role of the pastor in praying for the people and leading prayer in worship? Finally, how did the changed approach to prayer affect the people? Was it harder to learn the new prayers? Did they pray more often or less often? Was the quality of their praying altered? Did they feel closer to God, more accepted by God? Did the 'new' ways make the faith more meaningful?

Firm answers to some of these questions are probably not possible for historians. Others will await the next chapter. But in order to get started, we need to make some sense of the state of affairs in late-medieval spirituality. Thankfully, a variety of authoritative sources all point in the same direction, namely to a remarkable shift in piety in the late medieval period.

Many of the perceived abuses and excesses which led to the call for reform were a late-medieval development. Kieckhefer summarizes:

> Perhaps the most significant development in late medieval Christianity was the rise of devotionalism. In the last centuries of the Middle Ages, devotions of all kinds flourished in unprecedented profusion: pilgrimages, veneration of relics, Marian devotions, meditations on the passion of the Christ, penitential exercises, and more. Development of the Rosary was essentially a late medieval phenomenon. The Stations of the Cross, which attained their modern form by the early sixteenth century, arose out of devotional practices of the late Middle Ages. Eucharistic devotions, often connected with the feast of Corpus Christi, likewise stem from this age. The image of the Sacred Heart, in literary and artistic manifestation, can be traced to the last centuries before the Reformation. Devotional literature proliferated even before the invention of printing, and all the more afterward.[22]

Other authors confirm these generalizations. For example, the first known instance of the elevation of the host was around 1200 in the diocese of Paris. The word 'transubstantiated' was first made official in 1215 at the

---

[22]   Richard Kieckhefer, 'Major Currents in Late Medieval Devotion', in *Christian Spirituality: High Middle Ages and Reformation*, ed. Jill Raitt (New York: Crossroad, 1987), p. 75.

Fourth Lateran Council. Circa 1246 the Corpus Christi celebration began. By the end of the thirteenth century indulgences were being granted for veneration of the host.[23] Soon afterward the appearance of the body of Christ on the crucifix became more graphic and bloody, 'The feast of Corpus Christi grew more elaborate and, during the terrible Black Death, processions wound through the streets of towns and villages with the Eucharist carried in a golden monstrance accompanied by incense and the ringing of bells'.[24] Vandenbroucke states that mystery plays on the passion proliferated and indulgenced prayer increased.[25] Devotion to some 25,000 saints has been documented. Alexander of Hales first defines the *thesaurus meritorum*, a treasury of the accumulated merits of Christ and the saints which can pay for the sins of the living. The saints are thus to be adored, for they can function as mediators.[26] The first known instance of Mary as co-redemptrix arises from a fifteenth century hymn.[27] Vandenbroucke, a Benedictine scholar, views the divorce of lay piety from clerical – priests said their own prayers at mass while the people quietly recited others – as one of the chief culprits for the emotionalism, superstition, individualism, affectivism, sentimentality and pietism with which he charges his own tradition.[28] Holmes entitles a section of his survey 'The Fifteenth-Century Demise' of prayer.[29] This is not to say that no lay education or preaching took place, nor that attention to prayer was lacking (actually, prayer books proliferated at this time), nor that late medieval practices were monolithic.[30] Indeed, there was much hope for a reform from within the

---

[23]   Kieckhefer, *Major Currents in Late Medieval Devotion*, p. 97.

[24]   Jill Raitt, 'European Reformations of Christian Spirituality (1450–1700)', in *The Blackwell Companion to Christian Spirituality*, ed. Arthur Holder (Malden, MA: Blackwell, 2005), pp. 123–4.

[25]   François Vandenbroucke, 'Lay Spirituality from the Fourteenth to the Sixteenth Century', in *The Spirituality of the Middle Ages*, eds. Jean LeClercq, François Vandenbroucke and Louis Bouyer (London: Burn & Oates, 1968), pp. 486, 489–91, 497.

[26]   Carl A. Volz, *The Medieval Church: From the Dawn of the Middle Ages to the Eve of the Reformation* (Nashville, TN: Abingdon Press, 1997), p. 158.

[27]   Vandenbroucke, 'Lay Spirituality', p. 494.

[28]   Vandenbroucke, 'Lay Spirituality', pp. 495–7. Vandenbroucke speaks of a superstitious fear of Satan and suggests that the Inquisition arose in part to quell witchcraft and devil worship (pp. 486–7).

[29]   Urban T. Holmes III, *A History of Christian Spirituality: An Analytical Introduction* (New York: Seabury Press, 1980 [2nd ed. Morehouse Publishing, 2002]), pp. 83–8.

[30]   Kieckhefer, *Major Currents in Late Medieval Devotion*, pp. 77–8; Volz, *The Medieval Church*, pp. 228–9; Vandenbroucke, 'Lay Spirituality', p. 492; Irena Backus, 'The Apocalypse and Prayers of the Saints', in *Oratio: das Gebet in patristischer und reformatorischer Sicht*, eds Emidio Campi, Leif Grane, and Adolf Martin Ritter (Göttingen: Vandenhoek & Ruprecht, 1999), p. 174.

Church.[31] Even though recent scholars have justly disputed certain of the above generalizations, there is little doubt that they conform to the general view Farel had of the spiritual situation in which he was raised. We will explore further details regarding the movement from late-medieval to early modern spirituality as the following analyses warrant it.

We do well to avoid the mistake of reading the rhetoric of some of the early humanist-influenced Reformers against scholastic theology and superstitious practices as though they were thereby characterizing the entire Middle Ages prior to them, or – if they were so doing – as though they were correct. It would seem that the excessive rhetoric of some of the humanists of the early modern era, where it fits the facts, applies mainly to the late-medieval period.[32]

Farel's dissatisfaction with established Church doctrine and practice began under Jacques Lefèvre d'Etaples, who led the group of reform-minded humanists at Meaux. After some seven or eight years amongst this group, Farel encountered the limits of 'reform from within' when a disciplinary order from Bishop Guillaume Briçonnet came down. Farel decided that, for him, reform would have to take a more radical route. He journeyed to Basel where Johannes Oecolampadius was preaching reform.

The polemical context of prayer: Disputation of Basel (March 1524)

Attempting to promote reform, Farel gained government approval for a public disputation in Basel and posted 13 theses in Latin to be argued on 3 March 1524.[33] Interestingly, as a result of disagreement between the university and the bishop who opposed Farel, and the city magistrates who

---

[31]   'Reform' was widely discussed positively within the Catholic Church in France during the 1520s, and heresy was just one among the many 'abuses' to be eradicated. See David Nicholls, 'Heresy and Protestantism, 1520–1542: questions of perception and communication', *French History* Vol. 10, No.2 (1996), p. 190.

[32]   See Charles B. Schmitt, 'Aristotle as a Cuttlefish: The Origin and Development of a Renaissance Image', *The Aristotelian Tradition and Renaissance Universities* (London: Variorum, 1984), pp. 60–72; James H. Overfield, *Humanism and Scholasticism in Late Medieval Germany* (Princeton: Princeton University Press, 1985); Overfield, 'Scholastic Opposition to Humanism in Pre-Reformation Germany', *Viator* 7 (1976), pp. 391–420; Erika Rummel, 'Et cum theologo bella poeta gerit: The Conflict between Humanists and Scholastics Revisited', *Sixteenth Century Journal* Vol. 23, No.4 (1992), pp. 713–26; David V. N. Bagchi, 'Sic et Non: Luther and Scholasticism', in *Protestant Scholasticism*, eds. Carl R. Trueman and R. Scott Clark (Carlisle, Cumbria: Paternoster, 1999), pp. 3–15; John Van Engen, *Sisters and Brothers of the Common Life* (Philadelphia: University of Pennsylvania Press, 2008), p. 8.

[33]   This work, and Farel's satirical *'Determinatio Facultatis Theologiae Parisiensis'* (Basel, 1524) are his only Latin works. Otherwise he published in French.

had more interest in reform, the city government ended up ordering the dispute to take place, and further, that all citizens – especially ecclesiastics – must attend.[34]

The fourth thesis concerns us here. Farel argued,

> Long-winded prayers, (*verbosiores preces*) which are against the command of Christ and not according to Christian patterns, cannot be prayed or instituted without danger. Thus, it will be better to pay out to the poor whatever is offered in these matters and not to contribute to the funding of so many evils.[35]

Unfortunately, no record of the disputation's proceedings is known, but judging by the reference to things given for the praying of these prayers and the possible benefits for the poor, it appears that Farel has in view memorial masses endowed by the laity (individuals or corporations), to be carried out by the priests, that is, prayers for the dead.[36] These endowments were called chantries, and the masses performed were low masses performed by chantry priests. The literature terms them variously as funerary, requiem or memorial masses.

Late-medieval rise in chantries

Thomas Lambert relates the rapid rise in the number of chantries in nearby Geneva in the fifteenth and early sixteenth centuries, both those which simply paid a priest to perform extra masses, and those which resulted in the erection of dedicated altars and even new buildings or attachments to the existing cathedral. By 1516–18 the diocese around the city of Geneva counted some 1435 endowed chantries. The cathedral of St. Pierre itself

---

[34]   For a French translation of the original decree, see Aimé–Louis Herminjard, *Correspondance des Reformateurs* (Geneva: H. George, 1866), Vol. 1, pp. 195–8. See also K. R. Hagenbach, *History of the Reformation in Germany and Switzerland Chiefly*, trans. Evelina Moore, (Edinburgh: T&T Clark, 1878), p. 331; and *Guillaume Farel: Biographie Nouvelle*, p. 123. On the strategic importance of religious disputations in the nearby Pays de Vaud, see Michael Bruening, *Calvinism's First Battleground: Conflict and Reform in the Pays de Vaud, 1528–1559* (Dordrecht: Springer, 2005), pp. 137–141.

[35]   'Quae *contra praeceptum sunt Christi verbosiores preces, et non secundum Christianam formam regulatae sine perculo orari non possunt, nec institui: ut praestiterit quae in haec conferuntur pauperibus erogari, et non tantorum fomenta malorum fovere ...*' Herminjard, *Correspondance des Reformateurs*, Vol. 1, p. 194. A photocopy of the 20x33 cm. placard, reduced in size, can be viewed as plate 1–1 at the end of the *Actes du Colloque Guillaume Farel*, Tome II.

[36]   Indeed, Kirchhofer translates this part of the thesis rather freely, as follows: 'It is better to give to the poor the money which is paid for prayers on behalf of the dead'. Kirchhofer, *Life of William Farel*, p. 18. See also Kirchhofer, *Das Leben Wilhelm Farels*, Vol. 1, p. 21.

housed 100 chantries by 1536, in addition to its 23 altars.[37] Geneva was not unique in this regard.[38] Since one of the legal requirements for founding a chantry stipulated that sufficient funds had to be set aside for both its institution and maintenance, Farel could argue that this practice denied the poor much of what they might have received. In fact, Farel argued exactly that five years later in his *Summaire*, stating, 'By the mass the poor, the widows, and orphans are destroyed. For by it the Church of the Pope gains all the goods of the world'.[39] Another 16 years later, in 1545, he wrote a prayer for confessing sins and included, 'What a great number of foundations! And all this is done from the substance of the poor widows, orphans, and the blood of the poor people! All this cries out for and demands vengeance upon us'.[40]

The idea that the poor were being robbed because of the multiplication of chantries was, of course, not unique to Farel. Speetjens traces the early sixteenth century shift from the predominance of bequeathing masses said for one's soul after death (memorial services/chantries) to bequeathing the money to the poor, and notes places such as Leiden where this change even preceded the Reformation.[41] Other authors in the same volume examine this shift in England.[42] For the most part it was a shift that coincided with and was driven by Reformation currents, since one no longer needed to concern oneself with reducing time in purgatory, nor was it necessary to 'buy' the prayers of others, as it were, by using one's riches to bequeath more abundant and more elaborate chantries for one soul.

---

[37] Thomas A. Lambert, 'Preaching, Praying and Policing the Reform in Sixteenth-Century Geneva' (Ph. D. diss., University of Wisconsin–Madison, 1980), pp. 77–8, 90–92. As an example of the excesses of late-medieval piety, Lambert relates that when a large number of funerary masses were commissioned, one priest might rush the altar to perform his mass before the other was finished, lest he lose his mass fee (p. 92).

[38] 'All types of memorial foundations had been gaining popularity during the last decades of the fifteenth century, and slowly started to decline after 1510, and fell rapidly from 1520 onwards'. Annemarie Speetjens, 'Medieval Transformations of Piety in the Low Countries', in *Pieties in Transitio*, eds. Robert Lutton and Elisabeth Salter (Aldershot: Ashgate, 2007), p. 124.

[39] *Summaire*, Fol. D i (p. 118).

[40] Guillaume Farel, *Forme d'oraison pour demander a Dieu la saincte predication de l'Evangile* ... (Geneva: Jehan Girard, 1545), p. 67. This prayer will be examined in Chapter 4.

[41] Speetjens, *Medieval Transformations of Piety*, pp. 124–6.

[42] For example, Sheila Sweetinburgh, 'The Poor, Hospitals, and Charity in Sixteenth-century Canterbury', pp. 59–73.

The rosary and 'muttering'

The expression *verbosiores preces* literally means 'more abundantly-worded prayers' but one must not think that Farel is opposing long prayers as such. He himself was quite capable of lengthier prayers, as his paraphrase of the Lord's Prayer demonstrates. The prayers of many words must refer to the multiple repetitions of short prayers said in all the mass celebrations, prayers which, in Farel's estimation, were usually repeated mindlessly and thought to be beneficial by virtue of being spoken. Farel could argue against both clergy and laity practices in this regard. Although, '[t]he laity considered the clergy to be the specialists in prayer', yet the laity also undertook *verbosiores preces*.[43] In pre-Tridentine times, the priest performed the mass behind the rood screen while the worshippers in the nave were expected to repeat their short prayers quietly, that is to repeat the Lord's Prayer, *Kyrie Eleison*, Hail Mary, etc. while using their rosary beads to count the number. The priest used his *Breviary* for the official daily prayers, but the people used their *Book of Hours*.[44] After Geneva accepted the Reformation in 1536, and after the consistory was established in 1541, they had to deal with a great number of cases of 'muttering' (*barbotement*), that is, with those who attended the Reformed worship services but maintained the old practice of quietly saying their prayers in Latin, thus distracting others from the sermons.[45] The consistory's concern post-1541, and surely also Farel's concern here in 1524, has everything to do with the connection between the heart and the mouth. Abundantly-worded prayers were not spiritual if the heart was not engaged. As we shall see, Farel's style of praying and his admonitions regarding prayer will have everything to do with the moving of the affections toward the love of God and one's neighbour.

Thesis four of Farel's disputation at Basel thus combines an inner and an outer spirituality, the proper outer being love for the poor, and the inner, by implication, being that prayer in which the human spirit is activated by

---

[43]   Lambert, 'Preaching, Praying and Policing', pp. 95, 97–8.

[44]   Roger S. Wieck, 'Prayer for the People: *The Book of Hours*', in *A History of Prayer: The First to the Fifteenth Century*, ed. Roy Hammerling (Leiden: Brill, 2008), pp. 389–416. See also François Vandenbroucke, 'Lay Spirituality', pp. 497–8.

[45]   '*Barbotement*', translated as 'muttering' by Kingdon and others, is a negative word connoting the idea that such prayers 'carried no real meaning to those who said them, and were repeated in the superstitious hope that God will be pleased simply by hearing a prayer even if it could not be understood by the petitioner'. Robert Kingdon, 'Worship in Geneva Before and After the Reformation', in *Worship in Medieval and Early Modern Europe*, eds Karin Maag and John D. Witvliet (Notre Dame, IN: University of Notre Dame Press, 2004), pp. 49–50. For examples of consistory exhortations regarding muttering, see *ibid.*, pp. 42–5. cf. Lambert, 'Preaching, Praying and Policing', p. 102.

the divine Spirit to be lifted up to God. Ozment, who thinks of the 13 theses as preparatory for Farel's *Summaire*, rightly points out their very practical approach to living the Christian life, a life which Farel viewed as spiritual and in which prayer was key.[46]

The cultural context of prayer: Preface to the French New Testament (August 1524)

L'Epistre Chrestienne Tresutile was written to promote the reading of the scriptures in the vernacular, serving particularly as a promotion for Jacques Lefèvre's translation of the complete New Testament into French.[47] Addressed in its heading to 'all who are beginning to read Scripture', its more immediate addressee in the text of the letter is an otherwise unidentified *ma treschere seur*, acknowledged respectfully with *vous*. This literary device plays on the ambivalence of *vous*, permitting Farel to address both his sister in the faith and all who want to read scripture in French. It also allows the readers to look over the shoulder of a French noblewoman, as it were, while she reads a letter full of spiritual counsel about how to feed her faith with scripture and thus live out the evangel. It is the first known letter of its kind in French and was published anonymously.

Although Gilmont once listed its Farelian authorship as doubtful in his exhaustive bibliography of Farel,[48] Denommé and Kemp, with the collaboration of Gilmont, have since returned to the defense of Farel's authorship.[49] They argue on the basis of internal and external

---

[46]   Steven E. Ozment, *The Reformation in the Cities: The Appeal of Protestantism to Sixteenth-Century Germany and Switzerland* (New Haven, Conn.: Yale University Press, 1975), p. 68.

[47]   Lefèvre's complete New Testament in French appeared first in 1523, according to Higman, *Piety and the People*, p. 92. Lefèvre had first published the Gospels, writing his dedicatory exhortation on 8 June 1523, and then the rest of the New Testament with its dedicatory exhortation on 6 November 1523. The complete New Testament must have been assembled by the printers immediately, but it could not have been well-known until April 1524, when Lefèvre published a new and revised edition. See Eugene F. Rice, Jr., *The Prefatory Epistles of Jacques Lefèvre d'Etaples and Related Texts* (New York and London: Columbia University Press, 1972), pp. 449, 457. See also Henry Heller, 'Reform and Reformers at Meaux: 1518–1525' (Ph.D. diss., Cornell University, 1969), pp. 305–6.

[48]   See Gilmont for the previous scholarship (for example, Tricard, who subscribed to Farelian authorship). Jean-François Gilmont, 'L'Œuvre Imprimé de Guillaume Farel', *Actes du Colloque Guillaume Farel* (Geneva: 1983), p. 140.

[49]   Isabelle C. Denommé and William Kemp, avec la collaboration de Jean–François Gilmont, 'L'Épistre Chrestienne tresutile (c. 1524), Un écrit de Guillaume Farel? Présentation et edition', in *Le Livre Évangelique en Français avant Calvin*, eds Gilmont and Kemp (Turnhout: Brepols, 2004), pp. 43–69. After an introductory section on the question of authorship (pp. 43–51), Denommé and Kemp have published a critical edition of the letter

considerations, such as many parallels to Farel's other writings and several circumstances in Farel's life that match the letter.[50] The reason for Gilmont's categorization as 'doubtful' in 1983 hinged on his reconsideration of an invoice sent to Farel (dated 28 August 1524) from the bookseller Jean Vaugris of Basel wherein some 200 copies of Farel's prayer book, *Le Pater Noster*, were billed at a cheaper rate per copy than 50 copies of 'letters' in the same invoice.[51] Gilmont reasoned that these 'letters' could not refer to *L'Epistre Chrestienne* because their higher price indicates that they had to be longer than *Le Pater Noster*, whereas in fact *L'Epistre Chrestienne* is shorter. Thus, the invoice can no longer function to support Farelian authorship. This is the one argument that Denommé and Kemp do not overcome.

It seems to me that three responses can be advanced. First, prayer books were purposefully printed inexpensively so as to find wider distribution.[52] In the late-medieval period prayer books were popular in every sense – aimed at the people and heavily consumed by them. Second, the cost per letter had to be greater than the cost per prayer book since there were fewer letters printed, with the result that the setup cost had to be recovered in fewer items. Although it is true that the labour for typesetting was low, the number of copies in this case is extremely low, if we follow Higman's deduction that a 'modest average of 750 copies per edition' held for French religious printing in the period 1511 to 1551.[53] One should also consider the option that higher quality paper was used for the letters, especially if 'letters' does refer to *L'Epistre Chrestienne*, which was addressed secondarily to a woman of nobility.[54] Finally, contrary to Gilmont's claim in 1983, the two works are actually the same size, both at three quires of eight folios, the last quire ending in both cases at folio four verso![55] Besides this answer to Gilmont's reasoning, we can also point

---

(pp. 52–69). Although their conclusion on Farel's possible authorship speaks tentatively of trying '*d'apporter, sinon une réponse, du moins quelques esquisses de solution*' (p. 51), their actual arguments vouch quite strongly for Farel (pp. 44–7, 50).

[50]   Denommé and Kemp, *L'Épistre Chrestienne*, pp. 43–51

[51]   See Herminjard, *Correspondance des Reformateurs*, Vol. 1, p. 279. See also a letter from Anemand de Coct to Farel on 2 September 1524 which mentions the same 200 copies of 'Orationes' with 50 copies of 'Epistolis' (Vol. 1, p. 281).

[52]   See the editor's introduction to Luther's works on prayer. Martin Luther, *Devotional Writings II* (Vol. 43 of *Luther's Works*; ed. Helmut T. Lehmann, Philadelphia: Fortress Press, 1968), p. 7. See also Heller, *Reform and Reformers*, p. 69.

[53]   Francis M. Higman, *Piety and the People: Religious Printing in French: 1511–1551* (Aldershot: Ashgate, 1996), pp. 4, 22.

[54]   On the recipient of the letter see Denommé and Kemp, *L'Épistre Chrestienne*, pp. 47–8, and my discussion below.

[55]   Gilmont states that the letter was only 20 folios whereas the prayer book was about 30. The markings in the critical editions clearly shows otherwise, and the fonts are similar.

to further internal evidences favouring Farel, not noted by Denommé and Kemp. These include phrases common in the undisputed writings of Farel, such as, 'the good Jesus', 'poor souls', 'the sweet Jesus', 'the good God', 'this good Lord', 'his good Spirit', 'his great kindness', and the name 'Jesus' without any other titles such as Christ.[56] We therefore hold Farel to be author of *L'Epistre Chrestienne*.

Use of the vernacular

As early as the second page, Farel states his prayer for 'his very dear sister', that she might:

> come to the reading of the very dignified word of God, casting all your heart upon this good Lord by humble prayer made with the firm faith that he will give you his good Spirit, according to the unshakeable truth of his promise to us.

Here, in his concern for spirituality in the vernacular, Farel mentions in one breath both the word of God and prayer. His views reflect his changing cultural–religious context: the shift from Latin to the vernacular.[57] In Farel's view, just as God should be heard in the native tongue of the French, so they also should let God hear them in their native tongue. One needs to use the language of one's birth in order fully to involve the heart in religion – both for hearing and praying. Later Farel singles out the problem of the people (indeed, even many priests) not understanding the ecclesiastical ordinances because the priests are, 'saying everything in Latin of which the simple people understand nothing. This is contrary to the commandment of God who commands that those who pray or speak in the church should either be silent or speak things people understand'.[58]

Recent scholarship on late-medieval literacy mainly confirms Farel's observation. Some decades ago Thompson set out to debunk the common view that only the clergy read and wrote Latin; however, his study restricted itself mainly to the nobility, stating up front that, 'the illiteracy of the common people is not open to question'. He also concluded that many an ecclesiastic was indeed ignorant of Latin while many laypersons understood

---

Gilmont, *L'œuvre imprimé*, p. 140.

[56]   '*Au bon Jesus*', '*povres ames*', '*le doulx Jesus*', '*le bon dieu*', '*ce bon seigneur*', '*son bon esperit*', '*sa grande bonté*', all of which occur already on the first page of the letter (a2r [p. 54]), and are repeated variously throughout. Farel also frequently uses '*affin que*' and '*veu que*'. Lefèvre certainly spoke of the sweet Jesus and the good God. For a few examples, see Heller, *Reform and Reformers*, pp. 172, 308. See also Rice, *The Prefatory Epistles*, p. 450.

[57]   Nicole Bériou 'Conclusions', in *La prière en latin, de l'Antiquité au XVIᵉ siècle: formes, évolutions, significations*, ed. Cottier (Turnhout: Brepols, 2006), pp. 487–500.

[58]   Denommé and Kemp, *L'Epistre Chrestienne*, b7r (p. 64).

it.[59] More recently, Moulton's edited volume broadly demonstrates the movement from Latin to the vernacular. Here too the connection between wealth and literacy holds. Also, Protestant devotional practices correlate well with an increase in vernacular literacy.[60] Wieck thinks the average medieval person understood more than we usually grant, since French and Italian have many Latin cognates and since Psalms were used. People would become familiar with them over time, he argues. But one still wonders how many people understood the Latin liturgical readings apart from the tedious process of translation in their minds. Wieck's conclusions, however, are also qualified by speaking of most 'literate' people, which was, in fact, a minority.[61]

Erasmus had strongly critiqued using Latin in church liturgy already in 1522.[62] Practices, however, did not quickly change; although Karlstadt had already celebrated the mass in German in 1521 and Oecolampadius began publicly to read the New Testament in German in 1522,[63] Luther, Zwingli and Bucer waited until 1524–5 to conduct worship in the vernacular. It was one thing to offer translations of scripture in the vernacular as Lefèvre and Luther did; quite another to change what the worshippers experienced in the divine liturgy.

Farel's insistence on French for scripture and prayer thus stands at the fountainhead of French Protestant thought, and would fast become one of its motifs. All of Farel's writings would be in French, and Calvin would follow by strongly influencing the French language itself.[64]

Attracting the nobility

Remarkable for *L'Epistre Chrestienne*, however, is the fact that Farel appears to be writing to someone well-placed who, because educated, would have been able to use a Latin Bible. Without being able clearly to identify the recipient of this letter (Denommé and Kemp explore several possibilities, with Marguerite of Alençon as most likely), we nevertheless must appreciate that even in the case of those French persons who learned Latin as a second language, Farel insists on the French text as the foundation

---

[59]   James Westfall Thompson, *The Literacy of The Laity in The Middle Ages* (New York: Burt Franklin, 1960), p. 196.

[60]   Ian F. Moulton, ed., *Reading and Literacy in the Middle Ages and Renaissance* (Turnhout: Brepols, 2004), pp. xi, xiv.

[61]   Wieck, 'Prayer for the People', pp. 390–1.

[62]   Jean–François Courouau, 'La Réforme et les langues de France', *BSHPF* 154 (Oct–Dec 2008), p. 509.

[63]   *Guillaume Farel: Biographie Nouvelle*, p. 142, n. 3.

[64]   That is, all of Farel's writings save two from 1524.

for a much more robust spirituality.[65] Farel's references to his 'very dear sister' occur four times. His third reference – to my mind quite purposively, to connect with her noble birth – draws comparison to 'a prince so noble and so very excellent', namely, 'our Chief Jesus'. A page later Farel calls Jesus 'King' and 'Captain', and speaks of believers reigning with him, but here he sticks to the term 'chief' or 'head':

> [F]or I am certain that if you are a Christian woman – as truly you are – loving none but God, then Satan will greatly assault you'. [*But, he adds,*] 'My very dear sister, the word of God cannot lie. It prophesies to us: They persecuted me, and so they will you, for the disciple is not above the master [Mt 10:24, Jn 15:20]. Indeed, you (*vous*) will be persecuted and mocked within your house and outside it by all the world, and some will speak evil about you, for if a prince so noble and so very excellent as our Chief Jesus was mocked, rebuked and persecuted, so also will be his members.[66]

Interestingly, Farel later states that both he and she are among the so-called 'laity',[67] a statement which may help confirm the dating of the letter, since Farel appears to have taken on the office of administering the sacraments later that year.[68] Finally, although among the laity, he has somehow been in the habit of teaching her, 'And for this reason, remember for yourself the rule that I so frequently inculcated in you: Do only what the Lord God commands you; add nothing, subtract nothing'.[69] Although we do

---

[65]   Pertinent here is Thompson's statement that French and Flemish noblewomen were probably given enough Latin education 'to enable them to follow the services of the Church and understand the most frequently used psalms'. Thompson, *Literacy of the Laity*, p. 147.

[66]   'Car je suys certain que si estes Chrestienne, comme vrayement estes, n'aymant autre que dieu, que satan vous livera grands assaulx'. Denommé and Kemp, *L'Epistre Chrestienne*, b4r–b4v (p. 62). Scripture references were inserted by Denommé and Kemp (p. 53).

[67]   'Et par cecy est grandement à reprendre la bestialité des ennemys de Jesus, qui dissent que les simples gens et laiz, comme ilz nous appellant, ne devoient pas lire la saincte scripture ne traicter la saincte parole de dieu'. Denommé and Kemp, *L'Epistre Chrestienne*, b8v (p. 66).

[68]   Oecolampadius wrote to Zwingli on 21 November 1524, 'Excusat se Farellus, coactum se ad sacramentorum administrationem accessisse; proinde mihi satisfecit'. 'Farel finds justification in that he was forced to take up the administration of the sacraments. This suffices for me'. *Huldrici Zuinglii Opera*, eds, Melchior Schuler and Johannes Schulthess (Zurich: Friedrich Schulthes, 1830), Vol. 7, p. 369. See also the appendix of Farel's 1542 *Summaire*, translated below, where Farel claims the authority of the lawfully-ordained Oecolampadius. Farel also relied upon the local prince, Duke Ulrich of Montbéliard. See also *Guillaume Farel: Biographie Nouvelle*, pp. 132, 144; Kaltenrieder, *Liturgies of Guillaume Farel*, pp. 45–6.

[69]   Denommé and Kemp, *L'Epistre Chrestienne*, c3v (p. 68). Farel's exhortation matches the observations in Chapter 2 above about the contrast of divine and human wills as a theme in Farel's œuvre.

not know just who Farel was teaching and where, his statement about her enduring mockery 'within the house' may reflect personal knowledge of her circumstances.

Farel's letter to the readers of the Lefevre's New Testament highlights the concern that would remain widespread among the Reformers – namely, to attract the nobility to reform. When the more common readers of Farel's preface would realize that he was addressing one more well-placed than they – one whom he had taught frequently – they would gain the sense that the evangelical message was finding its way among the nobility, and then would be more likely to entertain the same. On the other end, by publishing the letter, Farel would bind this noblewoman more tightly to the evangelical cause by publicly asking her to pray for his progress in the gospel and by setting her up as a model – her anonymity notwithstanding. A decade later, Farel's summary of the Dispute of Rive in 1535 and the proceedings of the Dispute of Lausanne in 1536 would both attest to Farel's public prayers made in the presence of the magistrates. The dream of magisterial reform shaped the pattern of French and Swiss Reform from the beginning.

Right reading of law and Gospel

This letter is true to its stated goal in the title, namely to set forth summarily the goal ('*consummation*') of all scripture. We find no introduction to the Bible, no summary of biblical history; rather, we find a summary of the frame of mind necessary for an edifying reading of the New Testament. Read rightly, scripture ought to bring the reader near to God, and anyone *coram Deo* will become prayerful in attitude. This is precisely what gives the letter its spiritual tone. One might favourably compare the letter to something like a later Puritan tract on the role of law and gospel which teaches what it means to rest entirely in Jesus Christ for the overcoming of the conscience's fear of condemnation, yet clearly with an accompanying emphasis on the love of one's neighbour. In order to be made stronger in the faith, this is the kind of reading one must undertake, and it requires heartfelt prayer.

Farel's prayer early in the letter speaks of coming to the reading of scripture with one's heart cast upon Jesus in humble prayer for the Spirit. Hereby he ties the Spirit and word together, and specifies the engagement of the heart in both the reading of scripture and the uttering of prayer. He continues stating his prayer for both his female addressee and the wider readership – that out of his great kindness God would open His heavenly kingdom to them, illumine their hearts to make them new creatures who will live completely in Jesus Christ, loving none other but Him.[70] The words 'live', 'love', 'kindness', and the epithet 'new creature' are all very positive. But the struggle with sin is pictured as equally real. Later, as Farel reviews the gospel and the law in third-person language, he turns to the need for the Spirit and the struggle of the renewed sinner to love God. In this context the pastoral tone that pervades the letter heightens with rhetorical questions reminiscent of the Apostle Paul's struggle in Romans 7, where one's heart knows the law is spiritual, but one's 'flesh' discovers its inability to keep it.[71] A few pages later the letter takes on the voice of the gospel, directly addressing the readers:

> O poor thief, who wanted to disrobe the Deity and wanted to make himself God in his pride – poor, damned, and despairing, who in accordance with a just judgement are condemned to be cast away into the gallows of hell, who have a rope around your neck, that is, your will, flesh, and lusts which have dominion in you since you do not have the Spirit of God in you – the very merciful God sends you grace and pardon, desires that the sentence not be executed and that you not die but have life and be delivered from the hand of the devil of hell ... and so [God] receives you to be with him, not only as servant, but as son and heir, with the gentle Saviour Jesus, who has become your brother, and whom the Father by his infinite kindness and clemency ... gave for you.[72]

The believer is assured that she is now received by God, 'with the gentle Saviour Jesus' made her brother, and 'the priceless sweetness of the ever gentle Jesus' as her own by the promises of God, with the result that she may be filled with joy.[73] Throughout the letter one encounters a deeply pastoral tone, a concern that the readers should put their faith in Jesus and his merits, that the readers should have confidence in Jesus' conquering of the world. For such consolation and courage to form and to have their effect in the church, the praying and speaking must be conveyed in the vernacular.[74]

As we have seen, the topic of prayer was unavoidable in the cultural and pastoral context of this letter, and certainly was not avoided. The letter ends with Farel's request, 'I pray you, remember me in your prayers,

---

[70]   Denommé and Kemp, *L'Epistre Chrestienne*, a2v (pp. 54–5).

[71]   Denommé and Kemp, *L'Epistre Chrestienne*, a5r–a5v (pp. 56–7); also noted in their introduction (p. 50).

[72]   Denommé and Kemp, *L'Epistre Chrestienne*, a7r–a7v (p. 58). Whereas Farel uses 'vous' for his addressee(s), here he puts 'tu' in the mouth of the glorious gospel as it addresses the lowly sinner.

[73]   Denommé and Kemp, *L'Epistre Chrestienne*, a7r–b2r (pp. 58–60).

[74]   Denommé and Kemp, *L'Epistre Chrestienne*, b7r (p. 64).

in order that [I] may be able with dignity to make progress in the holy word of God, in the honour and glory of the very holy kindness of God. Amen'.[75]

The pedagogical context of prayer: Farel's prayer book (August 1524)

We turn now to Farel's most popular work, his explanation of the Lord's Prayer and the Apostle's Creed. Aside from the preface, the work proper was thought to have been lost for many years, until a copy was found by Francis Higman around 1980 in the National Library of Austria in Vienna. He published a critical edition in 1982. In 2008 William Kemp announced the discovery of a second copy – a more luxurious printing, purchased in 1536 by the bibliophilic son of Christopher Columbus and kept in the Colombine Library in Seville.[76]

In this work Farel extends his role as teacher. Whereas *L'Epistre Chrestienne* teaches one how to read scripture edifyingly, *Le Pater Noster et le Credo* teaches one how to become more fervent in the kind of prayer that nurtures the right attitude for edification. Farel's *Le Pater Noster* does so by being a model of prayer and pedagogy – showing, not just telling. The most remarkable feature of this work on prayer deserves to be stated upfront: It is written as a prayer, in direct address to God throughout. In fact, not only is this the case with the exposition of the Lord's Prayer, but also of the Apostles' Creed which follows. Both are periphrastically explained in the form of a prayer. Indeed, one must consider whether one of the indices of Farelian authorship is this penchant for direct address, something we already noticed in his *L'Epistre Chrestienne* ('O poor thief', etc.). Could it be that this matter of form, which has a dramatic effect on the content, is one of the important things that made this work of Farel's so popular?

Replacing the Book of Hours

The popularity of Farel's *Pater Noster* has been amply documented by Francis Higman in at least four scholarly articles, in addition to his introduction to the critical edition. After having undergone modifications, Farel's work was incorporated by others into *Le Livre de vraye et parfaicte oraison*, a devotional manual that received royal approval in France in

---

[75]   Denommé and Kemp, *L'Épistre Chrestienne*, c4v (p. 69).

[76]   Jean-François Gilmont and William Kemp, 'Wigand Koeln libraire a Genève (1516–1545), éditeur du *Pater Noster* De Guillaume Farel', *Bibliothèque d'humanisme et renaissance*, Vol. 70, No. 1 (2008), pp. 131–46.

1528 and even Sorbonne clearance in 1549, when certain phrases were omitted or toned down. It saw wide distribution among Roman Catholics and evangelicals alike, an interesting case of trans-confessional piety.[77] It may even have spawned the first traditional Roman Catholic response to the 'new genre'.[78] Higman traces some 3 printings of the preface, 15 of the exposition of the Lord's Prayer, and 28 of the Apostles' Creed.[79] Nicholls remarks that printers showed a preference for these little manuals of piety and instruction.[80] They were good money makers.

'These little manuals' were thus known to Farel. In fact, he entered a genre – albeit with his own nuances and distinctive contributions – which was well known in his time and held great potential for publishing a bestseller. Late-medieval and early renaissance prayer books have been studied by several authors and must detain us here before we describe Farel's prayer book in detail. This will give us some needed context.

'Large numbers of relatively cheap devotional books survive', states Elisabeth Salter.[81] Higman notes a 'long medieval tradition of devotional poetry and prose (for example, many of the works attributed to Gerson)'.[82] Wieck specifies, 'From the mid-thirteenth to the mid-sixteenth century, more copies of the *Book of Hours* were commissioned and produced, bought and sold, bequeathed and inherited, printed and reprinted than any other text, including the Bible'. It was a bestseller because of the laity's desire to imitate the clergy in praying, because of its frequently illuminated manuscripts (beautiful colour pictures to aid in meditation), and because of its link to the burgeoning cult of the Virgin.[83] Pertinent to Farel's context, we note that France by far led the way in producing these books and in beautifying them.[84] Wieck describes the *Book of Hours* as a prayer book containing the 'Hours of the Virgin' also known as the 'Office of the

---

[77]   Francis M. Higman, 'Histoire du livre et histoire de la Réforme', *BSHPF* 148 (2002), p. 848; cf. David Nicholls, *Heresy and Protestantism*, p. 201.

[78]   Francis M. Higman, 'Theology for the Layman in the French Reformation 1520–1550', *The Library* Sixth series, Vol. IX, No. 2 (June 1987), p. 112. Later in this chapter I will address the phrase 'new genre'.

[79]   Francis M. Higman, 'Luther et la piété de l'Église Gallicane: *Le Livre de vraye et parfaicte oraison*', *Revue d'histoire et de philosophie religieuses* 63 (1983), pp. 91–111. See also Higman's introduction to his critical edition of Farel's *Le Pater Noster*, p. 26.

[80]   David Nicholls, *Heresy and Protestantism*, p. 200.

[81]   Elisabeth Salter, ' "The Dayes Moralised": Reconstructing Devotional Reading, *c.* 1450–1560', in *Pieties in Transition: Religious Practices and Experiences, c. 1400–1640*, eds. Robert Lutton and Elisabeth Salter (Burlington, VT: Ashgate, 2007), p. 145.

[82]   Higman, 'Theology for the Layman', p. 109.

[83]   Roger S. Wieck, *Time Sanctified*: The Book of Hours *in Medieval Art and Life* (New York: Braziller, 1988), p. 27.

[84]   Wieck, *Time Sanctified*, p. 28.

Blessed Virgin Mary' and a sequence of prayers to Mary, preferably to be prayed hour by hour throughout the course of the day. These also typically contained the Penitential Psalms to help one resist the Seven Deadly Sins, and the Office of the Dead, prayed to reduce friends' time in purgatory.[85] Up to the thirteenth century these books usually contained the 150 Psalms but then people began to commission their prayer books without the 'cumbersome Psalter'. Thus was born the *Book of Hours* as we know it.

> By the late fourteenth century, the typical *Book of Hours* consisted of a calendar, Gospel lessons, hours of the Virgin, hours of the Cross, hours of the Holy Spirit, the two Marian prayers called the '*Obsecro te*' and the '*O intemerate*', the Penitential Psalms and Litany, the Office of the Dead, and a group of about a dozen suffrages; any number of accessory prayers complemented these essential texts.[86]

Vandenbroucke notes how these prayer books belonged to the popular spirituality of the late-medieval era, 'divorced as it had become from the Divine Office'.[87]

The early Reformers – Farel coming in only second to Luther – attempted to secure a more complete conversion of the masses also by replacing the *Book of Hours* with a Protestant alternative. Surveys of Reformation history rarely explore this reform of prayer in any detail, let alone its continuity with the late-medieval era. Erasmus's editors, for instance, complain of a 'collective amnesia' with respect to Erasmus's spiritual writings.[88] We will list a number of texts and individual studies to illustrate early Protestant attention to prayer, leaving further detail until after we have explored Farel's prayer book.

Although generalizations about late-medieval piety such as those above do hold, efforts to reform spirituality did pay close attention to piety at a popular level. Jean Gerson (1363–1429) for example, purposefully sought to reach a wider audience by using French for his promotion of a deeper interior (mystical), piety.[89] Coming closer to the sixteenth century, two popular preachers made their mark and wrote prayers: Gabriel

---

[85]   Wieck, 'Prayer for the People', p. 389.

[86]   Wieck, 'Prayer for the People', p. 390.

[87]   Vandenbroucke, 'Lay Spirituality', p. 492. Vandenbroucke goes on to describe the *Book of Hours* just as Wieck does.

[88]   *Collected Works of Erasmus*, Vol. 69 (Toronto: University of Toronto Press, 1992), pp. xi–xii.

[89]   *Jean Gerson: Early Works*, trans. and ed. Brian Patrick McGuire (New York: Paulist Press, 1998), pp. xiv–xv, 75. See also Daniel B. Hobbins, 'Gerson on Lay Devotion', in *A Companion to Jean Gerson*, ed. Brian Patrick McGuire (Leiden: Brill, 2006), pp. 41–78. Compare with Daniel Hobbins, *Authorship and Publicity before Print: Jean Gerson and the*

Biel (1420/5–95) made a Latin paraphrase of the Lord's Prayer,[90] while Girolamo Savonarola's (1452–98) exposition of Psalm 51 in the form of a prayer – written days before his execution in 1498 as his mangled arms and hands healed from torture – became a major bestseller, with translation into most European languages.[91] Luther would later publish editions of it. Between 1380 and 1560 the Societies of Modern Devout (*devotio moderna*) permeated especially the northern European world, where Thomas of Kempen's *The Imitation of Christ* became a bestseller. Biel belonged to the Modern Devout. These societies, although rejected as societies by the Reformers, nevertheless influenced their spirituality.[92] Erasmus, who was educated by the Brethren of the Common Life for ten years, was to be a key figure in the development of Protestant spirituality, even though he remained in the established Church.[93]

Luther's foray into the prayer book genre began in 1520, with his *Eine Kurze Form des Paterunsers*, incorporated into his *Betbüchlein* in 1522. In this work he included a German paraphrase of the Lord's Prayer, in order to provide a positive counter to the existing prayer books.[94] Here, by including explanations of the Apostles' Creed and Ten Commandments also, he set the standard for what would become the steady diet of Reform-minded teachers, in place of the complex catalogues of sins and the numerous hourly prayers of the existing prayer books. Like the late-medieval prayer books, Luther's became an inexpensive runaway bestseller, with numerous German editions in multiple printings and early Dutch and Italian translations, though none in French (except for Farel's use of Luther on the Creed, as we shall see).[95]

In 1523 the humanist Erasmus – the father of the biblical paraphrase genre[96] – also published an extended paraphrase of the Lord's Prayer,

---

Transformation of Late Medieval Learning (Philadelphia: University of Pennsylvania Press, 2009), pp. 148–50.

[90]   Translated into French in 1547–48 by Claude d'Espence. See Francis M. Higman, *Lire et Découvrir*, p. 100.

[91]   Girolamo Savonarola, *Prison Meditations on Psalms 51 and 31*, ed. and trans. John Patrick Donnelly (Milwaukee: Marquette University Press, 1994). See also *Selected Writings of Girolamo Savonarola*, trans. and ed. Anne Borelli and Maria Pastore Passaro (New Haven, CT: Yale University Press, 2006), pp. xvi–xviii, xxxi; Lauro Martines, *Fire in the City* (Oxford: Oxford University Press, 2006), pp. 94–100.

[92]   Van Engen, *Sisters and Brothers of the Common Life*, pp. 5–10, 315–20.

[93]   Van Engen, *Sisters and Brothers of the Common Life*, pp. 151, 319–20.

[94]   *D. Martin Luther's Werke* (Weimar: Nachfolger, 1897), Vol. 7, pp. 220–9. See also Helmut T. Lehman and Gustav Wiencke, eds, *Luther's Works*, Vol. 43, pp. 29–38.

[95]   *Luther's Werke*, Vol. 7, p. 195–8; *Luther's Works*, Vol. 43, pp. 7–8.

[96]   Irena D. Backus, 'Prière en latin au 16e siècle et son role dans les Eglises issues de la Réforme', *Archiv für Reformationsgeschichte* 93 (2002), p. 70.

intended to serve as a new kind of prayer book. Erasmus, however, stuck to Latin. He divided the work into seven parts for the seven days of the week.[97] In 1524, a few months after Farel's *Le Pater Noster*, Erasmus published, 'On Praying to God', a lengthy essay covering all the rubrics of prayer.[98]

In February 1524 Jacques Lefèvre, Farel's teacher, wrote *Vne epistre comment on doibt prier Dieu,* etc. This letter introduced seven Psalms in French translation with the argument that God intends for believers to pray in their own language. He quotes both Colossians 3:16 and First Corinthians 14:19 – the obvious connotation being that Latin prayers are improper for those who do not understand them.[99] The latter text, in particular, was to become commonplace among the Reformers in this discussion.

Farel's *Le Pater Noster et le Credo* was the first such work in French, printed in August 1524. After him many other Reformers would try their hand at providing prayers for the faithful. Many were built upon the Lord's Prayer; some were in the vernacular, others were not. The way to ensure a wider audience generally was to publish the prayer in Latin so that scholars in other places could readily translate it into their own languages.[100] One can readily appreciate, however, the more powerful appeal of a prayer originally composed in one's own tongue by an adept native speaker. Taking the various expositions chronologically, we may note Luther in 1520ff., Erasmus in 1523, Lefèvre in 1524, Farel in 1524, Hubmaier in 1526, Schlaffer in 1527, Brunfels in 1528, Schütz Zell in 1532 (published in 1558), Olivétan in 1533, Tyndale in 1535/6, Capito in 1536, Calvin in 1545, Vermigli in 1546, Viret in 1548, Melanchthon in 1559 and Beza in 1595. All of these authors have received some attention in recent scholarly literature.[101] These writings – and the list does not at all

---

[97]   See Erasmus, *Collected Works* Vol. 69 (*Spiritualia and Pastoralia*), pp. xi–xii. The prayers, with introductions, are found on pages 1–151. Their translated titles and dates are: *Prayer to Jesus, Son of the Virgin* (1499); *Paean in Honour of the Virgin Mother* (1499); *Prayer of Supplication to Mary, the Virgin Mother, in Time of Trouble* (1503); *The Lord's Prayer* (1523); *Liturgy of the Virgin Mother Venerated at Loreto* (1523); *Prayer to the Lord Jesus for Peace in the Church* (1532); and *Some New Prayers* (1535).

[98]   Erasmus, *Collected Works* Vol. 70 (Spiritualia and Pastoralia), pp. 141–230.

[99]   Eugene F. Rice, Jr., *The Prefatory Epistles of Jacques Lefèvre d'Etaples and Related Texts,* pp. 468–70. Both Lefèvre and Briçonnet were interested in developing lay piety. Henry Heller, 'Reform and Reformers at Meaux: 1518–1525', pp. 69, 208, 304.

[100]   Backus, *Prière en Latin au 16ᵉ siècle,* pp. 50, 70.

[101]   Backus studied Brunfels, Erasmus, Capito, Vermigli, Melanchthon and Calvin for their Latin prayers. See Backus, *Prière en Latin au 16ᵉ siècle,* pp. 43–71. On Brunfels, see also Marc Lienhard, 'Prier au 16e siècle: regards sur le Biblisch Bettbüchlin du Strasbourgeois Othon Brunfels', *Revue d'histoire et de philosophie religieuses* Vol. 66, No.1 (Jan–Mar 1986), pp. 43–55. Hubmaier and Schlaffer's prayers can be found in Leichty, ed., *Early Anabaptist*

claim to be exhaustive – show that prayer held the attention of Reformers throughout the sixteenth century. We turn, then, to investigate Farel's prayer book in more detail.

Farel's prayer book

In Farel's little manual, the exposition of the Lord's Prayer is, according to Higman, from Farel alone, whereas his praying through the Apostles' Creed 'has mostly exploited the exposition of Luther in the *Betbüchlein*'.[102] In his introduction to the critical edition, Higman gives the impression that Farel faithfully follows Luther's exposition of the Creed after having supplied his own introduction.[103] Indeed, the flow of the text follows Luther, and, of course, the structure of the Apostles' Creed. We do notice, however, writes Higman, several small changes which improve the thought (two examples are then supplied) and there are two additions which suggest some independent theological formulation on Farel's part.[104] Higman's appended notes single out seven places where Farel has made additions to

---

Spirituality, pp. 38–40, 109–10. Elsie McKee has analysed Katharina Schütz Zell's works on prayer. See 'Katharina Schütz Zell and the "Our Father"', in Emidio Campi, Leif Grane, and Adolf Martin Ritter, eds., *Oratio: das Gebet in patristischer und reformatorischer Sicht* (Göttingen: Vandenhoek & Ruprecht, 1999), pp. 239–47; and *Reforming Popular Piety in Sixteenth-Century Strasbourg: Katharina Schütz Zell and Her Hymnbook* (Princeton, NJ: Princeton Theological Seminary, 1994). For Tyndale, see Malcolm Yarnell, 'The First Evangelical Sinner's Prayer Published in English: William Tyndale's 'Here foloweth a treates of the pater noster'', *Southwestern Journal of Theology*, Vol. 47, No. 1 (Fall 2004), pp. 27–43. On Beza, see Manetsch, *Maister Beza's Household Prayers*, pp. 275–88. For Pierre Robert Olivétan, see his *Instrvction des enfans* (Geneva: 1533). For Pierre Viret, see his *L'Exposition familière de l'oraison de nostre Seigneur Jesus Christ* (Geneva: Jean Girard, 1548). On these works of Olivétan and Viret, see Francis M. Higman, 'Viret en anglais', *BSHPF* Vol. 144, No. 4 (1998), pp. 882, 885.

102   'de sa propre plume, and, a largement exploité l'exposition de Luther du *Betbüchlein*'. Francis Higman, *Luther et la piété de l'église gallicane*, p. 92. Higman specifies elsewhere that the commentary on the Creed, 'after the introductory pages, is translated from Luther's *Betbüchlein*, with some modifications to the text, and with a change from Luther's third-person form of reference to God'. Higman, *Theology for the Layman*, p. 109. According to Higman, Farel did not read German and must have had a helper, possibly Anémand de Coct. See *Le Pater Noster*, p. 18. Since Oecolampadius had earlier in the year translated Farel's 13 theses at Basel into German, he might also be a candidate. See N. Weiss, 'Guillaume Farel. La dispute de Bâle. Le conflit avec Erasme (1524)', *BSHPF* Vol. 69, No. 3 (July–Sept 1920), p. 119.

103   '*A partir de là et jusqu'à la fin de l'exposition, la version de Farel suit fidèlement le texte de Luther*'. Francis Higman, ed., *Le Pater Noster*, p. 16.

104   The two additions enlarge upon: a) the contrast between being able to choose only sin apart from grace, and being unable to sin under grace, in the sense that God's grace and Spirit cancel its effects; and b) the need for Christians to seek suffering in this life. Higman, ed., *Le Pater Noster*, p. 16.

Luther.[105] It appears to me that of the 297 lines of this prayerful exposition of the Creed, about 111, or one third, are Farel's own.[106] In this way we can appreciate that even in his exposition of the Creed, Farel develops his own approach rather than merely copying Luther.[107] Farel seems to have used a pre-1522 version of Luther's explanation of the Creed.[108]

Replacing the rosary

Farel directs that his prayer book be used, 'in place of the chaplet'.[109] Unfortunately, it is hard to determine to what extent Farel and those of his day would have distinguished '*chapelet*' from '*rosaire*', but if Farel was following technical usage, he would have been speaking of the most everyday set of prayers, a set of 50 Hail Marys, one third the length of the Rosary.[110] Whatever the case, rosaries and chaplets were a popular

---

[105]   Higman identified the following lines as additions from Farel: 362–9; 382–93; 401–3, 435–41; 457–62; 511–3; 565–76. One must also count lines 279–318, since these form Farel's own introduction, as Higman notes. The entire work encompasses lines 265–576 in the critical edition. Excluding the text of the Creed at the beginning (265–78), this makes it 297 lines long. Higman has identified 84 of these lines as additions from Farel. It is doubtful, however, whether lines 435–41 should count as an addition. *Le Pater Noster*, pp. 66–8.

[106]   In addition to those Higman references, I am adding lines (in some cases parts of lines), 322–4, 327–9, 339, 351–4, 357, 359, 371–5, 380, 419, 466–8, 493–4, 520, 531–2, 534–6, 546–549. It should also be noted that here and there Farel drops a line or two of Luther. For Luther's 1522 edition, see *D. Martin Luthers Werke* (Weimar: Nachfolger, 1907), Vol. 10, No. 2, pp. 388–95. See also *Luther's Works*, Vol. 43, pp. 29–38.

[107]   W. G. Moore carefully studied the German influences on the French Reformation, highlighting Luther's important place. Yet he was also careful to distinguish translation as such from the movement of ideas. Thus, he writes of Lutheran ideas being given expression in French form. In this context he highlights the eloquence of Farel. W. G. Moore, *La Réforme Allemande et la littérature française: Recherches sur la noteriété de Luther en France* (Strasbourg: Publications de la Faculté des Lettres, 1930), pp. 169–70.

[108]   On the Creed, Luther's 1522 edition adds only six words to that of 1520, 'unnd also die gepott gottis erfullen'. Farel does not translate these words. In light of the ending of Farel's *Pater Noster*, '*La plenitude de la loy c'est dilection*', an ending also found in his *L'Epistre Chretienne* (also from 1524), '*La plenitude de la loy, dilection*', and argued within that letter, it seems Farel would have translated the words if he had them before him. See *D. Martin Luthers Werke*, Vol. 10, No. 2, p. 392.

[109]   '*S'ensuite l'exposition de ceste orayson faicte en forme d'orayson, pour lire du chapelet, quant on aura loysir*'. *Le Pater Noster*, a4r, lines 72–4 (p. 40).

[110]   Littré defines a '*chapelet*' as, '*Objet de dévotion en forme de collier, fait de grains enfilés et composé de cinq dizaines d'avés, au lieu que le rosaire est composé de quinze dizaines d'Avés; à chaque dizaine est un plus gros grain sur lequel on dit le Pater*. Emile M. P. Littré, *Dictionnaire de la langue française* (1863–73), *sub* chapelet. Smolenski critiques the ambiguous usage of the term today and argues – contra Littré, it would seem, and relying on twentieth century developments – that technically the rosary is considered a species of the genus chaplet. Whatever the case, both rosary and chaplet originate from the concept of a

late-medieval development that imitated the monastic practice of reciting the Psalms. Taking the number 150 from the Psalms in the *Breviary*, 150 Hail Marys were chanted instead, in combination with repetitions of the Lord's Prayer and the *Gloria Patri*. Thus, the rosary became the poor man's imitation of the priests saying their 150 Psalms – the 'poor man's breviary'. So, if the *Book of Hours* was 'dumbed down' one step from the official *Breviary*, the rosary was simplified yet further, at least in terms of the literacy required. In addition, in Farel's day the number of mysteries to be meditated upon while chanting the rosary was being reduced to 15 instead of 150, for easier memorization (each 'mystery' was an event from Christ's life, death or resurrection).[111] Nevertheless, the rosary generated its own series of supporting publications which might even be considered competition for the *Book of Hours*.[112] Because people possessed their own prayer beads – even handed them down, as attested by wills of the period – the rosary, like the *Book of Hours*, did not require one's presence at mass for its use.[113] Thus, Farel's reference to the '*chapelet*' suggests that he has a prayer book for the broadest sweep of the populace that they can use as frequently and easily as their chaplet beads.

It is an interesting question whether Farel at this time would imagine any liturgical use for his text. Would Farel in 1524 have people go to mass and use his prayer book in the nave while the priest was conducting his liturgy beyond the screen? In 1524 he was not yet sent out by Berne, had not led any locales to live 'alone according to the gospel', and so was not yet leading evangelical worship outside the established Church. Farel offers no critique of the mass in the Disputation at Basel, nor in either of his 1524 publications. Denommé and Kemp note this with regard to *L'Epistre Chrestienne* as confirmation of its early dating.[114] Higman contrasts Farel's 'essentially non-polemical' teaching publications of 1524 with the 'attack'

---

garland, then extend to stringed beads used to count prayers, and then to the accompanying prayers and meditations. See Anne Winston-Allen, *Stories of the Rose: The Making of the Rosary in the Middle Ages* (Pennsylvania: Pennsylvania State University Press, 1997), pp. 4–5, 100–3, p. 164, n. 12; Joseph Therese Agbasiere, 'The Rosary: its history and relevance', *African Ecclesial Review* Vol. 30, No.4 (Aug. 1988), pp. 242–54; Stanley Smolenski, 'Rosary or chaplet?' *Homiletic and Pastoral Review* Vol. 86, No. 1 (Oct. 1985), pp. 9–15.

[111]   *New Catholic Encyclopedia* (New York: McGraw–Hill, 1967), Vol. 12, pp. 668–9.

[112]   These handbooks typically included stories relating the benefits of praying the rosary, the precise wordings to be followed, and pictures to aid in meditation. Winston-Allen, *Stories of the Rose*, pp. 122–7, 134–6.

[113]   R. N. Swanson, *Religion and Devotion in Europe, c. 1215–c. 1515* (Cambridge: Cambridge University Press, 1995), p. 87.

[114]   Denommé and Kemp, *L'Epistre Chrestienne*, p. 44.

and 'destroy' tactics of the 1529 *Summaire*, also against the mass.[115] Indeed, it was not till 1534 that Marcourt – with Farel's cooperation, it seems – would publish the notorious placards. Whether Farel envisions a role for his prayer book in the people's liturgy is hard to say, but we can confirm that Farel wants to replace the chaplets and rosaries, and that he raises the bar in terms of the expected level of popular literacy.

Replacing mere 'muttering'

In line with this expectation of increased literacy, Farel's introduction speaks against the mere 'muttering' of the lips, using the same root of the word that recurs in the Geneva consistory's minute books of the 1540s.[116] Prayer, then, although it begins with the lifting up of the spirit to God, includes the understanding as well, and comes to expression when one is 'thinking all the words which are in the spoken prayer'.[117] Farel intends this to be taken as a contrast to the rosaries and chaplets which encourage the worshipper to repeat the set words but to meditate sequentially on a different set mystery for each decade of Aves. Farel considers this a disjunction; one's words and thoughts need rather to be in one line, for this is 'to the honour of the one to whom we are praying'.[118] In addition to the remarks above in connection with the Disputation of Basel in 1524, we can also note Farel's judgement in Chapter 21 of the 1529 *Summaire*, on good works, where he writes of those 'who murmur, who do nothing but mutter the words without understanding. They honour God with their lips, but serve him in vain, following the doctrine and commandments of man'.[119] One could say that although Farel advocates a religion of the

---

[115]   Francis Higman, 'Farel's Summaire: The Interplay of Theology and Politics', in Jean-François Gilmont and William Kemp, eds., *Le livre évangélique en français avant Calvin* (Turnhout: Brepols, 2004), pp. 83–5. Note, however, that Farel certainly has a polemic in mind when he directs his prayer book to be used in place of the chaplet. Higman's argument about the turning point is correct as regards particular doctrines – here, the doctrine of the mass – but it is rather debatable to say that the Reform movement changed from positive to polemical in the late 1520s (see pp. 83–5). The entire movement was polemical by definition, and was so from 1517/18 onward. Higman's identification of the 1525 *Brief Recueil de la substance et principal fondement de la doctrine Evangelique* (an augmented translation of Melanchthon's 1524 *Epitome*) as 'something of an exception' because of its polemical tone also raises questions for his thesis about a change in tactics (pp. 73, 83).

[116]   'et non pas ainsy seulement barbouter des levres sans rien entendre', Farel, *Le Pater Noster*, a2v, lines 30–2 (pp. 36–7).

[117]   'en pensant tous les motz qui sont en la dicte orayson', Farel, *Le Pater Noster*, a2r, line 25 (p. 36).

[118]   'pour l'honneur d'icelluy que l'on prie', Farel, *Le Pater Noster*, a2r, line 25–6 (p. 36).

[119]   Farel, *Summaire*, Fol. D v (p. 136).

heart, he wants to avoid what he regards to be unedifying practices. His praying aims for the rational conjunction of words and thoughts.

Here Farel invokes the text which would often be used for the reform of worship – First Corinthians 14 – wherein the apostle Paul had written about the need for sounds uttered in the church to be edifying. Under this rubric we may also understand his chastizement of the pastors who have neglected 'the sheep of God' instead of instructing them in a language which is understandable.[120] All of the foregoing elucidates Farel's purpose in writing this little manual. He wants it to be accessible to those who do not understand Latin, whom he and Lefèvre often call 'the simple people'.[121] He wants them to be able to take it anywhere, hence it is a 'little booklet which can easily be carried in the hand by anyone'.[122] By means of these prayers the believers ought to find consolation for their souls. If they pray diligently, their very prayers will become the means by which the kingdom of heaven is opened, as Farel exhorts his readers:

> Therefore let each one devote himself to prayer for the infinite mercy of God, that it be his good pleasure to open to us the kingdom of heaven, by the true understanding of the Scriptures which he alone gives.[123]

We may summarize that Farel intends his prayer book to be used by all Christians (especially French evangelicals) at any suitable time, wherever they find themselves, with words and thoughts joined.

What is prayer?

Farel introduces his booklet with a description of prayer as 'one of the most noble fruits' produced by faith when that faith has regard only for the kindness, mercy and benevolence of God. 'Prayer' is here placed in parallel with the, 'lifting up of the spirit and understanding to God'.[124] He writes (now to quote more fully):

> And so when our faith has regard only for the depths of the goodness of God, depending on all the mercy and loving kindness of God, one of the most noble fruits which it produces is prayer – the lifting up of the spirit and

---

[120] 'jusques à maintenant les brebis de dieu ont esté tresmal instruictes, par la grand negligence des pasteurs, qui les devoient instruire de prier en languaige qu'on entendist'. *Le Pater Noster*, a2r–a2v, lines 27–30, (p. 36). Throughout the introduction the roots *entendre* (understand) and *instruire* (teach) recur.

[121] Farel, *Le Pater Noster*, a3r, line 47 (p. 37).

[122] Farel, *Le Pater Noster*, a2v, lines 42–3 (p. 37).

[123] Farel, *Le Pater Noster*, a3r, lines 50–54 (p. 38).

[124] Farel, *Le Pater Noster*, a1v–a2r, lines 13–16 (pp. 35–6).

the understanding to God. But because we do not know what we must pray, nor how, as it is written to the Romans, the good Jesus, who was so deeply humiliated for us, wanted to show us how we ought to pray, both as to form and manner. He commanded us that when we would pray, we ought to pray like this: 'Our Father who are'. And therefore all of us must speak this prayer with a very deep reverence and humility of heart, and a very great fervour of spirit, thinking through all the words which are in the spoken prayer. We must do so for the honour of him to whom we pray, yes, of him who gave us the form for praying like this. Until now the sheep of God have had very poor instruction in this, through the great negligence of the pastors, who need to instruct them to pray in a language which they comprehend, and not merely to mutter from the lips without any understanding.[125]

Farel here combines rational understanding with depths of passion. Both the proper orientation of the person's spirit and the full engagement of the mind are in view and it is hard to discern him giving more importance to one than to the other. Farel seems to expect believers to feel deeply moved when praying yet also to use words, such as those of the Lord's Prayer. Proper orientation of the heart depends on 'our faith', and therefore, by definition, this kind of prayer functions for believers only. The *Heidelberg Catechism* (1563) would later confess prayer to be 'necessary for Christians' because 'it is the chief part of the thankfulness which God requires of us'.[126] The basic idea that prayer is a fruit of faith and not faith's source thus remained mainstream in Reformed spirituality. In terms of the believer's perception of God's nature when they pray, Farel's approach is very positive, appealing to the contemplation of God's mercy with no word of fear for God's wrath. In Farel's view, believers should expect God to hear and to provide; prayer flows out of faith and hope.

Praying with zeal

The deep feelings which Farel advocates invite further study, especially since the Reformers are probably more well known for their cerebral emphases. On this theme, Farel keeps a variety of terms at his disposal, such as 'inflame', 'reverence', 'humility', 'desire' and 'zeal', as well as a variety of adjectives such as 'very', 'deep', 'strong' and 'great'. For instance, he stipulates the need for 'very deep reverence and humility of heart, and a very great fervour of spirit, thinking through all the words which are in the spoken prayer'.[127] Such reverence, he writes, arises out of 'honour of him to

[125]   Farel, *Le Pater Noster*, a1v–a2v (pp. 35–7).

[126]   Philip Schaff, *The Creeds of Christendom* (Grand Rapids, MI: Baker, 1993), Vol. 3, p. 350.

[127]   Farel, *Le Pater Noster*, a2r, lines 23–4 (p. 36).

whom we pray'. In humbly honouring him, Farel prays, 'I bend the knees of my heart before you'.[128] The title page of this work states that it is made in the form of a prayer, 'beneficial for inflaming the heart and spirit in the love of God'. Similar words occur in the introduction to the Creed, which he wrote as a prayer, 'to inflame faith in God'.[129] This word *'enflamber'* certainly speaks of zeal, yet it may, in a sense, be balanced with the word 'consolation', which appears close behind it in the title page of the prayer. It is supposed to be a zeal driven by God's love and expressing Christian love, so as to pursue and supply comfort for believers. Farel could be fiery in the face of opposition, but the same zeal could tenderly seek a contact point in the hearts of others to move them deeply. He wants their hearts inflamed just as he feels his own is. In line with this, Farel also prays that the governing of new affections according to the will of God might follow upon the slaying of the carnal affections of the flesh.[130] Prayer seeks grace for holy living. Farel's practice of prayer seeks to distance itself from mere external forms. It is indeed remarkable how often Farel's passionate rhetoric surfaces in all of his writings and moves him to prayer.

Farel grounds the kind of zeal he advocates in the nature of God. That is, because the one being addressed is so great, and since it is such a privilege to address him, Farel thinks people ought to pray humbly. He also makes regular appeal to the honour of God while addressing him in prayer. For instance, God's honour forms the ground for an appeal for pardon, namely that Christians, who are named after Christ, not carry that name in vain, but that God sanctify that name.[131] It is remarkable that Farel speaks of the believer's sin being committed not against God's holiness as such but against his 'holy benevolence' and 'divine power'.[132] In this sense the prayer portrays God as a God of love whose holiness is also kind. He mercifully desires to forgive and save Christians who are entirely lost on their own. These characterizations of God must also be intended to help move Farel's readers to pray often and cheerfully. Farel

---

[128]   Farel, *Le Pater Noster*, a4v, line 100 (p. 41).

[129]   Bodenmann draws attention to both of these, noting Beza's characterization of Farel's voice as animated with a zeal that would inflame his hearers, especially in the moment of prayer. Bodenmann, *Farel et le livre réformé français*, p. 25. What Bodenmann does not relate, is Farel's fuller text within the Creed, well worth quoting: '*jaçoit ainsy qu'il n'est nul besoing quant à toy, qu'aulcun descouvre son coraige, c'est à dire la foy, l'esperance, la fiance, et l'amour qu'il a en ta justice, bonté et misercorde; toutefois, quant à nous, il est fort besoing de souvent exciter, esmouvoir et enflamber nostre dormant, lasche et froit coraige, ou esprit, par fervente meditation de cueur, laquelle soit aydee par oraison de bouche, procedante de l'ardant desir de l'esperit*'.

[130]   Farel, *Le Pater Noster*, a6v, lines 154–62 (p. 43).

[131]   Farel, *Le Pater Noster*, a5v–a6r, lines 130–2 (p. 42).

[132]   Farel, *Le Pater Noster*, a5v, lines 126–8 (p. 42).

provides a model of such zealous praying by his own manipulation of rhetoric in the published prayer.

In *Le Pater Noster* abundant use of '*très*' and of adjectives for God demonstrate this passion of Farel, as do his articulations of the believer's absolute dependence on God's mercy, and his abundant confessions of sin.[133] Even more abundant, however, are his confessions of and allusions to God's mercy, kindness, sweetness, love, desire to forgive, and desire to convert sinners.[134] Farel will pray that God wants to be called 'our Father' in order that we might not doubt that God wishes to give believers everything out of his tender mercy.[135] Thus, while Farel's God is almighty, he is not distant; he most certainly hears all the prayers of his people. One of the most poignant expressions of Farel's prayer is reserved for the end, when believers pray that God would deliver them 'from the eternal sorrow of hell, in which no one will be able to praise you, nor confess your name or your kindness'.[136] Farel is teaching the French evangelicals how those should pray who confess God's initiative and sovereignty in salvation: they should appeal to the glory and praise of his holy name. Further, Farel gives his readers the sense that the worst punishment imaginable is the denial of the opportunity to praise God. Following this, the prayer makes its request in one final formulation, 'And because it is your holy will that sinners be converted and live in you, and with you, I pray you, O almighty Father'. [137] Evidently Farel wished to style his prayers in a very positive framework. He presents God in all his mercy and kindness, his desire to impart salvation and restore sinners to communion with him. These emphases must have helped make this prayer as popular as it was.

Interpreting the Lord's Prayer

Not all of the Reformers interpreted the petitions of the Lord's Prayer in the same way.[138] Farel reads all of the prayer with a very strong sense of God's greatness over and against human sin and weakness. God is the one who always lives 'full of jubilation and delight', in other words, God is

---

[133]   Restricting ourselves to the *Le Pater Noster* proper, excluding *Le Credo*, we will simply list the words by line number: *tresmisercordieux* (99, 138), *trescher* (138, 148), *tresbening* (118, 223), *treshumblement* (244). Other expressions such as *grande misercorde* could be listed (for example, 77). Confessions of sin occur in varying degrees (83–5, 87–9, 122–3, 127–8, 137–47, 174, 214–7).

[134]   In fact, these are too abundant to list exhaustively. See, for example, lines 77, 86–7, 89–91, 95, 109, 112–9, 125–6, 166–72, 197–9, etc.

[135]   Farel, *Le Pater Noster*, a4v, lines 90–1 (p. 40).

[136]   Farel, *Le Pater Noster*, b2r, lines 252–4 (p. 47).

[137]   Farel, *Le Pater Noster*, b2r, lines 254–6 (p. 47).

[138]   See Backus, *Prière en latin au 16e siècle*, pp. 62–9.

not disturbed by any imperfection. Given Farel's rising concern for gospel preaching in 1524, it is perhaps predictable that he spiritualizes the fourth petition (for daily bread). The prayer can be read in full in Chapter 5 (we here summarize Farel's interpretation of most of the petitions).

Farel first meditates upon God being Father, which makes him the source of all good, both in creation and in redemption. This leaves no room for human boasting, since everything humans possess or enjoy is a gift. Farel specifies that the requests of this the Lord's Prayer are uttered according to God's command, thus assuring God, himself, and his readers that this prayer must be pleasing to God.

Praying for the hallowing of God's name evidently requires an extended confession that the believer has not hallowed God's name; else, why pray for this?

Praying for the coming of God's kingdom is very personal. Farel glosses this as the need for the present personal obedience of the believer to the rule of this kingdom's King.

Doing God's will appears to mean praising and thanking God unceasingly. Here Farel does not make a distinction between God's prescribed will as expressed in the Bible and God's hidden will by which all things come to pass, although his rhetoric leans to the latter. Later Reformed authors would clearly opt for the former. Farel thinks of the angels and blessed souls in heaven doing God's will (your will be done, on earth as it is in heaven) particularly in terms of constantly praising God, rather than carrying out particular commands of God. He explains why believers should always do God's will by praising him: it is because God's will is always good, especially inasmuch as God provides compensation for those who suffer while trusting in him.

Obtaining daily bread becomes another occasion for Farel to seek more divine teaching, both via preaching and via the eucharist. Here Farel appears to opt for a non-transubstantiation understanding of the sacrament although without any polemic as such, for he speaks of the precious body of Christ being given 'for us in a covenant under the species of bread and wine to confirm our faith'.[139] The need for physical food and drink is not ignored by Farel, but clearly put in second place. One must first seek God's kingdom and have care and worry for one's salvation. The material things of life are freely promised to such believers per Matthew 6:33, which Farel quotes.

Remarkably, the theme of our corrupt wills over against God's perfect will, his love and his righteous commands appears in Farel's paraphrase of

---

[139]   Farel, *Le Pater Noster*, a8r, lines 195–7 (p. 45). Note Farel says that Christ's body is given for us, not to us. Further, he states that the sacrament confirms faith rather than saying that it gives grace.

the opening address (our Father in heaven) and every petition that follows except for the fourth.[140]

Interpreting the Creed with Luther

Although we have restricted most of our detailed study of the themes of prayer to *Le Pater Noster* proper, it may be remarked that in *Le Credo* Farel's additions to Luther are in line with the earlier prayer in the *Pater Noster* section. He emphasizes the following four ideas:

- First, the believer's absolute dependence on God – that without God's grace and Holy Spirit, the believer can do nothing but sin, whereas any good in the believer stems entirely from the work of God, so that no one is to trust in their own accomplishments, powers, etc.[141]
- Second, the believer's total submission to God, such that the believer seeks only God's glory and praise, whatever the circumstances.[142]
- Third, he states the need to seek suffering at the present time in connection with sanctification.[143]
- Fourth, Farel elaborates regarding the reception of the keys of the kingdom by all the church, and not just by Peter.[144]

A number of these additions may be termed rhetorical, as when Farel piles up the kinds of things believers might trust in but should not, and when he provides a balanced list of positive and negative circumstances in which the believer's faith in God must stand firm, as well as when he prays about the evil powers.[145] His introduction has been somewhat elaborated on already in this essay; the peroration returns to the confession of the Trinity with which the introduction ended, doing so in the context of a final prayer that Farel writes in the first person singular. He asks for faith and trust in order to maintain his confession until God delivers him from this mortal life into the perfect confession, love and eternal praise of God.[146]

---

[140]   See Chapter 2 of this work.

[141]   Farel, *Le Pater Noster*, b5r–b5v, b6v, lines 351–4, 383–92 (pp. 52, 53–4).

[142]   Farel, *Le Pater Noster*, b5v–b6r, lines 362–9 (pp. 52–3).

[143]   Farel, *Le Pater Noster*, c1r–c1v, lines 457–462, 466–468 (pp. 57–8).

[144]   Farel, *Le Pater Noster*, c3v, lines 546–9 (p. 61).

[145]   Farel, *Le Pater Noster*, b5v, b6r, lines 352–4, 365–9, 372–5 (pp. 52, 53).

[146]   Farel, *Le Pater Noster*, c4v, lines 565–75 (pp. 62–3).

Closeness to God

It may be noted, finally, that Farel addresses God in the *tu* form, not the *vous* form. Lefèvre's translation of the New Testament, which appeared around the same time as Farel's *Pater Noster*, also uses *tu*.[147] Higman, commenting on another work elsewhere, relates that the Reformers 'seem almost always to have preferred the "tu" form' in their prayers. *Tu* was always used in the Lord's Prayer. Some of the traditionalist doctors used *vous* in their prayers, but not all.[148] As one charting the course for the French Reformed writings, Farel's use of *tu* is not new, but fits within his context.[149] It also fits Farel's sense of closeness to God – near the end he specifically calls Jesus 'our brother', as he also did in *L'Épistre Chrestienne*.[150] Indeed, Higman identifies the personal relationship of believers to God as the first of three central themes of Farelian spirituality, together with the total dependence of the believer on God and the cleansing of the heart by the Holy Spirit.[151]

Farel's passion to teach prayer conveys itself throughout *Le Pater Noster et le Credo*. Using the most basic texts, Farel wants to teach the entirety of the faith by means of prayer. This may sound odd, for prayer is supposed to epitomize an upward spirituality. The point is that the upward spirituality is only real when it learns by practice how rightly to address this God it ought to know, a practice learned by the outward movement of one more practiced instructing another. Upward and outward spirituality can be distinguished, but not separated. Even a cursory read of Farel's prayer takes away the grounds for any who might argue that Farel has turned prayer into a cold, classroom tool. Most would agree that his pedagogy seems warm and lively.

---

[147]   *La Saincte Bible en francoys, translatée selon la . . . traduction de Saint Hierome*, trans. Jacques Lefèvre d'Etaples (Anvers: Martin Lempereur, 1534).

[148]   Higman, *Theology for the Layman*, p. 114, n. 8.

[149]   For comparison, Calvin's only French letter to Farel (1540) uses the *vous* form rather than *tu*. This is likely Calvin's expression of respect for a man 20 years his senior (in spite of Calvin's strong reprimands in the letter!). See Francis M. Higman, 'Calvin and Farel', in Wilhelm H. Neuser, ed., *Calvinus Sacrae Scripturae Professor* (Grand Rapids, MI: Eerdmans, 1994), p. 223.

[150]   Note that these are lines originating in Farel, not Luther: '*mesmement tous les merites de ton benoit filz Jesus nostre frere*'. *Le Pater Noster*, c3v, lines 534–535 (p. 61). cf. '*Jesus, qui s'est fait ton frere*'. [Farel] *L'Épistre Chrestienne*, a7r (p. 58).

[151]   '[L]*e rapport personnel du croyant à Dieu*', '*la dépendance entière du croyant envers Dieu*', '*la purification intérieure du croyant par le Saint Esprit*'. Higman, ed., *Le Pater Noster*, p. 15.

Farel's contribution

What was unique about Farel's prayer book? We have seen that both Luther (1520) and Erasmus (1523) offered paraphrases of the Lord's Prayer before Farel did, though none paraphrased the Apostles' Creed in the form of a prayer. Also, a distinction between Luther and Farel on the one side and Erasmus on the other, holds, for the former constructed their paraphrases much more as the personal plea 'of the believing soul to God'.[152] Savonarola's meditations on Psalms 51 and 32 [31] were also paraphrasing and personalized prayers. The genre of sustained address to God reaches back, of course, to the illustrious *Confessiones* of Augustine.

Farel's prayer book was the first paraphrase of the Lord's Prayer and Apostles' Creed of any confessional allegiance to be written entirely in the French language. His integration of the heart and spirit with the praying lips was new for many of his readers, although not disconnected from certain streams of late-medieval piety. Farel contributed directly to the revamping of prayer among the French evangelicals, both in France and Switzerland, since his publications reached many.

One may also reconstruct the history of popular instruction in an inverted formation: If late-medieval lay piety was on a trajectory of imitating the complex *Breviary* with the simpler *Book of Hours* and the even simpler rosary, early Reformation piety was on the opposite trajectory. Farel urges evangelicals to replace their chaplet and rosary prayers with his prayer book. His prayer book is more complex in terms of its concepts, its effort to unite lips and heart, and its departure from the practice of set hourly texts. But it is simpler than the *Book of Hours*, in the sense that it sticks only to the Lord's Prayer and the Creed.[153] Five years later, in 1529, Farel will be writing his *Summaire* and in 1537 his *Confession de la foi*, but in 1524 the inversion is just beginning. Like Luther's *Betbüchlein*, Farel's prayer book then may be viewed as a step towards the more involved Reformed catechisms that were to follow, where the Creed, Commandments and Prayer would almost invariably be explained – a rather Catholic approach, one might add, in view of early Church practices. It is interesting that the earliest German and French forays into this genre were both paraphrases, encouraging a warm piety. The later *Heidelberg Catechism* would follow this model in its explanation of the Lord's Prayer. Luther and Farel stand

---

[152]   Irena D. Backus, *Prière en latin au 16ᵉ siècle*, p. 47.

[153]   Even the Anabaptists Hubmaier and Schaffler use the Lord's Prayer. The first supplies a meditation that follows its structure; the second ends his freely composed prayer by quoting it. See Liechty, *Early Anabaptist Spirituality*, pp. 38–40, 110.

at the headwaters of the great Protestant concern to educate the people deeply in spiritual things.[154]

Free prayer?

One very interesting question that does not receive much attention in literature on prayer has to do with free prayer versus the use of set texts. Clearly there is a shift taking place. Farel does not openly advocate free prayer, yet he himself is undertaking that very thing and recommending that his prayer be used in place of chaplets, rosaries and, presumably, also the *Book of Hours*, since he said to use his prayer 'whenever one has the time'. Old makes the point that the Reformers did not seek to abolish the office of daily prayer, but to restore it to the people – hence the office of all believers.[155] He notes a rubric in *The Strasbourg German Church Service of 1524* which 'gave a German collect but allowed that a prayer "given by God's Spirit" might be used in its place'. A 1526 Strasbourg Psalter asked the worshippers to pray silently that the preaching might be efficacious.[156] Backus writes about Luther: 'The Lord's Prayer excepted, Luther objected in principle to all formal prayer, judging that people should be able to speak to God *ex tempore*'. Nevertheless, and perhaps contradictorily, he directs that the content of Christian prayer should be derived from the Bible, especially the Psalter.[157] In 1535 Luther wrote an extremely practical guide for prayer, and described his own practice of dwelling on the various petitions of the Lord's Prayer as he prayed. 'Occasionally', he stated, 'I may get lost among so many ideas in one petition that I forego the other six'.[158] Luther exhorted his readers to take such experiences for the guidance, indeed, the preaching of the Holy Spirit. In other words, he recommended

---

[154]   Russell describes how Luther preached and published on the Lord's Prayer repeatedly in the period 1516–22. William R. Russell, 'Luther, Prayer, and the Reformation', *Word and World* Vol. 22, No. 1 (Winter 2002), p. 51.

[155]   Hughes Oliphant Old, 'Daily Prayer in the Reformed Church of Strasbourg, 1525–1530', *Worship* Vol. 52, No. 2 (March 1978), p. 123.

[156]   Old, *Daily Prayer in Strasbourg*, pp. 133–4.

[157]   'L'oraison dominicale exceptée, Luther récusait en principe toute prière formelle, estimant que l'homme devait pouvoir s'adresser à Dieu spontanément. Toutefois, aussi contradictoire que cela puisse paraître, Luther admettait en même temps que le contenu de toute prière chrétienne devait être puisé dans la Bible et notamment dans le Psautier'. Irena D. Backus, *Prière en latin au 16ᵉ siècle*, p. 47.

[158]   Martin Luther, 'A Simple Way to Pray', *Luther's Works (Devotional Writings II)*, Vol. 43, p. 198. Note that he begins this treatise by explaining that when he grows cold or joyless in prayer, he returns to prayer by rote: he takes his 'little psalter' and says 'quietly to myself and word-for-word the Ten Commandments, the Creed, and, if I have time, some words of Christ or of Paul, or some psalms, just as a child might do' (p. 193).

free prayer. In the 1520s Luther and Farel seem to be recommending the same, although not as directly.

The late-medieval to early modern transition in spirituality

The conversation of early modern Reformers with late-medieval practices is complex. For instance, in continuity with the past, Luther includes the liturgical calendar and accounts of the passion in his prayer books.[159] Again, even free prayer was of course not a *de novo* idea. Mystics assumed its use. Wieck reminds us that the late-medieval *Book of Hours* was like an automobile that could be personally accessorized, '[T]here was a nearly inexhaustible array of ancillary prayers that people, depending on their piety and their pocketbook, felt free to add [to their commissioned prayer books]'. But when we look at the examples of added prayers, we see that they remained by and large set texts – seven requests to our Lord, seven prayers to St. Gregory, etc.[160] Post-Tridentine Roman Catholic decrees would maintain this practice, warning against devising one's own prayers.[161] Many reformers would blame the popular use of repeated, precise formulae for engendering superstition. Yet, later in the sixteenth century an impressive quantity of books of Catholic prayers in French would appear, some containing new prayers. Thus, although the lines of continuity and discontinuity cross and mix, the general historical patterns of a shift in late-medieval spirituality and a subsequent shift in early Protestant spirituality do hold.

Given Farel's reputation as a fiery Reformer whose rhetorical power came into its own in the midst of verbal disputations, it is fascinating to trace the use of Farel's *Pater Noster* into non-Reformed contexts. One slightly toned-down version even received Sorbonne clearance.[162] Higman refers this partly to Farel's 'irenic side'.[163] If we take into account the fact that Farel's rhetoric was far more often employed to comfort and strengthen believers than to oppose non-evangelicals (compare his frequency of preaching the gospel to the believing church to his occasions for disputation, and the former will far outweigh the latter), then this irenic side should not be so surprising. Farel should be thought of as a man of very deep affections who could pour out his heart in words and muster his passions either for or against a person or idea. Thus, if Farel

---

[159]   Backus, *Prière en latin au 16ᵉ siècle*, p. 47, n. 16.

[160]   Roger S. Wieck, *Prayer for the People*, p. 409.

[161]   Bruno Petey-Girard, 'Bible et tradition liturgique dans les prières Françaises de la fin du XVIe siècle', *Bibliothèque d'humanisme et renaissance* Vol. 64, No. 2 (2002), p. 355.

[162]   Higman, 'Histoire du livre et histoire de la Réforme', p. 848.

[163]   Higman, *Le Pater Noster et le Credo*, pp. 8–9.

wrote a passionate prayer but avoided polemical issues, a Roman Catholic could make use of it.[164]

It is the nature of the case that a committed Roman Catholic could use a prayer such as Farel's *Le Pater Noster* while a committed Protestant could not as easily reciprocate. On the one hand, Roman Catholics could personally use non-polemical Protestant prayers, so long as these did not prevent them from also continuing their prayers to the Virgin and the saints. The Protestant polemic with the Roman Catholic Church could not be expected to, and certainly did not, appear in every Protestant prayer, especially not when the base text – the Lord's Prayer – was held in common. On the other hand, the Protestant was troubled by much of the context, the form and the additions introduced by Roman Catholic prayers. Especially troubling for the Protestants were the additional persons to whom and through whom Roman Catholic prayer was offered, the seeming mindless repetition of prayer, the perceived 'blind superstitions' associated with prayer, the idea that various intermediaries besides Christ could make one's prayers efficacious, the motives for prayer such as getting one's loved one out of purgatory, the dedication of prayers to saints, statues and popes, the use of material and visual objects to aid prayer, and the idea that prayer was a good work which could secure penance for temporal punishment for sins. Farel also opposed the practice of meditating on the mysteries in one's mind while repeating other formulaic words with one's lips. Since, Protestants generally argued, all Roman Catholic liturgical prayers – and many personal ones – of the late-medieval period participated in these associations, Protestants felt the need to develop their own tradition of prayer. These conditions help to explain how in one sense Protestant prayer introduced simpler prayer practices yet stated its aim for a deeper and more complex involvement of heart and mind. They also show how certain prayers enjoyed cross-confessional use, even in the context of Reformation polemics.

Two later published prayers of Farel would be filled with polemics from start to finish. Among other writings, we shall examine these in the next chapter. In this chapter we have seen that Farel's focus on prayer stands in continuity with his context inasmuch as it was an age steeped in devotionalism and piety. Yet what he contributed needs to be categorized as distinctly evangelical in its setting and in its deliberate omissions. Farel made a running start at publishing on spirituality in 1524. This emphasis on spirituality represented well the man himself, and thus he would maintain this emphasis throughout his life.

---

[164]   See Backus, *Prière en latin au 16ᵉ siècle*, pp. 69–70.

CHAPTER 4

Farel's Upward Spirituality: Unceasing Prayer (1529–45)

Theodore Van Raalte

The confessional context of prayer: *Summaire* (1529)

The *Summaire* was introduced in Chapter 2. To review, it is a 42 chapter summary of the evangelical faith, the first of its kind in French, presenting the essential points of the gospel teachings in a chapter format with a table of contents.[1] The *Summaire* has been called the first French evangelical 'dogmatics'. It falls somewhere between a confession of faith and a dogmatics – too short for a text in dogmatics and never adopted by the churches as a confession. Thus, we use the phrase 'confessional context of prayer' somewhat freely. In this work positive gospel teaching and negative rejections of Roman Catholic doctrines and practices stand side by side. Chapter 24, entitled, '*De priere et l'oraison*' concerns us here. Prayer is also mentioned or alluded to in Chapters 9, 19, 20, 22, 26 and 40. The spiritual emphases in this document build upon what we have already seen, strongly emphasizing one's internal state in prayer – to the point that one might suggest mystical influences.

Farel opens Chapter 24 by defining prayer:

> Praying is an ardent speaking with God in which man does not know what to say or ask. But the Spirit who is with the faithful prays for us with great groanings which one could not even speak. In prayer the mouth is really not required to speak, but the heart only. For our Saviour Jesus taught us that when we pray we should say 'Our Father who are in heaven, etc'. This does not mean that we should only say these words with our mouth, that with these we would have what we ask, for that would be as the superstition of the enchanters. But [Jesus teaches us] this very beautiful prayer in order that in our heart we should

---

[1]   Higman remarks, 'It is characteristic of Guillaume Farel that he should perceive the need for something which did not yet exist: a systematic reference work which would order the 'new' teachings in an accessible form, in French, and with that fundamental reading aid, a Table of Contents'. Francis Higman, 'Farel's Summaire: the Interplay of Theology and Politics', in Jean-François Gilmont and William Kemp, eds, *Le livre évangélique en français avant Calvin* (Turnhout: Brepols, 2004), p. 74.

think of God as it says: that he is our God and that in true faith and in good conscience we go to him. In it we lift our hearts to heavenly things and ask only that which is contained in this very holy prayer. By it we understand that all that we ask that is not contained in this prayer is not the will of God. [2]

In line with his emphasis on the priority of the heart, Farel later specifies, 'Never let the tongue speak to pray if the heart is not with God'.[3] Similarly, he records a warning against mindless 'muttering'.[4] The context of chaplets, rosaries and the *Book of Hours*, noted above, forms the background for Farel's statements. He now comes to just the opposite point of view regarding common lay perceptions of prayer: instead of 'muttering' with the lips regardless of one's thoughts, Farel allows ceasing lip movement altogether to be concerned with thoughts only. His reasoning is also theological: true prayer involves the movement of the Holy Spirit within the believer. The 'true' stuff is internal first, then external, although in the case of private prayer it need not even become external. Mental or silent prayer alone fulfils all the requirements for personal praying.

Lefèvre and his 'especial friend'

Farel's emphasis on the internal and spiritual accords well with the evangelical phase of Jacques Lefèvre's life, the humanist master who, Farel recounts, had once so fervently and devoutly said his masses with Farel by his side.[5] Farel met him between 1509 and 1512. Around 1518 Lefèvre seems to have turned away from prayers to the saints and the use of material objects of worship, leaving incomplete a hagiography on certain saints to devote himself exclusively to scripture study.[6] The influence of the Modern Devout seems probable in Lefèvre's new emphasis, although direct lines are hard to trace.[7]

---

[2]   Farel, *Summaire*, Fol. E ii (p. 150–52).

[3]   Farel, *Summaire*, Fol. E ii (p. 154).

[4]   The word is '*barbottant*', a variation of '*barbotement*'. Farel, *Summaire*, Fol. E ii (p 154). This word also occurs in Chapters 21 and 42, *Summaire*, D v (p. 136), K viii (p. 318). Since context determines meaning, note the following in Chapter 21: '*et aux barbotteurs qui ne font que murmurer parolles sans entendement, honnorantz Dieu des leures, auquel ilz servent en vain suyvantz la doctrine et commandementz des homme*'.

[5]   Farel writes about this in, *Epistre a tous seigneurs* ... in *Du Vray usage de la Croix* (Geneva: Fick, 1865), p. 170. See also Sheila M. Porrer, *Jacques Lefèvre d'Etaples and the Three Maries Debates* (Geneva: Droz, 2009), p. 50, n. 151. See also Carlos M.N. Eire, *War Against the Idols* (Cambridge: Cambridge University Press, 1986), pp. 168–77.

[6]   Eire, *War Against the Idols*, pp. 174–5.

[7]   Philip Edgcumbe Hughes, *Lefèvre: Pioneer of Ecclesiastical Renewal in France* (Grand Rapids, Mich.: Eerdmans, 1984), pp. 35–8; Margaret E. Aston, 'The Northern Renaissance',

Interestingly, Lefèvre's change may also owe something to his student Farel. We learn this from Lefèvre's contribution in 1518 to the debate about the identity of the various Marys in the gospels. He includes there a lengthy quotation about a friend's earlier advice on the difference between worshipping God and venerating the saints.[8] This 'especial friend and intimate of mine' – whom Porrer suggests may have been Farel – had related to Lefèvre how to worship in spirit and truth by lifting his heart up to Christ when worshipping in places of pilgrimage before relics, crucifixes and altars. In this way, this friend argued, Lefèvre would not venerate the things but use them merely as pointers to Christ. The friend provided Lefèvre with concrete examples by telling him what words he might think while praying to Christ in the presence of an image or relic. If this friend was Farel, the emphasis on the manner of praying certainly fits what we know of the later Farel. His appeal to the *sursum corda* – lifting up one's heart to Christ and heavenly things – already shows itself, and its presence in Chapter 24 of *Summaire*. One would indeed expect that Farel's 1524 initial foray into publishing on prayer builds on prior sustained attention to personal prayer is then not new. This appears to be the very thing Lefèvre remembered of him.

One of the interesting arguments Lefèvre's 'especial friend' used to diminish the importance of the visible relics and their promotion was their participation in mortality. He stated that rather than pay too much attention to them now, he looked ahead with the hope of seeing 'all these things more happily, in that renewed life immortal'.[9] In a similar way Farel, in his 1530 *Epistre a tous seigneurs, et peuples et pasteurs*, speaks three times about how he and Lefèvre discussed the coming renewal of the world, although here the reference appears to refer not so much to the second coming of Christ as to the reformation of the Church.[10]

If Lefèvre in 1518 was writing about Farel's views prior to that time, we gain some insight into the evolution of Farel's thought. His movement from the 'gross idolatry' of which he speaks in his *Epistre a tous seigneurs* did not end at once, but first involved a spiritual use of the material objects

---

in Richard L. DeMolen, ed., *The Meaning of Renaissance and Reform* (Boston: Houghton Mifflin, 1974), pp. 82–90, 95–6. For the Modern Devout attitude on mental prayer, see, for example, John van Engen, *Devotio Moderna: Basic Writings*, pp. 289–90.

8   Sheila Porrer, *Jacques Lefèvre d'Etaples and the Three Maries Debates*, pp. 243–52.

9   Porrer, *Three Maries Debates*, p. 243. See also n. 81.

10   Guillaume Farel, *Epistre a tous seigneurs*, in *Du Vray usage*, p. 170. Porrer, *Jacques Lefèvre d'Etaples and the Three Maries Debates*, p. 51, n. 152 points to a passage of Lefèvre in the *Three Maries Debate* (p. 385) wherein he encourages 'true devotion and veneration' in place of 'foolish devotion ... which posterity will roundly reject (if the Church is to be renewed by a new influx of the Holy Spirit and by celestial favour, as not a few men have predicted in our time)'.

before finally rejecting them altogether in his 1529 *Summaire*. His polemics against these can be found in Chapters 19 and 27, on the mass and on the adoration and worship of the saints, respectively. In Chapter 24 on prayer Farel polemicizes against the idolatry of praying to any other, obviously referring to prayers to saints and Mary.

The Spirit and the new man

A study of Farel's spiritual view of prayer in *Summaire* should also turn to his chapter on the Spirit and the new man, Chapter 9. He calls the Holy Spirit, 'the movement and affection which God gives to man, the Renewer'.[11] Here Farel writes of the Spirit subduing human 'presumption and rashness', bringing believers in submission to the word of God, and making them steadfast against all the world's vanity and lies. He states, 'Much better would it be to know this by experience than by a book'.[12] He continues, 'Nevertheless, [the Bible] is written for the elect, in order that they might passionately desire and pray that the Spirit be given to them to make them into new men'.[13] Farel here treats the scriptures instrumentally, as a means of gaining the Holy Spirit. Yet, the very same Spirit makes the believer, 'humble and obedient to the pure word of God', and 'directs him to hold only to the pure word of God'.[14] There is a reciprocal movement: The Spirit gives the word and from within directs God's elect to the word, while the word causes the elect to desire the Spirit all the more to make them new and obedient. Farel envisions neither the Spirit without the word nor the word without the Spirit.[15] Also, no mere intellectual virtues are in view; rather, the believer's very affections are led and moved by the Holy Spirit.

As a fruit of the same Spirit, the right use of the law follows in the life of the believer. This view of Farel also permeates the *Summaire*.[16] We have also observed that Farel locates prayer in the same place: it is a fruit of faith, or an expression of thankfulness by one who already enjoys salvation.

---

[11]   'L'Esprit est le mouuement et affection que Dieu baille à l'homme le renouuellant'. *Summaire*, B v (p. 70).

[12]   Farel, *Summaire*, B vi (p. 72).

[13]   Farel, *Summaire*, B vi (p. 74).

[14]   Farel, *Summaire*, B vi (pp. 70, 72).

[15]   Calvin's emphasis on the same should thus not be isolated from his fellow and prior reformers. See B. B. Warfield, *Calvin as a Theologian and Calvinism Today* (Philadelphia: Presbyterian Board, 1909), pp. 14–7; J. Faber, 'The Saving Work of the Holy Spirit in Calvin', *Essays in Reformed Doctrine* (Neerlandia, AB: Inheritance Publications, 1990), pp. 282–91.

[16]   See Charles Partee, 'Farel's Influence on Calvin: A Prolusion', *Actes du Colloque Guillaume Farel*, pp. 179, 181.

Direct address in the Summaire

It is rather striking that in this chapter-by-chapter setting forth of doctrine Farel cannot avoid the mode of second-person direct address. The *Summaire* begins in what one might expect of a manual of doctrine: a third-person presentation of what must be believed. However, Farel does not maintain this. In Chapter 29 he moves to three rhetorical questions on the number of souls seduced by the papacy. A paragraph later he addresses his readers directly, 'Christians, pull yourselves away' from the pope who lays on a heavy burden, and 'come' to Christ who took our burden.[17] In Chapter 35, entitled 'The Power of Pastors', Farel argues that the entire power of pastors lies in properly teaching the people the simple word of God. He mourns the fact that all kinds of what he considers to be foolish books are available while the true word is not allowed to be read by the simple people for whom God intended it. In the emotion of his rhetoric, Farel addresses the sun and the earth regarding this horror. Then he turns directly to God and inserts a prayer consisting of some 13 rhetorical pleas that God grant justice. These pleas express such a longing, convey such zeal, and hold God to his word so fiercely, that it would have been hard for an evangelical to be unmoved when reading them. This brings Farel to direct his admonitions against those who deny the scriptures, in the form of four questions and two statements to the effect that it would be better if they had not been born. Finally, he ends with, 'Rise up, O God . . . make the trumpet of the holy gospel to be heard'.[18] In terms of teaching prayer, once again we encounter Farel teaching by example. Direct address to others and direct address to God seem to bring out Farel's most powerful rhetoric and most moving emotions.[19] Even the *Summaire* testifies to this.

The pastoral context of prayer: *Deeply Devout Prayer* (Metz, 1542)

Farel's zealous rhetoric in Chapter 35 of the *Summaire* for an increase in gospel preaching finds much lengthier expression in a 1542 prayer entitled, *Oraison tresdevote en laquelle est faicte la confession des pechez,*

---

[17]   Farel, *Summaire*, F vii (p. 200). See also Chapter 27, where Farel had already exhorted the 'Christians' directly.

[18]   Farel, *Summaire*, H ii–H iv, pp. 240–8. Note here the recurring emphasis on mission.

[19]   Direct address also occurs in Chapter 38 on marriage, speaking to believers and addressing the magistrates. Chapter 39 speaks to fathers. Chapter 41 addresses the champions and warriors who go out with the word of God as their sword. Chapter 42 reads like a sermon, complete with a host of imperative verbs.

des fidelles qui ainsi crient après Dieu.[20] In what follows we first examine the historical context of the prayer, then delve into its contents in 1542, before looking at the additions made in 1545. Finally, we finish with a consideration of Farel's motives in publishing these prayers. The recent publication of the first volume of the critical edition of Farel's works greatly helps us determine the provenance and dating of the prayer.[21]

Historical context of Oraison tresdevote

The 'Deeply Devout Prayer' arose out of the suppression of the Reform in Metz. It was written to help evangelicals seek from God the gospel's progress. Metz was a large city, once more eminent than Paris, situated between French and German influences, and rightly considered key by Farel, Bucer, Calvin and others. In the early sixteenth century Metz housed its cathedral, 20 churches and 30 convents.[22] Henri Strohl writes that for 40 years Farel's affections for the inhabitants of Metz were undiminished. 'He came to Metz for the first time in 1525, for the last time in 1565 just before his death, and there in 1542 he made a decisive visit for the establishment of Protestant worship in that city'.[23] For about one year, from the end of August 1542 to September 1543, Neuchâtel gave up their pastor to Metz. Securing freedom of worship for the Metz evangelicals became the entire focus of Farel. At first things seemed hopeful: Gaspard de Heu, favourable to the evangelical cause, had been elected as Chief Eschevin (a kind of mayor) in March 1542. However, his fellow aldermen, the Council of Thirteen, did not share his enthusiasm. Things came to a head in September 1542 when de Heu led Farel and 600 evangelicals out of town for preaching to a nearby chateau in Montigny which was under the protection of the Smalcaldic League. The Council of Thirteen then locked the gates against their own mayor and the party of evangelicals. Intense negotiations between Strasbourg, Berne, Metz, the Smalcaldic League and

---

[20]   Guillaume Farel, *Oraison tresdevote en laqulle [sic] est faicte la confession des pechez, des fidelles qui ainsi crient après Dieu* ([Strasbourg: J. Knobloch, 1542]). For identification of the publisher, see *Guillaume Farel: Biographie Nouvelle*, pp. 40, 43.

[21]   This prayer was traditionally dated to 1543 but Olivier Labarthe and Reinhard Bodenmann have now decisively demonstrated that in fact Farel composed it in 1542. See Guillaume Farel, *Œuvres imprimées*, Tome I: *Traités messins* eds. Reinhard Bodenmann and Françoise Breigel with Olivier Labarthe (Geneva: Droz, 2009), pp. 27–9.

[22]   *Guillaume Farel: Biographie Nouvelle*, p. 472.

[23]   *Guillaume Farel: Biographie Nouvelle*, p. 471. Strohl's essay remains authoritative for Farel's important role in these developments in Metz. He recounts Farel's work there around 1525 on pages 473–83, Farel's work in 1542–43 on pages 489–503; and Farel's triumphant visit in 1565 on pages 510–1.

even the emperor Charles the Fifth ensued.[24] Bucer, Melanchthon and Calvin each joined the fray in various ways. Farel wrote his prayer sometime in the midst of all the negotiations, protestations and interventions.

Labarthe has narrowed the composition of the prayer to between 2–23 October 1542, with publication prior to Christmas 1542.[25] The traditional dating, going all the way back to Jean Crespin's *Histoire des martyrs*, had Farel compose the prayer after Easter 1543 when the troops of the Duke of Guise had scattered the evangelicals of Metz. However, Farel is entirely silent about this notable event and several others between October 1542 and March 1543. Whereas the 1545 version of the prayer does speak of these events, the earlier version does not, which would be inexplicable if they had just occurred.[26]

After Farel's prayer was published, the evangelical cause in Metz did not at all improve. From January 1543, several of the evangelical bourgeoisie of Metz were imprisoned, exiled, deprived of their possessions and allowed to be molested by Burgundian troops in the city. Records show that a good number of merchants were pro-evangelical. In March about 200 residents of Metz went to Gorze to celebrate the Lord's Supper for Easter. When they were about to begin their second service a detachment of soldiers under Claude de Guise set out to frighten them and obtain loot. An old man was killed defending his purse and seven women were held for ransom, although not harmed. Two women, however, died fleeing when they failed to swim across a river.[27] Strohl writes that 'Farel consoled his companions in misfortune by his fervent prayers and his exhortations, and by singing Psalms with them'.[28]

These events at Gorze triggered a spate of publications from Farel between 1542 and 1544, the first of which was the prayer under consideration here.[29] Written and published from Strasbourg, Farel

---

[24]   Charles the Fifth later stayed in Metz for three weeks to observe the success of the repression of the evangelicals in the city. Comité Farel, *Guillaume Farel*, p. 502.

[25]   The prayer reacts to an event of 3 October 1542. Then, in a letter dated 23 October 1542, Farel informs Calvin of his intention to show him the manuscript for his approval. Farel, *Traités messins*, p. 29.

[26]   Farel, *Traités messins*, pp. 27–8.

[27]   *Guillaume Farel: Biographie nouvelle*, pp. 492–3, 495.

[28]   'Farel réconforta ses compagnons d'infortune par ses prieres ferventes et ses exhortations et en chantant avec eux des psaumes'. *Ibid.*, p. 495.

[29]   In addition to the prayer, Farel signed his 120 page *Epitre envoyee au duc de Lorraine* on 11 February 1543 from Gorze. Early that summer two public appeals, 24 and 32 pages respectively, went out to Caroli, who had entered Metz in Farel's absence to advance the Roman side of the debate. In 1544 Farel published his 64 page *Epistre exhortatoire a tous ceux qui ont cognoissance de l'Evangile* (Geneva, 1544), and his 16 page *Epistre envoyee aux reliques de la dissipation horrible de l'Antechrist* (Geneva, 1544).

launches straight into prayer for 54 octavo pages without any introduction regarding the purpose or use of the prayer. Its purpose is more fully laid out in the following seven page request to the established Reformed churches to pray for their fellow believers who do not enjoy freedom of worship. Farel explains that they thought the word would have its way among them, that they would institute the church in Metz, but it 'all went up in smoke'.[30] He follows this with a short request to the princes and lords for freedom of worship. The booklet ends with a paraphrased versification of Psalm 120 in 7 stanzas with an 11–11–10–6 metre accompanied by a melody. In 1545 Farel reworked the prayer so extensively that he more than doubled the length of the book.[31] Obviously the issue of helping the persecuted believers pray was close to his heart.

Bodenmann and Labarthe are inclined to believe that Farel most likely dictated the prayer to an amanuensis. They point to several linguistic and stylistic indications.[32] Our own observations about the style of the prayer confirm this, as does Labarthe's narrowing of the time of composition to a window of about two weeks.

Before we turn to the prayer's contents, we note with Strohl, the final triumphant visit of Farel to Metz, undertaken shortly before his death at the age of 76. He was invited by the elders of the church in Metz to come and see the fruits God had granted there since the establishment of the church in 1561. Already in September 1561 the church numbered 7000.[33] In 1564, some six months before Farel arrived, the Reformed church of Metz had gathered about 10,000 members for worship in one day when a prominent Protestant lord married the widow of a local count. Farel arrived there on Saturday, 12 May 1565 accompanied by three prominent men from Neuchâtel and preached the next evening to an innumerable crowd, 'with extraordinary comfort for all the congregation'.[34]

We will now first examine the 1542 edition of the prayer written for Metz, and then some of the additions Farel makes in 1545.

---

[30]   Guillaume Farel, *Oraison tresdevote*, c6v–d1v. In the prayer and letter Farel never mentions Metz by name but does speak of *'monsieur le maistre Escheuin'* (c7r), *'ceste paoure ville'* (b7v), and of the people fleeing *'de la ville'* (b8v). He tells the churches that *'Helas tout est alle comme en fumee'* (c8r). He adds, however, that the intercessions made for them have not been without fruit, since they continue to hold to the faith and are able to receive the word by going out of the city (c7r, c8r).

[31]   Farel, *Forme d'oraison pour demander a Dieu la saincte predication de l'euangile* (Geneva: Jehan Girard, 1545). Note that the prayer of this title contained in *Du vray usage de la croix de Iesus-Christ* (Geneva: Fick, 1865, pp. 278–88, has been severely abridged, containing only about ten per cent of the 1545 prayer.

[32]   Farel, *Traités messins*, p. 23.

[33]   *Guillaume Farel: Biographie Nouvelle*, p. 507.

[34]   *Guillaume Farel: Biographie Nouvelle*, p. 511.

Trinitarian structure

What is the structure of the prayer? We ask here a rather rational question of a rather affective prayer. Like many free prayers – especially those full of fervour – Farel's prayer does not readily exhibit a clear structure. Repetition occurs, particularly in confessing sin and asking for the hearing of the pure word of God. Nevertheless, it is possible to discern a chiastic structure addressing each of the persons of the Trinity sequentially with the plea for the giving of the word. First Farel pleads with the Father (a2r–b8r),[35] then the Son (b8r–b8v), and then the Holy Spirit (b8v–c1v). He then returns to the Son (c2v–c3v), and ends with the Father (c3v–c5v).[36] We are convinced that Farel did this consciously, as his 1545 additions to the prayer will demonstrate. The chiasm lends itself to regarding the Father as overall cause, director and end; the Son as the one who glorifies the Father by serving as mediator to fulfil the Father's plan; and the Spirit as the life power at the heart of both of the other persons, who proceeds from both and glorifies both.[37] If thought of as a 'V' instead of the chiastic 'X', the structure puts the Spirit closest to the world, as the one who brings all the divine gifts down and carries believers up to God spiritually. Throughout this structure, Farel's central plea is unmistakable: that God grant the church pure gospel preaching, faithful preachers and the right use of the sacraments. Every person of the Trinity receives this petition. On the other hand, many other petitions more closely follow the particular incommunicable attributes of each divine person and the activities in which each one is most prominent. As we now examine the prayer's contents, we will first roughly follow the order of the prayer itself and then probe some of the themes more deeply.

Praying for pastors, preaching and sacraments; confessing sins

Farel opens the prayer in this way:

> O Lord God and Father, full of mercy, have pity on us and lend your ear to our cry. We are compelled to lift up [our cry] to you, our only refuge, help and consolation in this great distress. We are pressed by the dreadful famine of your word, lacking the lawful food for our poor souls, deprived of good and

---

[35]   It is possible that sometimes Farel may have the whole Trinity in view as 'Father' and not just the first person.

[36]   The only transition point that is not transparent is the shift from addressing the Holy Spirit to the Son.

[37]   In the New Testament see, for example, Romans 11:36, 'For from him [as Father?] and through him [Son and Spirit?] and to him [as Father?] are all things. To him be the glory forever! Amen'.

faithful pastors who carry out their office and duty just as you, O Lord, have commanded. Rather, we are in the hands of those who do not care for you or for your flock and who do not pay attention to your law or your word, and do nothing with the goal of serving, esteeming, honouring, and adoring you by a true and living faith as you require.[38]

Exposing the Roman Church's faults does not lead Farel to self-justification or to the plea for its destruction, but rather to the confession of corporate sins. He considers that the Church – himself and the believers in Metz included – has deserved this famine, and therefore the grounds for his appeal can only be the mercy of God, the promises of God and the reputation of God. This also allows Farel to remind God of his own perfections:

For we have offended you too much by the grossest idolatry, comparing you to the work of human hands – you Lord, who are almighty, all good, and all wise; you who see, understand and know everything, who give life and being to all that live and subsist, and who have life from none other than yourself.[39]

As Christoph Burger has pointed out, other evangelical themes also pervade the prayer.[40] Thus, righteousness by works is ruled out. Law and gospel are contrasted. A true and living faith is sought. The mass is opposed to Christ's satisfaction and the Reformed understanding of the Lord's Supper. Throughout, the form of prayer is maintained, yet the polemics of the Reformation come through clearly. For instance:

If the works that you commanded, O Lord, cannot give life, righteousness and salvation, and can in no way bring back the sinner from his sin, nor purge and cleanse him because of the evil and sin which is so great and so rooted in man – to such an extent that it is impossible, being so corrupted, that he have the purity that the law commands or that he perfectly perform that which it

---

[38]   'O *Seigneur Dieu & Père plein de misercorde, aye pitie de nous, & exauce nostre cry: lequel sommes constrainctz de leuer a toy, nostre seul refuge, ayde, & consolation en la grosse destresse, de laquelle nous sommes pressez par l'espouvantable famine de ta saincte parolle, n'ayant la droicte nourriture de noz paoures ames, priuez de bons & fidelles Pasteurs, qui facent leur debuoir & office, O Seigneur, ainsi que tu leur as commande, & sommes es mains de ceulx, qui ne se soucient ne de toy, ne de ton troppeau, & qui ne regardent ta loy, ne ta parolle: et ne sont rien afin que tu soyes seruy, prise, honnore, & adore en vraie & viue Foy comme tu le demandes'*. Farel, *Oraison tresdevote*, a2r.

[39]   '*Car trop t'auons offense par tresgrosse ydolatrie, te comparant a l'œuuraige de la main de l'homme, toy Seigneur, qui es tout puissant, tout bon, & tout saige, qui voys, qui congnois, & qui scais tout, qui donne vie & estre a tout ce qui est viuant & qui subsiste: & n'as vie ne estre d'autre que de toy mesme'*. Farel, *Oraison tresdevote*, a2v. See also b6r.

[40]   Burger, *Farels Frömmigkeit*, pp. 151–4.

demands – how can the abominations invented by so cursed an antichrist be able to save, justify, purge and cleanse the sinner?[41]

When confessing sins before God and seeking forgiveness – which occurs periodically throughout the prayer – Farel recounts some Old Testament history as proof that God punishes persistent sin. He recalls the Noahic flood, Sodom and Gomorrah, the ten tribes of Israel going into captivity, the two tribes of Judah suffering the same, and finally the Jews rejecting Jesus and his gospel.[42] This brings him to the early Church and gives him opportunity to remind fellow evangelicals that judgement awaits those who avoid reform at present. He does this by noting that the early Church in the West, in Judea, Egypt, Asia and Greece did not abide by the word of God and did not remain in a 'true and living faith working through love'. Their apostasy explains why they are now under the tyranny of Mohammed, writes Farel, and provides an example for the Church at present to move it to return to 'the purity of the gospel'.[43] The threat of Islam was never far from the minds of sixteenth century European Protestants and Roman Catholics alike.

Theology and spirituality

There are many indications of how Farel's view of God influences his spirituality. He never suggests any *quid pro quo* framework. Rather, Farel asks God the Father forgiveness in the evangelical way, 'for the love of Jesus your beloved Son', and 'in accordance with the merit of Jesus and in accordance with your righteousness and holiness'.[44] He asks that God do for the evangelicals in Metz what he did in New Testament times for Jerusalem when he gave grace to that 'murderous city' so that they still heard the word.[45] Even more, everything about faith and salvation rests on

---

[41]   'Si les œuures que tu as commandees, O Seigneur, ne peuuent donner la vie, iustice, & salut, & ne peuuent aulcunement retirer le pecheur de son peche, ne purger & netoyer a cause du mal & peche qui tant est grand & si enracine en l'homme: tellement quil est impossible, estant tant corrumpu, quil ayt la purete que la loy commande de quil parface ce qu'elle demande: comment les abominations inuentees d'vn si mauldict antechrist pourront sauluer, iustifier, purger, & netoyer le pecheur?' Farel, *Oraison tresdevote*, a7r.

[42]   Farel, *Oraison tresdevote*, b1r–b2r.

[43]   Farel, *Oraison tresdevote*, b2r. In the 1545 edition of the prayer Farel here inserts some second person pronouns, an 'O God', and an 'O righteous Lord'. He must have realized that the 1542 version here loses the sense that it is prayer.

[44]   'pour l'amour de IESVS ton trescher Filz … selon le merite de IESVS, & selon ta iustice & sanctite'. Farel, *Oraison tresdevote*, b6r.

[45]   Farel, *Oraison tresdevote*, b6v.

God, even the desire that he and his fellow praying believers have for the increase of the gospel. Thus, he prays:

> O Lord God, will you not have pity on us? Alas, Lord, look upon us in pity and grant only that the desire that we have by your grace to hear your holy word – which comes from and is from you – not exist without obtaining that which we in such a manner desire, O good God.[46]

With such a view Farel can also plead that God not abandon what he has begun. 'Alas, Lord, will you grant such a beginning and such an entrance into knowledge of you, to neglect and abandon us?'[47]

Further, since Farel regards his own faith to be God's gift, and since he knows that he once thought and practiced differently, he trusts that God can change the hearts of those who oppose the evangelicals. He writes, 'We do not want evil to come to anyone, but that all be filled with your blessings and graces'. Again, 'Do we not ... with holy prayers seek [our neighbours'] salvation?'[48] He seeks the conversion of the priests, on the analogy of the apostle Paul's conversion, asking God to forgive them in grace.[49] As Burger points out, Farel wants the greatest number of lost souls reached by the gospel and rescued from the papacy.[50]

Grounded in God's Trinitarian glory

Like many later Reformed theologians, Farel finds the deepest ground for his petitions in God's own glory: This occurs in petitions to all three persons. To the Father he says, 'O Lord, grant that we know that you have worked it and that all the honour and the glory be given to you'.[51] Again, he asks for the conversion of civil leaders, 'to the end that you may be praised, served, and worshipped everywhere'.[52] To the Son he says, 'Look

---

[46]   'O Seigneur Dieu n'auras tu point pitie de nous? Helas Seigneur regarde nous en pitie, & ne permets que le desir que nous auons par ta grace d'ouyr ta saincte parolle: lequel vient & est de toy, ne soyt sans obtenir, o bon Dieu, ce que tant nous desirons'. Farel, Oraison tresdevote, b6v. See also b7r where Farel repeats to God three times that the evangelicals' desire for the salvation of their neighbours must be a gift from God.

[47]   'Helas Seigneur, nous auras tu donne tel commencement & telle entree en ta congnoissance pour nous laisser & abandonner?' Farel, Oraison tresdevote, c4r.

[48]   Farel, Oraison tresdevote, b7r.

[49]   Farel, Oraison tresdevote, c5r.

[50]   Burger, Farels Frömmigkeit, p. 159. This becomes even clearer in the 1545 version.

[51]   'Ha Seigneur qu'on congoisse que tu y as besongne, & que tout l'honneur, & la gloyre te soit rendue'. Ibid., c4v.

[52]   Farel, Oraison tresdevote, c5v. See also Forme d'oraison, 4 (new for 1545), 'Brief, ie n'ay autre chose, sinon que de me humilier deuant Dieu, & donner louange à son souuerain

to your honour and glory, look to your holy promises, O God, O our God'.[53] Again, recalling Luke 10, 'Is not this harvest great, O Lord Jesus? Is it not for you?'[54] To the Spirit he says, 'Glorify Jesus, because his glory is yours and the Father's'.[55] The last words of the prayer are, 'For the love of Jesus your Son fill all with your Spirit in order that all praise, glory and thanksgiving be given to you forever. Amen'.[56] What Old says generally of the Reformers in his study of the Strasbourg liturgy between 1525 and 1530 holds true also for Farel: 'Their whole understanding of prayer was based on the perception that prayer is essentially the work of the Holy Spirit in the body of Christ to the glory of the Father'.[57] This closing serves to highlight the Trinitarian schema of the prayer and the sovereignty of God.

Within the prayer Farel's rhetoric reaches higher when he implores God to grant the pure word, lest those who have begun in him should return to 'popery'. Surely, says Farel, you do not want us to serve your adversary more![58] Similarly, in his request to the churches he speaks of those facing death without the consolation of the pure word by faithful pastors.[59] His own possible death also figures: 'Will I die without hearing your holy word preached openly?'[60] Earlier, Farel made another memorable plea about God giving physical food to animals and to those that hate God: 'O good Lord, will you have more pity on the beasts than on those who sigh after your word which is our true food? Will you be more merciful and more inclined to give us ... food for the body than food for the soul? O Lord, are not our souls more dear than our bodies?'[61] He heightens this further when

---

Nom, qui voit, congnoist, & entend tout'.

[53]   Farel, Oraison tresdevote, c3v. See also Farel's 1552 edition of Summaire, where he inserts a new definition of prayer which highlights prayer's link to the promises of God. 'Praying is an ardent speaking with God from whom man asks and begs that which he has promised; that is, to aid his people, delivering them, forgiving them, saving them. In prayer, man declares God's power and magnifies his name and reign' (italics ours).

[54]   'Ceste moyson n'est elle point grand o Seigneur IESVS? N'est elle point a toy?' In the next sentence Farel uses an epithet we have seen in his earlier works, 'Ha doulx IESVS'. Farel, Oraison tresdevote, b8v.

[55]   'Glorifie le Seigneur Iesus, car sa gloyre est la tienne, & celle du Père'. Ibid, c1v. See also Burger, Farels Frömmigkeit, p. 153.

[56]   '[P]our l'amour de IESVS ton Filz: remplissant tous de ton Esprit: affin que toute louange gloyre action de graces te soyt donnee eternellement AMEN'. Farel, Oraison tresdevote, c5v–c6r.

[57]   Hughes Oliphant Old, 'Daily Prayer in the Reformed Church of Strasbourg, 1525–1530', Worship Vol. 52, No. 2 (March 1978), p. 126.

[58]   Farel, Oraison tresdevote, c3v.

[59]   Farel, Oraison tresdevote, c7v.

[60]   Farel, Oraison tresdevote, b7v.

[61]   Farel, Oraison tresdevote, c2r–c2v. See John 6.

he returns to Jesus and reminds him of his words to the Samaritan woman at the well about providing her with living water that would remove all her thirst. Farel then appeals: 'O good Saviour, although our faith be too small to come to you, yet let us come to you to ask you for this true water and for a drink'. Just as Farel spiritualizes 'daily bread' in the Lord's Prayer, so here he asks for the bread from heaven. He adds, 'Will you be so angry with us that you not hear us, you who heard the Canaanite woman? O Lord, give us some of the crumbs that fall from the children's table!'[62] With such a high view of spiritual things, Farel also prays about the believer's pilgrimage 'from this earthly city to the eternal city'.[63]

Finally, we return to the Trinitarian structure of the prayer by noting that the concepts that appear within the prayer do match the particular person of the Trinity being petitioned. Thus, in the sections addressed to the Father we especially notice appeals that focus on the sovereignty of God, his providence, his justice as Judge, the ordained way of salvation, salvation history and its present day lessons, his grace and forgiveness in Christ, and the plea that this Sovereign move the hearts of the earthly sovereigns. The plea that people know God's will also goes to the Father. To the Son Farel twice addresses the plea to remember the suffering he once endured so that he will not abandon his people. Since Jesus himself said to pray the Lord of the harvest to send workers into his harvest (Luke 10), Farel does just that. Farel also makes use of Jesus' words in John 4 to the woman at the well and John 6 about the heavenly bread. He alludes to other words of Christ from the gospels when he speaks of the leaven of the Pharisees, the crumbs from the children's table, and the shepherdless sheep. Farel addresses the Holy Spirit in line with the Nicene Creed, 'O Holy Spirit, true life-giver for poor souls'.[64] He follows this with mentions of the Spirit's inspiration of the Apostles, his gift of the word in many different languages at Pentecost (in contrast to the present use of Latin, of course), and his power to teach truth over against confusion, and give light over against darkness. From John 16:8 Farel takes the words of Christ about the Spirit's work and prays the Spirit to do this very thing, namely, to convict the world of sin, judgement, and righteousness. Here too Farel addresses the Spirit as divine, calling him 'Lord' and later pleading, 'O God, O God, shall we perish?'[65] In this way Farel shows himself fully

---

[62] Farel, *Oraison tresdevote*, c3r–c3v. See Matthew 15.

[63] Farel, *Oraison tresdevote*, c5r.

[64] Farel, *Oraison tresdevote*, b8v. Nicene Creed, 'We believe in the Holy Spirit, the Lord and Giver of life'.

[65] Farel, *Oraison tresdevote*, c2r. That Farel continues to address the Spirit here is evident from his use of '*Seigneur*' in connection with John 16:8, and his continued use of lie–truth and darkness–light themes. Although it is not as clear that Farel continues addressing

Trinitarian, something that Caroli – his sometime friend but now sworn opponent who had at the time entered Metz to help the Council of Thirteen – should have noted well, since in 1537 Caroli had charged Farel and Calvin with Arianism.[66]

The unity of the Godhead appears not only from the closing words noted above, but also from the fact that each are conspicuously addressed as 'Lord' and 'God', in the plea that the Spirit glorify Jesus because Jesus' glory is the Spirit's and the Father's also, and in Farel's early confession that 'when we lost Jesus our Saviour, no longer being in him nor for him, we were deprived of the Holy Spirit who unites us to him, and causes us to be in him by faith'.[67]

Singing for comfort: Psalm 120

Farel's use of Psalm 120 at the close of his 1542 *Oraison tresdevote* deserves some attention because of the crucial role of song in the 'culture of persuasion', in the spirituality of the Reformation.[68] Kaltenrieder argues persuasively that Farel should be given more credit for the start of congregational singing among the French speaking evangelicals, since the first publications of songs came in 1532 and 1533 from Farel's printer Pierre de Vingle in Neuchâtel.[69] His arguments are supported by Farel's words to the Geneva Council in 1535 summarizing the Dispute of Rive. Farel criticized the Latin Introit and Kyrie Eleison for being in Latin and being sung only by priests, and argued that all the faithful should instead assemble and 'all sing a Psalm in their language which they understand, praising God'.[70]

Farel's context for using Psalm 120 in 1542 was very similar to Luther's use of the same Psalm in 1524. Luther had used Psalm 120 in his 'Christian Letter of Consolation to the People of Miltenberg' whose city had been

---

the Holy Spirit further in c2r–c2v, yet even his appeals about daily bread may be brought to the Holy Spirit, who, in scripture, also gives life to all physical creation (Psalm 104:27–30).

[66]   Bernard Cottret, *Calvin: A Biography*, trans. M. Wallace McDonald (Grand Rapids, MI: Eerdmans, 2000), p. 125.

[67]   '[E]n de laissant *IESVS nostre Saulueur n'estans plus en luy ne a luy, priuez du S. Esprit qui nous conioinct a luy, & nous faict estre en luy par Foy'*. Farel, *Oraison tresdevote*, a4v. The Spirit is clearly addressed as '*Seigneur Dieu*' (c1r), since before and after this Farel directly prays to '*O sainct Esprit*' and '*O sainct & bening Esprit*'.

[68]   See Andrew Pettegree, *Reformation and the Culture of Persuasion*, pp. 40–75.

[69]   Andre Emile Kaltenrieder, 'The Liturgies of Guillaume Farel: Their Meaning and Relevance', (Ph. D. diss., Rhodes University, 1980), pp. 141–4.

[70]   Théophile Dufour, 'Un opuscule inédit de Farel. Le résumé des actes de la Dispute de Rive (1535)', *Mémoires et documents publiés par la Société de l'histoire et d'archéologie de Genève* (Geneva: J. Jullien, 1886), pp. 225–6.

forcibly re-Catholicized. Luther provided a translation of the Psalm into German followed by a brief commentary. The psalmist calls on God in trouble, claiming that he is a man of peace while others around him lie, deceive and promote violence. Luther emphasizes for the 'Lutherans' (as their opponents in this dispute were already calling them) that the battle is a spiritual one, not physical.[71] He ends by addressing the question of why the 'word of God' is not spreading as rapidly as he and others would like, when he says:

> I can blame [this] on nothing but our own indolence in asking for sharp arrows and hot coals. God has asked us to pray for his kingdom to come and his name to be hallowed, that is, for his word to make more Christians and to help them grow strong. However, since we let matters rest as they are and fail to pray earnestly, the arrows are dull and weak, the coals are cold and ineffective. The devil is not very much afraid of us ... Let us now turn the tables on him, vex him, and avenge ourselves. That is to say, let us call upon God without ceasing until he sends us marksmen equipped with sharp arrows and coals.[72]

Parallels between Luther's concerns and Farel's are obvious – praying for the progress of the gospel and for faithful, preaching pastors. Farel's spirituality also joins Luther's generally in promoting song, although Luther in 1524 did not offer Psalm 120 in song. Psalm 120 is not exactly an imprecatory Psalm, but it does assert the kind of punishment God will exert against those who hate peace and practice lies.

The version Farel uses is not original to him. The text was composed by Jean Ménard, included in the *Psalmes de David* from Antwerp in 1541 as text only, and in *La manyere de faire prieres* from Strasbourg in 1542, again as text only.[73] It appears that Farel's 1542 prayer is the first place that we encounter the melody of the Psalm in publication, a well-known melody from the Swiss Romande.[74] In 1545 Farel no longer included the Psalm, perhaps because it was to become available in the Strasbourg Psalter of that year together with its melody. It is of course possible that the printer Knolboch suggested the addition, but given what we know

[71]	Martin Luther, 'A Christian Letter of Consolation to the People of Miltenberg', *Luther's Works* ed. Helmut T. Lehmann (Philadelphia: Fortress, 1968), Vol. 43, pp. 105–7.

[72]	Luther, 'A Christian Letter', pp. 111–2. Luther's references to the arrows and coals are drawn from Psalm 120, where they are instruments the Lord will use in punishing deceitful tongues.

[73]	See Pierre Pidoux, *Le Psautier Huguenot* (Basel: Baerenreiter, 1962), Vol. 1, pp. 110–1; Vol. 2, pp. 7, 25, 29–30. *La manyere de faire prieres* was also published in Geneva in 1542 but this edition does not include Psalm 120.

[74]	Farel, *Traités messins*, pp. 33–4.

about Farel's use of Psalm singing to comfort the people of Metz in 1542, the inclusion of Psalm 120 was likely his own contribution.[75]

The pastoral context of prayer II: *Form of Prayer* (Neuchâtel, 1545)

New edition in 1545: Forme d'oraison

In late 1544 Farel reworked his '*Oraison tresdevote*' and published it in early 1545 as '*Forme d'oraison*'.[76] In doing so he provided us with an interesting case study in sixteenth century authorial editing. Just as Calvin is said rarely to have changed his views or substantially subtracted from the contents of the *Institutes* over its various editions, so here Farel hardly drops so much as a word of the original text.[77] Rather, he inserts huge sections of text at points – to the order of some 34 pages in one place and 24 in another – without losing any of the 1542 prayer. Many other smaller additions occur, from several lines to a couple of pages.[78] In a few places Farel changes a pronoun from third to second person to make it more clear that he is addressing prayer to God. All in all, the entire work goes from 56 octavo pages to 156. Besides the new title page with new scripture quotations, the only things dropped are the closing song (Psalm 120) and the marginal notes (which included scripture references and summary phrases in the 1542 version).

---

[75]   '*Farel réconforta ses compagnons d'infortune par ses prieres ferventes et ses exhortations et en chantant avec eux des psaumes*'. Strohl, *Guillaume Farel: Biographie Nouvelle*, p. 495. Bodenmann suggests that since Knolboch was the printer of the two earlier text-only versions of Psalm 120, it was probably the case that he had not yet received the musical notation from Jean Ménard. He also notes that in March of 1542 some 600 copies of *La manyere de faire priers* had been seized in Metz. Thus, by including the Psalm Farel was supplying something the evangelicals there lacked. Farel, *Traités messins*, p. 34.

[76]   Farel's letter to the reader was signed on 11 January 1545. Guillaume Farel, *Forme d'oraison pour demander a Dieu la saincte predication de l'euangile* (Geneva: Jehan Girard, 1545). Note that the prayer of this title contained in *Du vray usage de la croix de Iesus-Chirst* (Geneva: Fick, 1865), pp. 278–88, has been severely abridged, containing only about ten per cent of the 1545 prayer.

[77]   This is noted by Bodenmann also. '*Aucuns phrase du text 1542 n'a été sacrifée au cours du remaniement de 1545. Seuls de rares mots significatifs de l'édition première ont été omis ou remplacés par d'autres en 1545*'. Farel, *Traités messins*, p. 24.

[78]   Additions to the 1542 text are found in the new work as follows. First, a 30 page opening letter to 'All hearts inflamed with desire …'. Second, in the prayer itself the major additions encompass pp. 37–71 and 102–26. Smaller sections are inserted on pp. 35, 36, 72, 73, 75, 78, 81, 82, 83, 84, 85, 87, 91, 92, 93–5, 96–7 and 101. Third, a new section occurs in the request to the churches, pp. 137–8. Finally, the request to princes and lords receives 11 new pages, at pp. 142–53, and a section on p. 154. I have not included additions under five lines in this tally. See also Burger, *Farels Frömmigkeit*, p. 150, n. 2.

Farel's new title indicates more clearly that he is presenting the prayer for use by others, since he calls it 'A Form of Prayer' instead of a 'Deeply Devout Prayer'. Instead of quoting Psalm 90 on the title page, 'I am with you in trouble; call upon me and I will lend my ear to you', Farel quotes Psalm 79:8 9 where confession of sin leads to seeking God's help for the sake of the glory of his own name. This fits Farel's theology of prayer very well. Farel does not give any reason for his new title; it may simply be his desire for a fresh reception of the prayer – not only for the sake of sales but also to keep the people praying.

Since we are already familiar with the contents of the 1542 prayer, we will highlight only Farel's additions. This will begin with a clearer statement of how he envisions the use of his prayer. After reviewing the rest of his additions we will ask what these say about his spirituality. Finally, we will again explore the question of how these publications could persuade people to the Reformation cause.

Written as a proof of his affection

The first large addition to Farel's manuscript was an opening letter for those whose hearts were inflamed with the desire for the preaching of the holy gospel and the right use of the holy sacraments. In this letter he speaks very personally to the evangelicals of Metz – still without naming the place – about his deep affections for them, like a mother for her children.[79] For his part, he has never stopped praying for them to receive faithful pastors.[80] He would have liked to serve them with regular preaching but since he is prevented by Satan's schemes, he writes:

> I have laboured to stir you up to pray to our Lord and to move you better to holy prayer so that you will entreat the help of God in your present need and poverty, which is so great and so pitiful. I wanted to set in writing a request addressed to the Lord which is more pleasing and upright than any ever were. For he has never refused to grant a petition or request which is just and reasonable, one made to him in faith.[81]

---

[79]   This simile is drawn from First Thessalonians 2:7.

[80]   Farel, *Forme d'oraison*, pp. 3, 9.

[81]   '[I]'ay tasche de vous inciter à prier nostre Seigneur, & pour mieux vous emouuoir à la saincte priere, & à requerir l'aide de Dieu en la necessité & poureté, en laquelle vous estes, qui est fort grande & fort pitoyable: i'ay voulu mettre par escrit une requeste adressée au Seigneur, lequel est plus amiable, & plus equitable, que tous ceux qui onc furent. Car iamais il n'a refusé d'octroyer la demande & requeste iuste & raisonnable, qui luy a esté faicte en Foy'. Ibid, p. 7.

Farel's written prayer should be taken as proof of how deeply he desires their salvation and wants them to pray for what they need.

> You should take this [prayer] as a memento from one who desires your well-being and salvation in our Lord. After reading holy scripture you can read this and listen to it. It will stimulate you to pray and give you material to think more on the sins for which you have been under the Pope, sins which certainly go beyond all that one can say – in order that when you remember them, you may cry out for mercy …. And those in other places who with you desire the word, can also be somewhat moved by this. Even all who have not been utterly corrupted and perverted and who have not fully intended to make war on our Lord – as many as have been baptized in the name of the Father and of the Son and of the Holy Spirit – can be moved to desire that the true and pure doctrine be preached and received by reading or hearing this. This pure doctrine must be held onto by those who have received holy baptism and true faith.[82]

Like Farel's prayer of 1524, his central aim is to move hearts – to prayer, to confession, to reformation, to request the very things God has promised, in particular his word. Farel expects scripture reading to occur prior to reading his prayer; scripture has the pre-eminent place. Yet the relation is symbiotic, for these prayers in turn ought to seek more of scripture, the source of true teaching. His remarks about both reading and listening fit the sixteenth century context where reading was less likely to be private and more likely to take place aloud, but may also suggest a communal setting as large as a worship service. He addresses them, after all, as '*vous*'. Farel certainly wants the entire church to cry out for mercy together. He will be well aware of the communal confession of sin and scriptural words of pardon that belonged to Bucer's liturgy in Strasbourg. *Oraison tresdevote* and *Forme d'oraison* would both support this liturgical element.

The connection to baptism is new compared to 1542.[83] Farel has in view the vast majority of Western Europeans of the time, who had been baptized with the Trinitarian formula. He wishes that all of them would read or hear his prayer and join him in praying. This will move forward the programme of reform, causing the kingdom of Christ to come.[84]

Farel states in his introductory letter that the churches should believe that God will grant such prayers, for these prayers are in accord with his will, and a perfect faith that desires such things will obtain them.[85]

---

[82]   Farel, *Forme d'oraison*, pp. 30–31.

[83]   Farel, *Forme d'oraison*, pp. 30–33. Farel's words about daily renewal by the Holy Spirit and 'detesting' sin also seem to be new concepts compared to 1542. The word 'detest' occurs several times in the opening letter.

[84]   Farel, *Forme d'oraison*, pp. 135–6.

[85]   Farel, *Forme d'oraison*, pp. 2, 7, 11.

Sometimes, however, God waits until his children have no hope, humanly speaking, like Abraham who was promised a child through Sarah.[86] They are to pierce heaven with their prayers, trusting that God can change the hearts of others – such as their civil leaders – even in a moment, as he did with the apostle Paul.[87] Farel recounts the sad events of 1543 in Gorze, trying to comfort the evangelicals by noting how their just-celebrated Lord's Supper helped them at that time.[88] Three sample prayers are included in the text of the letter as ways in which evangelicals can 'Put this death of Jesus in your prayers, and pray to the Father that he would consider it'.[89] The *sursum corda* motif returns.[90] Farel also makes more explicit the teaching that he and his fellow evangelicals are in themselves no better than their opponents.[91] Summaries of the gospel and its comfort occur repeatedly, something Farel never tired of teaching. Farel's additions to the prayer proper concern us next.

Idolatry and the devil

The first large addition (pp. 37–71) comes in the first section addressed to the Father and goes into great lengths on idolatry. Its placement rightly belongs to the opening of prayer, where one might more firmly establish the nature of the God being addressed. Not only is God far above lifeless idols, even those praying are above these idols, says Farel. Thus, Farel slightly satirizes the bringing of a lifeless idol before a living child made in God's image, and the idea of a real man standing stationary without eating or drinking, solely to represent God. The latter, he says, would be an insult to the man, as it also is to the pure Virgin Mary.[92] In fact, making idols out of trees and stones apparently even perverts the order of nature and the final causality of trees and stones.[93] He ranges from the Old Testament to the New, with the *a fortiori* argument: If idols were prohibited in the Old, how

---

[86]   Farel, *Forme d'oraison*, p. 8.

[87]   Farel, *Forme d'oraison*, pp. 5, 12–13, 18. Farel's six page 'Request to the churches' which follows the prayer is only slightly changed from 1542, but the change acknowledges the passage of time. He writes (1542), how they have 'begun to pray for us in the name of our Lord' and adds (1545) 'Pray and persevere, O you holy assemblies and all believers, who in your prayers till now have recommended us to our Lord'. *Ibid*, p. 137.

[88]   Farel, *Forme d'oraison*, pp. 14–17. Compare Labarthe's comments on dating. See Farel, *Traités messins*, pp. 27–8.

[89]   Farel, *Forme d'oraison*, p. 20. These prayers occur at pp. 12–13, 19–20 and 20–21.

[90]   Farel, *Forme d'oraison*, pp. 23–4, 53.

[91]   Farel, *Forme d'oraison*, p. 25.

[92]   Farel, *Forme d'oraison*, pp. 39, 43–4, 60.

[93]   Farel, *Forme d'oraison*, pp. 44–5.

much more in the New![94] The true and living images of God are believers who have been made new creatures by a true and living faith, adorned with good deeds.[95] Such people learn to seek spiritual things because Jesus left us bodily in order to send us his Spirit.[96] In line with this, Farel criticizes those who claim contemporary sightings of Jesus which sanctify this or that place: they would have people think of comings of Jesus other than his first and second comings. This is a distraction.[97]

It is important to remember that Farel and his contemporaries from all traditions had a very lively sense of the spiritual world. If we remember the legend of Luther throwing an inkpot at the devil – probably only a legend, but still highlighting the lively sense of the devil's presence for Luther and others in early modern Europe – then perhaps one of the rather unusual additions to Farel's prayer is not as odd. It occurs after he has recounted how Satan fills the world with idolatry and 'horrible blasphemies'. Farel accosts the devil himself! 'O Satan, how you have worked with all deceit and by vain seduction! How the poor souls are perishing … !'[98] It seems an odd turn indeed, to speak directly to the devil while praying to God! Immediately after nine lines of addressing the devil, Farel turns back to God, '*Ha, Seigneur*', he says, only you know the extent of these abominations.[99] It seems, then, that Farel knew he had addressed the devil, yet left the prayer that way. Perhaps we need to think of him as being greatly caught up in 'heavenly places' or 'spiritual realms' where he believes angels and devils do their respective duties towards God and the devil. Standing among them, he trusts in God and shakes his fist at the devil. Farel does so without fear because he believes the devil is a fallen angel under the power of God. His rhetorical turn to the devil shows Farel as a leader in prayer who does not need precedent, but prays as he thinks is fitting. While Farel's move might seem quite odd to us, it at least holds together with all of this first large addition, under the rubric of idolatry. In Farel's mind, Satan's deceit stands behind the idolatry, just as, one could say, the apostle Paul tells the Corinthians in First Corinthians 10:19–20 that demons stand behind the idols.

---

[94]   Farel, *Forme d'oraison*, p. 43.

[95]   Farel, *Forme d'oraison*, pp. 49–50.

[96]   Farel, *Forme d'oraison*, p. 53.

[97]   Farel, *Forme d'oraison*, p. 56.

[98]   Farel, *Forme d'oraison*, p. 62.

[99]   We offer here a paraphrase.

Addressing the Son: Affirming the Trinity

The second major addition to the prayer occurs in the next section, where Farel prays to God the Son. The entire addition of 24 pages addresses only the Son, strongly confirming the Trinitarian chiastic structure which we have observed in the original prayer of 1542. This addition perhaps offers some balance to the large addition in the earlier section to the Father. Were one to compute the number of pages prayed to each person in the 1545 prayer, the result would be 69–70 pages to the Father, 26–7 pages to the Son, and 2–3 pages to the Spirit. Farel thereby leads the Reformed believers in primarily addressing the Father, while not neglecting to address the Son, and reserving a small place for prayers to the Holy Spirit. In doing so, he generally reflects scripture, where Jesus teaches his disciples to pray to the Father (Matthew 6:9; John 15:16; 16:23–8; see also Ephesians 1:17; 3:14; and Colossians 1:3), yet accepts worship of himself and receives some direct prayer (Acts 7:59–60; Revelation 22:20, see also John 14:14), while no examples exist of prayer to the Spirit, and he is said to direct glory to the Son and Father, not himself (John 16:13–15). The argument for prayer to the Spirit is a theological one, resting on the fact that prayer is a form of worship, and each of the persons of the Godhead are equally worthy of worship (see the Nicene Creed).

It is worth remarking that Farel rarely speaks of the oneness of God. He clearly holds that the three persons are one God, as we learn from *Le Pater Noster et le Credo* where he says:

> I believe that you are one only God in three persons: the Father, from whom proceeds all action; the Son, who is the counsel of the operation; and the Holy Spirit, who is the motion or movement, from whom all things have their energy and power to make our service to you agreeable. Such then is the faith, which is only one, yet divided into three principle parts, of which the first is properly attributed to the Father, the second to the Son, and the third to the Holy Spirit.[100]

Yet Farel focuses on the divine persons. Might one say that his is a very personal kind of spirituality? He fastens on the persons as more concretely knowable, and thus also avoids certain streams of mysticism. But note well that the unity of God is present in his form of address. If he is praying to the Father, he speaks of 'your Son' and 'your Spirit', whereas if he is praying to the Son, he speaks of 'your Father' and 'your Spirit'. Praying to the Spirit he says the Son's glory is 'yours and the Father's'.

---

[100]   Farel, *Le Pater Noster et le Credo*, b4r.

Questions of Trinity are of course connected to baptism, and it was in this connection that Farel spoke about the use of his prayer by all baptized people, as we saw above. Farel later builds upon the reality of baptism when admitting sin. He confesses, 'How we have caused your holy name to be mocked, and holy baptism which we have received, to be violated!'[101] In a further addition, Farel speaks of how those who have been baptized ought to live. Evidently, he considers the use of the sacraments to put the recipient under obligation to God.[102] This helps provide him a connection point to the vast majority of Europeans in his day.

The role of prayer in the Reformation

Why does Farel so persistently utilize prayer? What was the role of prayer in moving people to embrace reform? It is abundantly evident that we cannot ignore the role of prayer in the Reform spearheaded by Farel. We may go further and state that no study of the Reformation can ignore the major shifts in piety, which included a concentrated reform of the practice of prayer. But, limiting ourselves here to Farel, what were the benefits of his focus on prayer? How did his upward spirituality contribute to the establishment of Reformed churches?

The very fact that Farel dictated (or wrote) and published the 1542 prayer is remarkable in itself. His 1545 reworking of the prayer shows that his 1542 work was not undertaken on a mere whim of affection, and followed closely on a different 1541 prayer (republished in 1543) as well as his very popular 1524 prayer. Farel had thought about the matter deeply and determined that sustained prayer was essential to the progress of reform. In this determination he probably was not unique, but in terms of his publication record, he was. Who else was in the habit of publishing prayers of this kind? Others wrote household and family prayers, prayers based on the Lord's Prayer, prayers based on Psalms, short prayers for the classroom, and some liturgical prayers, but repeated writing of new prayers and published prayers the likes of Farel's from the 1540s – prayers which were pointedly designed to seek the Reformation of the Church, indeed, to mobilize evangelicals towards concerted prayer for further reform – were singularly uncommon.

---

[101]   Farel, *Forme d'oraison*, p. 54.

[102]   '*& comment doyuent viure ceux qui sont baptisez*'. Farel, *Forme d'oraison*, pp. 93–4.

Prayer, not the sword

Farel's prayers – especially the 1542 prayer written in the midst of persecution – represent for him the spiritual answer to the problems faced by the Church. By the very act of praying as he does and publishing the prayers, Farel exercises the sword of the word and points away from the sword of the magistrate. In all the alliance building, letter writing, appeals to the Smalcaldic League and the Emperor Charles the Fifth, Farel points the Church to God by way of prayer. Farel truly believes, like Luther, that the prayers of believers have more power than the sword of the emperor.[103] This does not contradict Farel's request to the lords and princes for freedom of worship nor does it preclude participation in the Smalcaldic League. After all, Farel believes that civil government exists to protect the Church. It was lawfully established by God to be distinct from Church government, yet also to help the Church. In his view, members of the civil government should also be true members of the Church.[104] But even if these lords and princes do not heed the evangelicals' requests, the God of the evangelicals will use their own prayers to sustain them in the faith, no matter what the opposition.[105] For their part, the evangelicals would always pray for the lawfully instituted civil government. Farel's prayers for them appear repeatedly in the liturgical forms of 1533 and in the prayers of 1542/5. At the same time, the style of his prayers and the fact that he published them for others to join him in prayer underlined for the civil authorities the passion of the evangelicals for their own pastors, churches, preaching and sacraments. Farel wanted them to know this, and thus addressed letters of request to them, both as part of these prayers and separately, in other publications. Farel distances himself from Anabaptists and names Rome as the source of their views on church and state, since they, like the Pope, judged that they did not need to be subject to civil government.[106] By engaging evangelicals in this kind of prayer, Farel wants them to access the one mightier than all earthly powers, the one who directs kings and princes, and to rely on him alone to change the hearts of leaders and people alike for the sake of his own glory. Farel's prayers thus represent the point of a deep theological conviction about the sovereignty of God.

---

[103] See Martin Luther's, 'On War Against the Turk', *Luther's Works*, Vol. 46, pp. 165–6, 171–4.

[104] '*Vous donc, nobles ... comme vrays membres de la saincte Eglise, & vrayement du corps de IESVS CHRIST, vous faictes seruir vostre puissance en l'honneur de Dieu, & au salut des ames: à fin, que selon la pure parolle d'Euangile elles soyent conduictes & gouuernées*'. Farel, *Forme d'oraison*, p. 153. See also pp. 154–5.

[105] Farel, *Forme d'oraison*, pp. 10–11, 138.

[106] Farel, *Forme d'oraison*, p. 150.

Farel's self-loving God

Like Farel's *Le Pater Noster et le Credo*, both *Oraison tresdevote* and
Forme d'oraison teach evangelicals how to pray when God is sovereign
and humans' sinning is deep-rooted. Given God's maximal greatness,
there is no higher object of desire possible in the world, not even for God
himself. Thus, it is praiseworthy that God should put his own glory as the
final cause of all things. Already in his 1529 *Summaire* Farel wrote about
God doing all things and especially granting forgiveness 'for the love of
himself'.[107] His 1533 liturgy (which in large part dates back to 1528/9)
twice speaks similarly about God deciding to erase our sins out of love
of himself.[108] All of the documents under consideration were intended for
popular consumption, meaning that this teaching was not restricted to
the ivory towers of the theologians at all. This idea – that God's deepest
motivation for acting is his own glory – was not new to the Reformed
at all, but did receive special attention by them and should therefore be
considered in our historical questions of persuasion and reform. How could
this teaching advance the Reformation? Misconceptions arise easily. For
instance, if God acts for his own glory, it would seem that the condition of
people on earth is irrelevant to his acting. Why would he act for them in
trouble any more readily than when they are doing well? Whether or not
these were real problems for Reformed spirituality, Farel never seemed to
have noticed any contradiction here. In his mind, all things serve the glory
of God, and although believers do not know how God has ordained all
things to fall out by his sovereign providence, yet they know what God
has revealed via the Old and New Testaments. This explains Farel's fierce
praying by which he holds God to his word. Farel is convinced that no
one can go wrong by praying for an increase of gospel preaching, faithful
pastors, and the right administration of the sacraments precisely because
the scriptures teach that God desires these very things. Similarly, Farel
understands the scriptures to teach that God especially hears the prayers
of those who have no hope left but him. If the scriptures teach that God's
heart moves in these ways, then it must be to his glory to seek such things.
For Farel this involves no contradiction: God alone is an end in himself; all
things and people should serve him according to his word.

---

[107]   Farel, *Summaire*, Fols. A viii v; B vii v; C i v; G i r; K iv v; L ii r (pp. 48, 78, 88,
206, 306, 322).

[108]   Farel, *Maniere et fasson*, D i and D vi.

Farel's God and late-medieval spirituality

How might the above theology fill a gap in the spirituality of late-medieval and early modern people in Christendom? This, after all, is a key question to ask when we consider why the Reform spread so quickly. As Benedict has pointed out, we need to consider theological and not just social questions here. We now offer a synthesis of the material we have considered thus far, in particular, how the variety of secondary sources described late-medieval spirituality and how Farel considers himself to offer something different.

Farel steers away from a spirituality which involves a God with whom people could bargain, whom they could make indebted to them, cajole and reach via material objects. He wanted a big God, one, he argued, far beyond human capacities, sensibilities, predictions, 'superstitions' and manipulations. This suggests that in doing so he supplies a felt need of many of his fellows. It seems that the Reformers' return to themes of God's power, decrees, wisdom and incomprehensibleness served the perceived need for many people of the time to feel that God was bigger than their physical suffering, political instability, and short lives. Furthermore, the theme of God's word captured the hearts of people whose learning was growing in part due to Renaissance humanism's rediscovery of the classics. The theme of God's faithfulness and commitment to his word captured the hearts of people who perceived that their clergy had by and large become a self-serving institution loyal first of all to themselves – men, it was commonly said, who often kept their vows of celibacy to the letter (they did not actually marry), but not at all in spirit. Farel's insistence that believers pray in line with what God has promised in scripture pointed them to a dependable, trustworthy, promise-keeping God. He wanted to instil such fierce praying in people that it would seem (to him, at least) impossible to engage in such prayer while at the same time living profligate lives. Farel's God, then, was thought to raise the bar of morality, something that a city such as Geneva seemed to be already looking for, Reformation or not. All of the above is of course an explanation after the event yet it fits the facts regarding the shift in spirituality that was occurring.

If we can further synthesize what Farel is trying to do, we see that he seeks to motivate the entire existing Church, not just the leaders, but every last believer whose heart is 'inflamed with desire' for the gospel. Even those who are not so inflamed but are at least baptized and ought to desire the gospel more should pray these thoughtful prayers.[109] According to him, they all have direct access to this almighty, sovereign, all-glorious, self-subsisting God. Their very own prayers are no less valuable to their salvation than the prayers of their priests, departed saints, or the loved

---

[109]   See note 83 above.

ones who will survive them. While their God is infinitely greater than they, yet they are empowered by him to enjoy direct access to him, just as direct as their pastors. Farel, as preacher of the gospel, offers to them his own thoughts and words for their praying minds and lips. Thus, the 'office of all believers' is taking back prayer from the clergy; the distance between clergy and laity is shrinking; and Farel is a servant (minister), not a priest. The people were, Farel argues, being deeply involved in their salvation in an intellectually and emotionally meaningful way. No longer is there to be a divine office with its breviary alongside the rosary – the so-called poor man's breviary. Farel believes that Christ's Spirit illuminates all believers without discrimination.

Farel's efforts to comfort the persecuted, defeat the papacy, gain freedom of worship and establish Reformed churches – all by means of one and the same prayer – were not possible without teaching. New teachings were being introduced (or old ones were being re-introduced), a fact which once again speaks to the need for renewed study of the intellectual history of the Reformation. We are reminded of the purpose of *Le Pater Noster*. There, Farel wanted to get back to basics by teaching the Lord's Prayer and the Apostles' Creed, yet to do so by means of prayer. The teaching component of prayer takes an even more prominent place in *Oraison tresdevote* and *Forme d'Oraison*. Where *Le Pater Noster* had very little of polemics, *Summaire* introduced them and the prayers of the 1540s are filled with polemics. *Le Pater Noster* found trans-confessional usage, but this would have been impossible with *Summaire* and these later prayers. The polemics are far too prominent. On the one hand Farel himself had developed; on the other hand the formation and consolidation of the Reformed churches needed continued justification. Thus, the prayers Farel writes seek the very things the evangelicals of Metz were not obtaining, and cry out against what he saw as departures from the truth. Farel does the latter by confessing his own and his readers' participation in these sins. Part of proving the need to confess these sins included teaching from the Old and New Testaments about the divine punishment because of the sins of the people of God in scripture. Similarly, Farel is not satisfied merely to state the emptiness of what he sees as idolatry; he takes the opportunity to list various abuses, to satirize, to draw on scripture's critique of idolatry and to speak of the scriptural alternative – worship in spirit and in truth.

Farel regularly justifies his petitions as he prays them, thereby constantly teaching in the context of prayer. That is to say, his prayers repeatedly remind God why God should respond positively to the requests. Here and there – but not often – Farel gets so involved in justifying the petitions that he forgets that he is praying. He begins simply to speak to the people as a teacher, instead of to God. A few minor corrections of the 1542 prayer, made in 1545, show that he noticed this after the fact. Nevertheless, in the large additions of 1545 he once or twice seems to fall into the same mistake again. Perhaps this is not surprising when the prayer became 100 pages long. Whatever the case, the combination of teaching and praying is an interesting development. While it occurred more widely with respect to the basic theological diet of reform-minded persons – the Lord's Prayer, Apostles' Creed and the Ten Commandments – Farel may be unique in publishing prayers on the more involved and polemical Reformation teachings.

Farel's view of prayer and his published examples also promote corporate unity in the evangelical faith and its spirituality. Above all, Farel desires a heartfelt faith, a deep spirituality. If others could more clearly lay out the dogmas of the faith, few could tug at the strings of the heart more strongly than Farel. He wanted to be a man of piety and to expend himself to develop an entire Church of like piety. He rarely loses sight of encouraging others to pray; just the opposite, he easily loses sight of his own purpose, for example, when writing *Summaire,* and starts praying when one would not expect it. In reading his letters we see that Farel knew some of his faults well enough and admitted them freely. He would be the first to say he was far from perfect. But by doing so he simply underlines the transparency and authenticity of his own character. Given his successes, we may conclude that a good number of people must have recognized his leadership and been comforted by his lively and heartfelt spirituality.

Authenticity and the office of all believers

By freely employing prayer, Farel was saying to the people of his day that he wished to live before the face of God moment by moment. He speaks in God's sight, invokes God's name and includes himself as a sinner seeking forgiveness with others. This kind of authenticity was designed to help evangelicals live *coram Deo* – before the face of God. At the same time it seems it was the source of Farel's boldness. He answered to no man in matters of faith. God, Farel thought, ruled him through the scriptures and made him fearless. It is not hard to see how Farel promoted himself as an agent of change, and helped embolden many to identify with and advocate for reform. He lived like one whose spirituality was not primarily inward and mystical, but upward – one who seemed to find himself lifted up to heavenly places where one can see the throne of God and shake one's fist at the devil.

Calvin once stated that he regarded Luther to be an apostle, that is, a teacher sent by God for a one-time task, a man without successors.

Apparently some people thought of Farel as an apostle as well. Doumergue comments that Farel objected to being addressed as '*L'Apôtre des Allobrages*' and told his friends to address their letters very simply, to 'G. Farel, Genève'.[110] What might have led people to ascribe apostleship to Farel? No doubt his boldness led them there.[111] But Farel's devoted energy to preaching and prayer would also sustain this ascription. In the New Testament when the apostles found themselves too busy with practical concerns of outward spirituality (care for the poor), they encouraged the Church to select other men to take care of these aspects while they would devote themselves continually 'to prayer and to the ministry of the word'.[112] Many of Farel's colleagues dedicated their lives to the ministry of the word, but we know of few who matched him in their dedication to prayer.[113]

Farel seemed to work hard to gain such colleagues, as his prayers for Metz demonstrate. Farel had to build a rather new kind of clergy in the midst of strong anti-clericalism. Blakeley relates that on the eve of the Reformation there were about 322–470 secular clergy in the 161 parishes, and 677 religious men and women in 11 religious orders occupying 43 monasteries and convents in the Pays de Vaud.[114] Taking Lausanne as an example, Blakeley figures that only about 1.6 per cent of their clergy converted. On the other hand, about 50 per cent of the laity converted, a figure which seems to underline the disconnect between clergy and laity.[115] What this meant for Farel was an extremely acute shortage of pastors. In 1528– 9 there were only three preachers in the Pays de Vaud, soon five more, and by the 1530s a dozen. But there were about 160 parishes dotting the countryside! By 1536, when Calvin arrived on the scene, about 40 men were serving these parishes.[116] This context helps us to understand Farel's repeated plea in prayer for more pastors, as well as his plea to fellow evangelicals to join him in this praying. The finger-shaking prophet who kept Calvin in Geneva in October 1536 was not doing anything out of the ordinary. He was in the business of securing pastors, and he did only

---

[110]   Émile Doumergue, *Jean Calvin*, Vol. 2, p. 168, n. 3.

[111]   Compare Acts Chapter 4, for example.

[112]   See Acts 6:4.

[113]   This is not to say that Farel ever loses sight of the poor. In his publications concern for the poor and weak appears repeatedly.

[114]   James J. Blakeley, 'Popular Responses to the "Reformation from Without" in The Pays de Vaud' (Ph. D. diss., University of Arizona, 2006), pp. 154–5.

[115]   Blakeley, 'Popular Responses', pp. 177–8.

[116]   Blakeley, 'Popular Responses', pp. 82–3. Compare Herman J. Selderhuis, *John Calvin: A Pilgrim's Life* (Downers Grove, IL: InterVarsity Press, 2009), p. 55.

what Oecolampadius had done for him in 1524 and what Bucer would later do for Calvin in 1538.[117]

Evangelicals grew to respect Farel as leader of the new kind of clergy. One can imagine that his ardent praying would have made them feel like he had their best interests at heart. They could have felt that he was entering the trenches with them, visiting those suffering from the plague, putting his life on the line to preach the gospel in unfriendly cities. Farel's 1533 liturgy is one of many imprints that underline the anti-clerical motif with an opening challenge to the reader, 'Test the spirits, whether they are of God,' taken from 1 John 4.[118] He was trying to empower the people, draw them into the circle of the clergy, and give them the tools to pray directly to God themselves. The 'office of all believers' reduced the need for so many clergy.

Prayer, persuasion and Reformation

Farel would not let us avoid the question: How much of the success of the Reformation finds its explanation in these unceasing prayers that went up to God? Historians cannot subject such things to the same cause and effect scrutiny that is restricted to the natural world, and so they tend to avoid study of prayer. But if the first reason not to avoid such study is simply because it is an historical reality that people in the sixteenth century prayed and that changes in prayer life correlated with reform, then surely the second reason one should not avoid it is because all Christians of the sixteenth century – whether Catholic, Lutheran, Reformed or Anabaptist – considered prayer truly to reach the throne of God and to contribute in some way to the progress of Christianity on earth. For these reasons our sociological models and our analyses of the process of reform should acknowledge the important role of prayer. Undoubtedly only those 'within' the faith can wholeheartedly affirm the role of prayer (as understood by the Reformers themselves), in their understanding of the why of the Reformation. But this should not prevent historians from acknowledging the integral place of prayer in the lives of reform-minded persons, in their personal ownership of the doctrines and practices of the Reformation, in their advocacy for ongoing Reformation, and thus, in the end, in the whole movement that we call the Reformation.

---

[117]   See Chapter 1 of this volume.

[118]   Compare Isabelle C. Denommé and William Kemp, *L'Epistre Chrestienne*, pp. 46, 66; Philip Benedict, 'Propaganda, Print and Persuasion in the French Reformation: A Review Article'. *Bibliothèque d'Humanisme et Renaissance* Vol. 69, No. 2 (2007), pp. 454–5.

PART II
Texts of Guillaume Farel
in Translation

CHAPTER 5

The Lord's Prayer and the Apostles' Creed (1524)

Translation and Introduction
by Theodore Van Raalte

Introduction

The following text was translated from Francis Higman's critical edition published by Droz in 1982. We thank Droz for their permission. Arabic numerals inserted into the text indicate the page numbers in the critical edition. The original folio markings for Higman's base text, the 1525 Basel printing of *Cratander* found in the Österreichische Nationalbibliothek in Vienna, are also included in square brackets. We did not consult the 1536 Geneva printing of Wigand Koeln recently rediscovered by William Kemp in the Biblioteca Colombina in Seville. No other copies are presently known, possibly an indication that Farel's prayer book was so popular that most copies were discarded because extensive use left them in a state of disrepair.

The text of the Lord's Prayer that Farel uses varies slightly in its wording of the fifth petition (forgive us our debts) from his 1533 liturgy, but this variation simply reflects the different versions of the prayer in the gospels.

Farel's creedal text varies slightly between this publication and his 1533 liturgy, but the differences are minor such as the presence or absence of a pronoun, preposition or conjunction. One change is interpretive; where 1524 uses '*son filz unicque*', 1533 uses '*son seul filz*'.

In place of '*la saincte eglise catholique*' Farel uses '*la saincte eglise universelle*'. This is consistent over both documents. Calvin's 1553 Catechism used '*catholique*' while 'La forme des prieres ecclesiastiques' of 1552 used '*universelle*'.

Farel wrote the text without entering any scripture texts in the margins, thus we have not added any, although the alert reader will pick up allusions here and there. The translation has, however, broken up some of Farel's long sentences – indeed, in the French language the concept of a sentence such as we are familiar with today was only just developing at the time.

Calvin would make an important contribution to this process.[1] We have also taken the liberty of adding the italicized subtitles to help the reader. For further bibliographic information about *Le Pater Noster et le Credo*, see Chapter 3 of this volume.

---

[1]   Francis M. Higman, *Lire et Découvrir: La Circulation des idées au temps de la Réforme* (Geneva: Droz, 1998), pp. 344–8.

[33] [A1r] **The Lord's Prayer and the Apostles' Creed in French, with a rather nice and helpful explanation of each one, made in the form of a contemplation – an ample prayer profitable for inflaming one's heart and spirit with the love of God**

Read O Christians, and you will find consolation!

[35] [A1v] *To all the faithful, greetings in Jesus Christ.*

Our heavenly Father, an ever-merciful God has, by his infinite goodness, desired to declare to us his holy will in order that we might certainly reach him. He has declared it by a great number of messengers – so many patriarchs and prophets – and finally, in the times of the revelation of the greatest and highest mystery, which had been hidden for time eternal, he sent to us his dearest Son, true God and true man, Jesus Christ our only Saviour and sole mediator. He came to abolish and destroy all our sins, and to establish us by his holy teaching in the true and living faith, a faith full of good works.

And so when our faith has regard only [36] for the depths of the goodness of God, depending on all the mercy and loving kindness of God, one of the most [A2r] noble fruits which it produces is prayer – the lifting up of the spirit and the understanding to God. But because we do not know what we must pray, nor how, as it is written to the Romans, the good Jesus, who was so deeply humiliated for us, wanted to show us how we ought to pray, both as to form and manner. He commanded us that when we would pray, we ought to pray like this: 'Our Father who are'. And therefore all of us must speak this prayer with a very deep reverence and humility of heart, and a very great fervour of spirit, thinking through all the words which are in the spoken prayer. We must do so for the honour of him to whom we pray, yes, of him who gave us the form for praying like this. Until now the sheep of God have had very poor instruction in this, through the great negligence of the pastors, who need to [A2v] instruct them to pray in a language which they comprehend, and not merely to mutter from the lips without any [37] understanding.

For, as saint Paul says, 'If I pray in a tongue, my understanding is unfruitful'. And therefore he commands, that whatever is spoken in the assembly of believers, which is the church, be spoken in a language that all can comprehend; otherwise we should remain silent.

Now if we had observed this command, never would such dark times have come upon us, for we should have prayed more in spirit and truth to the celestial Father himself in heaven, and not to creatures on earth, carnal and vain.

Therefore, to the end that everyone be able to pray in a way that he understands whatever he is saying, this little booklet, which anyone can easily carry by hand, contains the Lord's Prayer and the articles of faith found [A3r] in the Apostles' Creed, with a simple exposition of the two. Thus they can be more easily understood by simple people who are not studied in holy scripture. This booklet can also give them some access to that [38] table from which every Christian must obtain his reflection, and his rule for living.

Therefore, let each one devoutly pray for the infinite mercy of God, that it might be his good pleasure to open for us the kingdom of heaven, through the true knowledge of the scriptures which he alone gives and no one else, to the end that in all things and through everything we might be means and conduits for him and no other, and thus we might arrive in the promised land, in the city of the heavenly Jerusalem with all its joyful things. Amen.

[39] [A3v] The prayer made by our Lord Jesus Christ, recited by saint Matthew in Chapter 6, where Jesus Christ says: When you pray, do not speak a great deal, like the Gentiles do, who think that they must be praised for the multitude of their words. Therefore do not make prayers like theirs, because your Father knows what things you need before you ask him. You therefore should pray like this:

> Our Father who are in heaven,
> hallowed be your name.
> Your kingdom come to us;
> your will be done on earth as in heaven.
> Give us today our daily bread,
> and forgive us our debts,
> as we forgive our debtors.
> And lead us not into temptation,
> but deliver us from evil.
>   Amen.

Now follows the explanation of this prayer made in the form of a prayer, to be read in place of the rosary, when one has the time [40] [A4r]

Our Father in heaven

O our blessed God and almighty Father, how is it possible that we should be able to understand your great mercy and goodness, which you have shown to us in all the good things that you have done for us – in creating heaven and earth, and all creatures to serve and help us in all our needs, and most of all in restoring us by the incarnation, death and glorious resurrection of your dear Son, our blessed Saviour and Redeemer, Jesus Christ! We, the human family, who by the unbelief and offence of the first man, Adam, were made subject to death and eternal damnation! Above [A4v] everything, I am not able to marvel enough at the great goodness and love which you show us in this, that you wish to be called Father by us beggars, wretches and condemnable sinners. So gently do you receive us as your children, that we should not doubt in anything that out of your infinite mercy you wish to give us all [41] that we need from you, as you have shown us by your Son Jesus Christ, who says to us: 'Whatever you ask of my Father in my name, he will give it to you'.

In order that we might have an even greater trust in you, he says moreover: 'If you, who are evil, know how to give good gifts to your children, how much more shall my heavenly Father, who is good, give good things to those who ask for them'. Therefore, O ever-merciful Lord, I bend the knees of my heart before you, [A5r] and I speak according to your commandment: O our Father, who are in the heavens, not only now, but always, full of jubilation and delight, in whom we ourselves must abide and put all our trust, to whom we owe our creation, to whom we owe that we have been redeemed and delivered from our sins, to whom we owe all the good things and virtues that we have! We call you Father, in order that we might know that you are gentle and kind toward us, you who we say is in heaven. We call you Father so that when despising these earthly and fleeting goods, we might be able to lift our hearts up there, and ponder that through your blessing alone can we be made pure and [42] whole. We call you Father and we say you are ours, and not only mine, in order that we might understand that we need have nothing of [A5v] our own, for whatever comes to all from your kindness and liberty alone is all that believers have.

Be pleased then, O our most bountiful Father, to turn the eyes of your very wide mercy toward us your poor children, who are here on earth, full of earthly terrors, full of distress, full of sorrows and tribulations, especially always filled with sins, filled with unbelief and without trust in you. We pray that you be pleased to help our uncertainty, and strengthen our feeble trust. We pray that you be pleased graciously to pardon us all that we have wrongly done against your divine power by our unbelief, and whatever we have wrongly done against your holy goodness by our feeble trust. We pray this in order that we, who according to the name of your dear Son Jesus Christ are called Christians, [A6r] not carry this name in vain, but that your name be sanctified in us by true faith, sure hope, and perfect love in you, and toward our neighbour. Surely boasting does not belong to us, seeing that everything which is done well and praiseworthily

through us is the work of your grace, which you give us with your Holy
Spirit, whom we receive by faith.

Hallowed be your name

I confess however, O my ever-dear and most merciful Father, that I have
dishonoured your holy [43] name some 70 times by my lack of faith and
trust in you. I have shown this by complaining against you, and not bearing
with patience all that which you have sent to me. Nevertheless, you make
all things as good as they can be, so that despair of you and of your holy
goodness show me to be rather the son of your enemy, [A6v] the Devil
of Hell. I am more worthy to be called a son of eternal damnation than
your son or a Christian. But dearest Father, I do not want to distrust you,
but rather with all ardent courage, distrusting everything of my own, and
abiding entirely in you, I cry out through a firm trust in you – O our Father,
have pity on your disobedient and law-breaking children; remember their
weakness which prevents them from controlling themselves.

Your kingdom come

Therefore let your kingdom come, make your dwelling in our hearts,
and rule according to your holy will in all these our thoughts, desires,
affections, words and works, so that we are no longer able to act against
your holy will. Let all our human carnal and damnable affections be put
to death, abolished and destroyed to the extent [A7r] you know to be
necessary for your honour and our salvation.

Your will be done

Your will be done on earth, as in heaven, where all the holy angels and
all the blessed souls of the saints – men and women – give thanks to you,
forever praising you unceasingly. May we too, who [44] are here on earth
be able to give thanks to you always and to offer praise for your great
blessings and infinite grace which you work for us every day. May we
abide ever in your grace, especially rejoicing through faith out of your
grace, because from moment to moment you give us all that is needful for
us, all that is wholesome for body and soul.

Thus, the good things which we possess come from you, and they are
your powers which work through us, because all our willing, all our power,
is only sin and damnation.

[A7v] Seeing therefore that we can do nothing without you, that you
love nothing in us, except your grace and favour, govern us always according
to your holy will (for by the provocation of our own will, of the world,

and of the enemy from Hell we act only in rebellion against your holy will. Whenever something happens to us against our own opinion and foolish affection, we will certainly want our will to be done, and not yours. Yet yours can only be good and wholesome for us, since in compensation for this present misery, sorrow and tribulation you have promised us salvation and eternal rest, and in you alone we put our trust). Seeing therefore that from no other can we acquire anything acceptable to you, except from you alone, our so freely-giving and ever-merciful Father, do not withdraw your ever-merciful eyes – that is [A8r] to say, your holy grace and favour – from your children, but rule us always according to your holy will.

Give us this day our daily bread

And [45] give us today our daily bread from your divine teaching, and from the holy and sound words of the gospel and from the precious body of your blessed Son Jesus Christ. He gave it for us in a covenant under the species of bread and wine to confirm our faith. By this we believe, that through his death and suffering peace has been made between you and us, and that we have forgiveness of all our sins. Thus, by this divine bread we might be fortified against all unbelief and distrust, from which all sins go forth, and thus we might be able always to live and die according to your divine will.

As for the rest – that which we need to pass through this life – we depend and rely upon [A8v] everything in the promise, which you spoke by the mouth of your dear Son: 'Seek first and above everything the kingdom of God, and his righteousness, and everything else you need shall be added to you'. In this I discern your great bounty, by reason of which you promise us (without demanding) what of ourselves we are accustomed to be the more worried about, and show us that all our care and worry must be in the things concerning our salvation.

Forgive us our debts

But unhappily, O good Father, our wickedness is so great that we abuse the good things that you have given us through greed, avarice, wastefulness, pride and several other sorts [46] of sins. You give them to us not to hoard them but to distribute them everywhere whenever charity shows this to be [B1r] necessary. How ungrateful we are when we do not want to recognize that they come from you! As a result, we do not give thanks to you, inasmuch as we have been blind in ourselves.

Therefore, O our most bountiful Father, I prostrate myself and come into your presence humbly, praying that by your great mercy you would have pity on us and forgive us all our sins.

Moreover, I know by the teaching that your blessed Son Jesus Christ gave us that we cannot have remission of all our sins, unless we first have peace and harmony with our Christian brothers, freely forgiving them from a good heart all that they have done wrong against us. But I find within such evil and perversity, and such lust for vengeance, that from myself I am not able [B1v] at all to do it. Therefore I pray you, Father, with all my heart, that it please you to help me, to change my deceitful, hardened feelings by your goodness and mercy and by your Holy Spirit. Do so that I might be able perfectly to forgive all others, and to say with a good and sincere heart: Forgive us our debts and sins, as we forgive our debtors and all those who have wronged us.

Lead us not into temptation

To the end that we might be prevented from offending you more, and from doing anything against your divine will, indeed, that we might rather do your will through your assistance and help, I plead most humbly with you, that you not lead us into [47] temptation. By your divine aid, enable us to resist all the temptation of the devil, of the world and of our own flesh. Deliver us from that evil enemy, who, without ceasing, surrounds us and lies in wait, seeking us out, roaring like [B2r] a lion set to devour us. Deliver us also from his allurement with all manner of sins and evils. Deliver us as much from the past as from the present, and from the eternal sorrow of hell, for there no one will be able to praise you nor to confess your name and your goodness.

For yours is the kingdom, the power and the glory

And because it is your holy will that sinners be converted and live in you, and with you, I pray you, O almighty Father, that you bring us through this brief and dangerous life, seeking your honour and your glory alone by a firm faith, sure hope and perfect charity. May we in this way be found among the number of your holy elect and be placed by you and together with you in eternal life. Grant this all so that with all the angels and blessed souls we might give you unending thanks and praise forever. Amen.

[48] [B2v] Here follows the Apostles' Creed, containing the 12 articles of the faith

I believe in God the Father almighty, Creator of heaven and earth, and in Jesus Christ his only Son, our Lord, who was conceived by the Holy Spirit, born of the virgin Mary, who suffered under Pontius Pilate, who was crucified, dead and buried, and descended into Hell; on the third day he arose from the dead, he ascended into heaven, and sits at the right hand of God his Father almighty, from where he will come to judge the living and the dead. I believe in the Holy Spirit, the holy universal church, the communion of saints, the forgiveness of sins, the resurrection of the body, the life everlasting. Amen.

[49] [B3r] Now follows a very helpful explanation, to inflame faith in God, made in the form of a prayer

O my blessed God, although you know the secrets of my heart, and know that I cannot have even the smallest longing for you or the littlest faith or trust in you without your knowledge, yet I need to pray. Although you precede every good thought I have, because you are necessarily the giver, the source, and the fountain of all good thoughts and all other good things, the worker of all goodness, yet I need to pray. Although you have no need for anyone to tell you his desires, that is to say, the faith, hope, trust and love which he has in [B3v] your righteousness, goodness and mercy, nevertheless we have need frequently to pray. Our need is to excite, move and inflame our sleeping, lazy and cold desires and spirits by fervent meditation of the heart which is helped by the prayers of the mouth when they proceed from the ardent longing of the spirit.

For this reason, our exercise of faith in you is highly necessary [50] to attain to true righteousness; indeed, we cannot have it without faith. For, as you said by the mouth of your holy one, the just will live by his faith, and, whoever believes in you will not taste eternal death, because by this faith alone are we made acceptable to you. I pray you most humbly that it please you to give me your Holy Spirit who enables me to learn [B4r] how I must confess before your face the faith and trust which a true Christian must have in you.

I believe that you are the one and only God in three persons: the Father, from whom proceeds all action; the Son, who is the counsel of the operation; and the Holy Spirit, who is the motion or movement, from whom all things have their energy and power to make our service to you agreeable. Such then is the faith, which is only one, yet divided into three principle parts, of which the first is properly attributed to the Father, the second to the Son, and the third to the Holy Spirit.

But, my blessed God, not only do I believe that whatever is said or written concerning you in Holy scripture [51] is true, but I also put all my hope and trust in you alone. Without yearning for or confiding in anything else, I believe in you, confessing that mere acceptance of scripture is better called knowledge [B4v] than faith, and is really nothing but a dead faith.

I believe without any doubt that you will be and do for me just as you have said and promised in your true and holy word. And I believe that such a faith – yearning, confiding and venturing out entirely in you (just as you say), whether in life or in death – alone makes a person Christian. You grant him all that he asks in your name. And I believe likewise that no deceitful, double heart can have such a faith, because it is a living faith, such as you command in the first commandment, where you say: I am the Lord God, you shall have no other gods. In addition I believe that no one [B5r] can give me such a faith but you alone, my almighty God, and that by this faith, and through no other means, I am able to know the deity of your Son Jesus Christ, and of the Holy Spirit. Thus I believe in them as in you, O heavenly Father. This faith will be able to make me believe that you, Father, and your [52] Son, with the Holy Spirit, are one only essence, and moreover one God in three persons.

I believe in God the Father almighty

For the first part of the Christian faith, then, I believe in you, Father, God, the Almighty, Creator of heaven and earth: that is to say, I abjure the evil spirit, all idolatry and sorcery, all false diviners, and all unbelief or heresy. I do not place my trust in any man – not in myself; not in my virtue and good works, [B5v] however much they seem to be holy, great or numerous; not in my merits; not in my knowledge; not in my prudence; not in my riches; not in my power; not in any other thing that I can have or think of on earth; not in any creatures, however holy they may be, or in whatever place they may be, whether on earth, or in heaven. I solely place my trust, my hope, my comfort, and all my refuge in you alone, my infinite God, who created heaven and earth, who alone is almighty and above all creatures.

I place myself completely in your hands and infinite power, submitting all my life to your most holy and good will. Whatever can happen to me, whether prosperity or adversity, repose or tribulation, [53] honour or shame, riches or poverty, [B6r] sickness or health, life or death – in the end even salvation or damnation, I submit to you and seek nothing else but your glory and praise.

What is more, I am neither afraid nor terrified in any way by all the evil, perversity and guile of the devil and all his followers. I believe, O my almighty Father, that you are far above all of them, and that the doors of hell, that is to say, all the hellish powers, whether the devil, temptation or sin, are unable to do anything against such a faith and trust in you. I do not believe less in you if I am persecuted and abandoned by all the people of the world; if I am poor, ignorant, illiterate and little learned; or even if I lose all that I have in the world, I do not believe less and I do not trust less in you, my ever-merciful Father. Still, I am a sinner. Principally, however, I [B6v] trust and abide only in you, because I know and recognize that from myself, and without your grace and favour, and without your Holy Spirit, [54] I am unable to do anything but sin.

Being in your grace by the means of this faith, I am not able to sin – not meaning that in this life I am able to do something free of imperfection, but that your grace and your Spirit, which you give to this faith, abolish and destroy all the power of my deceit. They are the reason why my imperfection and iniquity have not been imputed to me, and why you conceal it as if it never existed.

Because my faith needs to navigate and pass over everything there might or might not be, it must overcome everything – sin, virtue and everything else, to the end that it abides entirely and purely [B7r] in you, just as your first commandment requires.

I also do not need you to prove yourself to me by any sign or miracle. I believe firmly in you, however long you delay or at least seem to have withdrawn from me, because you always help us, even if we do not always sense and perceive it. I do not prescribe anything to you – time, measure or manner, but I place everything in your divine will, with a true and lawful faith. Since then you are almighty, as [55] you certainly are, what could weaken me, or of what could I have a lack or poverty? Since you are the Creator of heaven and earth, and Lord of everything, where is the one who could take anything from me, or overwhelm me in any way? In particular, if you approve and apportion all things to me, how will they not come together [B7v] for good and for my service, seeing that they are all obedient subjects of yours?

Since therefore you are God, you can do everything, and you know how you will do the best for me. Since you are Father, you desire to do it willingly, and you do it from a good heart. Since I doubt none of this and since I place my trust in you in this way, I am considered by you and held to be your son, your servant and your heir, and thus you will do for me according to my faith.

I believe in Jesus Christ, his only Son

[56] Secondly, and with respect to the second part of the faith: I believe in Jesus Christ your only Son, our Lord, who was conceived by the Holy Spirit, born of the virgin Mary, and suffered under Pontius Pilate, crucified, dead and [B8r] buried, he descended into hell; on the third day he arose from the dead, he ascended into the heavens, he sits at the right hand of God his Father almighty; from there he will come to judge the living and the dead.

That is to say: I not only believe that Jesus Christ is your true and only Son in one eternal, divine nature, always without a begotten beginning, but also that all things are subject to him, and that according to his humanity he is constituted my Saviour. He is even Saviour of everything which, according to his divinity, he created with you, O heavenly Father.

I believe that no one can believe in you, nor come to you, whether by skill, by subtlety, by machination, by any work, or by anything that we can name in heaven or on earth, except only by and through Jesus Christ your only Son, that is to say, by faith and belief in [B8v] his Name.

I believe firmly that he was conceived for my benefit without any human work or fleshly act, without a physical father or male nature. Thus he could purge and make spiritual the criminal, fleshly, impure and damnable conception, both of me and of every human who believes in him, seeing that it is the benevolent [57] will of you his almighty Father. I believe that he was born for my benefit from the pure Virgin Mary, without any loss or shame either to her bodily or her spiritual virginity. Thus, according to the ordinance of your fatherly mercy he could come to make innocent and pure the sinful and damnable birth both of me and of all those who believe in him.

I believe that he bore his torment and his cross for my sins and the sins of all believers. By his torment [C1r] and pain, he has blessed, sanctified and made highly meritorious and beneficial all the torments, sufferings, tribulations and adversities that we could suffer in this world. Indeed, a good Christian must now long for suffering and tribulations in this mortal life, honouring them as most holy relics, soaked and dripping with the precious blood of your blessed Son Jesus Christ.

I believe that he died and was buried to slay, destroy and bury all my sins, and the sins of all believers, by which he has moreover killed and made [58] harmless bodily death, even making it beneficial and consecrated. For I know with certainty that my death will be the entrance into eternal life.

I believe that he descended into hell, to destroy and imprison the subtlety, violence and perversity of the devil, so that from now on the enemy [C1v] cannot overwhelm me. He has delivered me from the sorrows of hell, so that they too cannot overwhelm me.

I believe that on the third day he arose from the dead, to give new life to all believers. By this new life he has raised us with him by his mercy and Spirit, that from now on we may nevermore sin, but serve you alone with all power.

I believe that he ascended into heaven and that he has received from you, O my most blessed heavenly Father, all power and honour, above all the angels and all other creatures. He sits at your right hand, that is to say, he is King and Lord over all your possessions in heaven and on earth, and likewise in hell. And for this reason he is able to help me, and will help me, and all believers, in all our need, and will deliver us from all our opponents [59] and enemies.

I believe [C2r] that he will come down again from heaven in the last day of the judgement to judge the living and the dead, who from the beginning of the world until that day shall have been dead. All people, all the angels, and all the devils must appear before his throne of judgement, and they must see him there bodily, as he delivers both me and all his believers from bodily death, and from all imperfections and miseries, as he corrects and punishes eternally our enemies and opponents, and as he delivers us forever from their violence. All this he will do if we are found among the number of those chosen, as I fully expect to be.

I believe in the Holy Spirit

Thirdly, concerning the Christian faith: I believe in the Holy Spirit, the holy universal Church, the communion of saints, the forgiveness of sins, the resurrection [C2v] of the body, and the life everlasting.

That is to say: I not only believe that the Holy Spirit is one true God with you and your Son Jesus Christ, but I believe moreover that nothing can prevent me from believing in you. Nothing can prevent me from reaching you by means of your Son Jesus Christ who is the life – that is to say, by the means of his life, death and resurrection. Nothing can prevent me from obtaining anything else, because of the operation of the Holy Spirit, by which he [60] moves, invites, admonishes and attracts me and all those who are his, and makes them alive, holy and spiritual in your blessed Son Jesus Christ. Thus he carries them through your Son to you.

It is particularly by your Spirit that you work and give life to all things through and in Jesus Christ.

I believe that on the earth, as wide as the world may be, there is only one shared holy Christian Church. It is nothing else but the company of holy believing persons on earth. Being assembled by the [C3r] Holy Spirit, it is maintained, governed and daily increased by the sacraments and by your holy words as made visible through our good Master, your blessed Son Jesus Christ. I believe no one can have salvation unless he is found in this community and lives in peace and concord with it through a common faith, common teachings, common sacraments, and one hope and love. And I believe that no Jew, heretic, pagan or sinner will have salvation with that church, unless he first changes his ways, uniting with and conforming to it in everything.

I believe that in this Christian community all things are common property, and that no one has anything that is his alone. From this I know and am certain that all good works, prayers, vigils, fasts, alms, and all other good deeds [61] of the holy Christian community come as aid and help for me and for every [C3v] faithful Christian. All its good things – especially all the merits of your blessed Son Jesus our brother – must bestow strength and help in living and dying. Thus each one carries the burden of the other, as your holy servant Paul says.

I believe that in this same community, and not some other, there is forgiveness for all sins, and that outside it no one can have remission of sins, however many might be his works – whether they might be great or good or numerous. No one can be prevented from obtaining forgiveness of his sins – however great or numerous they might be. By means of this forgiveness the believer lives in this community, to which your blessed Son Jesus Christ has given the keys of the kingdom of heaven, of the forgiveness of sins. He said in the gospel to the apostles who would represent the multitude of Christians: Whatever [C4r] ye bind on earth will be bound in heaven. He also grants Saint Peter, who would represent the unity of the Christian Church, to understand the same when he says to him: Whatever you will bind on earth will be bound in heaven.

I believe there will be a resurrection of the dead. Every human body will be resurrected – the good as well as the bad – by the living Holy Spirit. The same flesh, which had died and [62] been buried, and through diverse means been corrupted, will come back and receive life. I believe that after the resurrection there will be an eternal life of the saints and an eternal death of the sinners. And I do not doubt any of this, but I know for certain that you, heavenly Father, by your dear Son Jesus Christ our Lord, together with and by the Holy Spirit, will ensure that all these articles here come to pass and are fulfilled.

Therefore, my most dear Father, I pray you by the merits of your dear Son Jesus Christ, that you desire to make me live and die with true faith and trust in you, in your Son and in the blessed Holy Spirit, one God in three persons. I pray that through this Spirit I may be able to know you, and in knowing you to love and fear you, until the time when it pleases you to deliver this mortal body from all that hinders me from perfectly serving you. Let me after this mortal life know, love and praise you without any hindrance, and perfectly rejoice in your goodness in life eternal. Amen.

Love is the fulfilment of the law.

CHAPTER 6

A Summary and Brief Exposition (1529/34)

Translation and notes by Jason Zuidema

[A ii] [Preface:] To all those who love our Lord and desire to know the truth, greetings

In these times when our Lord thinks it good to reveal his holy clarity and light on those who were in very great darkness, greater even than that which affected and was felt in Egypt, many cannot believe that they were in such great darkness. All confess, nonetheless, that there is much to say about the status of those who should be a model for others, but have not fulfilled their office in the desired manner. These false models have not, in any case, known the principal cause of their error, seeing the great blindness, trouble, and confusion in which the world has been surrounded and enveloped. They cannot understand nor believe that all could have changed or deteriorated to such a degree that nothing is pure as [26] it should be and that for such a long time no one resisted error or had any knowledge of the truth – seeing that in that period so many miracles were performed, such great Churches were erected and an innumerable list of those considered more than saints from the many religious orders had lived. Yet those who were considered to be of great repute were always put forward for even more advantage and honour.

All you who love the truth, understand this well and do not trust your own ways of understanding, your own wisdom, your own reason or your own prudence, but trust in God whose plan is unchangeable and whose word cannot be otherwise than it is. All that [28] which he foreordains by his servants must come to pass. Examine the scriptures and you will find that all needed [A iii] to happen just as it did – that a seduction such as this had to come about and that all needed to deteriorate and be destroyed, even more than we could believe.

So, do you see the reason for which you are incapable of believing that such an enormous deception could become dominant? You will know more by the revelation of God if you examine the holy scripture, but in reading be cautious not to twist it according to your own understanding so as to make it serve your own passions, or to throw out the food of the sheep, that is the word of God contained in scripture, nor to trample it under foot, nor to trouble all by treating your brothers cruelly with the word as if gouging them with your horns. Rather, use the word for that which it is intended – to give honour and glory to God alone without being attached to any creature. Do [30] not place your salvation in any other beside God or honour any other beside him. Act in a manner by which all is in the service of love, for the maintenance of friendship, peace and goodwill for all, in the measure in which it depends on you. Learn the goodness and gentleness of the Saviour and not the cruelty and rage of the Pharisees. Work for the destruction of the vices and of sin, and for the salvation of sinners with full gentleness. Administer difficult discipline, which is displeasing to the poor sinner, with great love, always digging out of and taking from scripture. For a very dangerous and deadly sickness must not be treated lightly, but with the right and appropriate remedies. Also in the area of salvation, in the care of the soul, one must only propose that which is absolutely certain, that which is taken from holy scripture alone. For scripture contains the decree and the will of God. No one should spare himself from helping his neighbour. Also, no one should reject the admonition or the counsel of another, but let him test it and keep what [A iv] is [32] good and reject what is bad – not taking or leaving according to his own desires, but as holy scripture directs.

For this reason, knowing that I am a debtor for what our Lord has placed in me and that I am responsible to all for the good, the salvation and the profit of each, not wanting ill for any, but desiring that all give honour and glory to God alone, I offer and present this book to all those whom our Lord has given to me. For the love of him who has loved us so much that he gave his only beloved Son for us, I pray that each might carefully examine all the contents of my little book according to God's law, according to the teaching of scripture, and with the ardent desire to know the truth in which God's honour is held. I pray the Father full of mercies that he desire and that it be his good pleasure to show more clearly his knowledge and understanding to our poor world, by dispelling the darkness of error by the sun of justice, our Lord Jesus, the true light and truth, and by illuminating by the Holy Spirit those who are pitifully blind and ignorant. From all [34] the parts of the world, all will then come to worship our Father in his holy tabernacle, at his mercy seat, in our Saviour and Redeemer Jesus. May the Father be served, worshipped and honoured in him and by him, according to his holy will by the working of the Holy Spirit alone. Amen. [38] [A vi]

Table of Contents[1]

---

[1]   This table of contents is produced on Av–Avi. The 'Preface', the chapter on 'Contrition' and the 'Conclusion' are all distinct sections, but not included in the table of contents. We include them in square brackets here for reference purposes.

1. God

God[2] is goodness, power, infinite wisdom, without beginning and without end, and unchanging truth. We know this well by the creation of the world in which nothing is useless and all brings profit.[3] Despite its being made from nothing and its great diversity, the world is nonetheless upheld by divine power and was so well ordered by the great wisdom of God. According to holy scripture, our God is so good that he made us in his image, giving us dominion over all the creatures.[4] Lost by disobedience and prideful presumption, this dominion was originally given by the great goodness of God who so loved the world that he gave his only Son.[5] By the effectiveness and power of the Father which is in him, this Son destroyed our death by an astounding wisdom. [A vii] He destroyed sin in his body which was made like ours unto sin.[6] Because of his obedience, he gave and restored a full life to those who were dead by disobedience. The plan and [40] unchanging command of God[7] were thus accomplished, and those

---

2   The 1542 text adds: 'God is a simple spiritual essence, indivisible and incomprehensible. No created reasoning could comprehend or understand him by considering him simply and in himself. We confess and believe that there is one and only God in three persons, the Father, the Son and the Holy Spirit in a unity of essence and nature. We confess that the Trinity of persons has true personal distinction and perfect unity of essence and substance, without confusing the persons or dividing the essence. We understand and believe this by faith, according to that which God has revealed by the holy scriptures which give testimony of this and not that which our understanding could fabricate. But considering him in what he has done, by which he manifests himself, we know him to be goodness, power and infinite wisdom....'

3   Gen. 1.

4   Gen. 3.

5   John 3.

6   Rom. 8.

7   Eph. 1.

ordained to life before the beginning of the world could rejoice in and have possession of this life. So understood and written on the heart, this certainty of life produces such an assurance in the great goodness of God that nothing can separate us from his love.[8] In fact, we live for God when we believe him and when we know him because he is eternal life: 'To know the only true God and he whom he sent, Jesus Christ'.[9] [42]

2. Man

Man is wicked, incapable, foolish, headstrong, ambitious, full of error and hypocrisy, inconsistent and changeable.[10] He only thinks of evil and sin – that in which he was born and conceived.[11] In all and everywhere he thinks only of himself, he values only himself and his interests. He wishes always to glorify his works, his faculties and his qualities.[12] He is full of ingratitude and disobedience. He keeps his inventions, his laws and his ordinances with more strictness and care than those of God. He cannot bear to be humiliated, dishonoured or hated, but wants rather to control God, his holy word, his law and his commandment. The more he presents the appearance of justice and holiness, the more he is full of all iniquity. For this reason he is damned, miserable and a liar. As a rotten root and a spoiled tree, he can only bear spoiled fruit.[13] All is thus corrupted in him because by the disobedience of the first man he can [44] only bear fruit for his death and condemnation. All his thoughts are evil because all the impulses of the thoughts of his heart are [A viii] only evil at all times.[14] For he is flesh and that which comes from his heart is evil and nothing but the desires of the flesh. [46]

3. Jesus Christ

Jesus Christ is the true Son of God, the arm, the power, the word and the wisdom of God.[15] As man, Jesus was chosen by God to be his holy temple, his habitation, his tabernacle, his holy of holies, his mercy seat where all

---

8   Rom. 8.
9   John 17.
10   Ps. 61.
11   Rom. 3.
12   Ps. 50.
13   Matt. 7.
14   Gen. 6 and 8.
15   John 1 and Isa. 53.

the treasures of his knowledge and wisdom are found. In him lives all the divinity, not in mere shadow or image, but in a real and true way.[16] In him is brought about and perfectly accomplished all the work of God. For by him all things are restored and made perfect in heaven and on earth because the fullness of life, of power, of virtue, of wisdom, of grace and of justice abide in him. Becoming obedient to his Father, born of a mother, a virgin, without the seed of man, subjected to the law, [48] Jesus never sought his glory or his will, but that of his Father. Jesus never spoke or acted to serve his own will, but always to serve that of his Father who was in him reconciling the world with himself.[17]

He, being just and innocent, humbled himself and was brought low unto death for us, the unjust and sinners, in offering his body and his blood for the purification of our souls.[18] By this death and sacrifice, by this beautiful gift of his Son, the Father wills that these poor souls be assured of their salvation and their life and that they be fully purified and washed of their sin.[19] Because of his love for himself and not of his love for us, nor for our works, merit or just actions, which are only abominations, the Father saves us, brings us to life, and adopts us as sons and heirs.[20] We become heirs with Jesus Christ of whom we have become members. [B i] His members are all those who have a true faith in him and are, for this reason, united and incorporated in the body of Jesus.[21] By the divine power which [50] dwells in the head, all hostile power is destroyed. By this perfect life and immortality our death is abolished. By this holiness, this justice, this purity and this infinite innocence which live in him, all our wickedness, sin and filth are destroyed. By this great power, we are put back into a more noble position than that in which we ever were before the sin of Adam in paradise – a position that is not terrestrial, but celestial. We are given a life not bodily, corruptible or capable of being lost, but spiritual, without corruption and which can never be lost.

He who knows and understands this with a living and true faith truly has eternal life. He no longer attaches himself to creatures or vain things, for he knows the Father through the Son. In the person of the Son, he knows and understands the great goodness of God and his infinite mercy. [52]

---

[16]   Eph. 1.

[17]   2 Cor. 5.

[18]   1 Pet. 3 and Heb. 7, 9, and 10.

[19]   Ez. 36.

[20]   Rom. 8.

[21]   1 Cor. 12.

4. The Law and its Power

True rule of the good life, the law of God shows humans their faults and how they are far from the way in which they should walk.[22] By its threats, the law makes clearly known the great harm which will come on its transgressors.[23] The law brings forth horror, the fear of a slave, anger and indignation.[24] Because it finds all men carnal and deprived of the Spirit of God, it gives sin and covetousness the occasion to show themselves, to multiply and to become worse.[25]

As a result all men under the reign of the law live under a curse because they cannot fulfil that which the law demands.[26] For the law is not accomplished by works, but by faith.[27] For this reason, the law[28] makes us understand that we should [B ii] seek Jesus Christ. For he is the goal of the law: the one who justifies all those who believe in him. There is no other means than Jesus to [54] escape the anger and indignation of God – an anger which is displayed for us in the law as the power and sting of sin. We are only delivered from its sting by Jesus Christ when we understand and believe that he bore the curse in our place.[29] [56]

5. The Gospel

The gospel is the real power of God for the salvation of every believer,[30] the consolation of the afflicted, the deliverance of the prisoner, the life of the dead and the lost, and a joy of heart far beyond all imagination.[31]

Who would not be joyful when he hears of the defeat and destruction of his enemy from whom he could not escape and who held absolute power over him? In the same way, who would not be joyful hearing that inevitable death and condemnation are changed for him to eternal life and salvation, that hell is changed into the kingdom of heaven, that horror in the company of devils is changed into citizenship in heaven and the adoption as children of God? This change is announced for us by the death of Jesus.

---

[22] Rom. 3.

[23] Lev. 26.

[24] Dt. 28 and Rom. 4.

[25] Rom. 7 and Gal. 3.

[26] John 6.

[27] Gal. 3.

[28] The 1542 text adds: '…as a pedagogue who does not want us to stay with it…'

[29] 1 Cor. 15.

[30] Rom. 1.

[31] Lk. 4.

By the power of the Father which is in him, Jesus saved us in taking away the enslaving fear of the threats of the law. For, there is no condemnation for those who are united to Christ.[32] In fact, they are delivered from their enslavement [58] to sin and death in which they were held by the law.[33] They now serve God and live for him whose sons they now are by faith, fully believing in the complete pardon given by Jesus, the powerful victor over our enemies.[34] His victory is ours and by him all belongs to us as it is announced to us in the good news which is the gospel. This gospel has restored all things for us and has given us everything – even more than we had lost.

So with a full faith [B iii] let us arm ourselves with his justice against our sin, with his life against our death, with his innocence against our iniquity.[35] By him we will obtain all the promises of God and a good so great that 'no eye has seen, nor ear heard, nor mind imagined how great is that which God has promised to us'.[36] [60]

6. Sin

Sin is a corrupted and depraved nature which lives for itself,[37] loves itself, fights against the law of God and hates it, loves the things of the flesh, hates those which are spiritual, understands nothing of the things of God, is full of all ignorance, and produces only that which leads to death.[38]

For sin is a spring so damned and so evil that it can only produce evil. The more the right way and the good are shown clearly to it, the more it rejects them and criticizes them.[39] If sin does not die and is not destroyed by the death of Jesus, it is said rightly that 'good is evil, evil is good and light is darkness'. As such it blasphemes the Holy Spirit, attributing to God injustice and declaring itself innocent. It accuses God and his Spirit. It condemns him for reigning, for it wants all the fame and honour.[40] [62]

---

32   Rom. 8.

33   Rom. 7.

34   Col. 2.

35   Isa. 64.

36   1 Cor. 2.

37   Rom. 7.

38   1 Cor. 2.

39   Matt. 12.

40   The 1542 edition adds: 'Sin resides in some as if sleeping or as dead, not making itself known … in others it disguises itself with the appearance of holiness … in others it manifests itself openly with great passion. All these kinds have the same source and root in the perverse and corrupted nature which manifests itself in different ways depending on which can bear the most fruit'.

7. Righteousness

Righteousness is the true image of God which displays the regeneration produced by the word of God, received by faith, and written in the hearts of the sons of God.[41] By it, man, dead in himself and having renounced himself in all things, loves God. He has his heart set on the holy law, pulled away from all terrestrial things and made to burn after heavenly things. For by his knowledge of God, man bears the fruit of life. He knows how to choose the good and to condemn and reject evil. He gives [B iv] all honour and glory to God, attributes all good, all salvation, all life to him. He rejects all other aid, confidence or anything that the clear and pure commandment of God does not contain.[42] [64]

8. The Flesh or the Old Man

The flesh is the old man, that is, any who by himself is slave and prisoner to sin. All that this man desires, wants, understands, is aware of, knows, decides and does – all this is the desire of the flesh, its will, wisdom, prudence, judgement and carnal work.

The covetousness of the flesh and the covetousness of sin are one and the same thing.[43] For they produce only hate, murder, envy, debauchery, pilfering, heresy, idolatry, blasphemy, perverse ideas and thoughts; in sum, that which resists and is in opposition to all that is good.

At the same time, the flesh directly opposes itself to the word of God. It accuses the word of injustice all the more because God does not act according to the will, the consideration and the opinion of the flesh. The flesh says: 'There is no God. There is no justice up there.[44] God does not pay attention or worry about things down here'. Other blasphemies against our Lord and his word spew forth and come from the flesh. [66] In another way, the flesh pretends it is not a false imitation.[45] It *seems* to have zeal for God and the desire to honour him, pretending to want to

---

[41]   1 Pet. 1 and Jer. 31.

[42]   The 1542 edition adds an extended discussion of justice. At one point Farel writes: 'by the Spirit of Jesus he is a possessor of him and of all that is in him. He is clothed with Jesus and made a member of his body. Because of Jesus' justice, purity, innocence and holiness the Father considers us as just, pure, holy and innocent – no matter how much sin resides in us. This sin displeases us and we wish to be delivered from it, but because we are clothed with Jesus and his justice, this sin is hidden and is not imputed or counted. For the love of Jesus our sin is fully remitted and pardoned'.

[43]   Gal. 5.

[44]   Ps. 13 and 72.

[45]   Matt. 7.

praise and magnify his holy name and saying that he should be served
with more sanctity and with more reverence. By this it invents new ways
to serve him outside of that written in the word of God – new sects, rules
and institutions that only simulate, imitate and show falsely the sanctity
and love of God.[46] For this reason, one must not follow with haste all that
seems to have a divine origin, both [B v] in our own hearts and in those
around us. But one must verify with care from what spirit it comes. For in
the same way that the angel of darkness transforms himself into an angel
of light, so can his ministers and, most clearly, the wisdom of the flesh.[47]
[68]

It is necessary, therefore, to prove by the holy scriptures of God and
to examine diligently all decrees, all remarks and instruction in order to
know what spirit brings them forth, either the Spirit of God or that of
the flesh. Remember the good intentions of Peter for which he was called
Satan,[48] also those of King Saul and the other kings wanting to worship
God on the high places or in the forests,[49] as did the patriarchs before
them – remark how the scriptures reprimand them. For, they acted entirely
according to the wisdom of the flesh. In all possible ways the flesh wants
to have lordship and domination. It wants to govern, direct and dispose by
its own pleasure, and be honoured and worshipped by all. [70]

9. The Spirit and the New Man

The Spirit is the movement and affection which God gives to man, by which
he renews man and gives him his grace, and justifies him by Jesus.[50]

This Spirit continually fights against the flesh and there is never peace
until the flesh is dead. Simple and pure, the Spirit knows God, the deep
things of God, the celestial things to which he pushes man so that he can
be the imitator of the goodness of God and can produce the fruit of life, all
gentleness, friendliness, goodness, compassion, chastity, patience, peace,
joy, love and generosity. The Spirit produces a firm hope in him who has
made everything, in whom he has all confidence and faith. This Spirit makes
that man not headstrong or presumptuous, but [B vi] humble and obedient
to the word of God. This God is true and does not change. For that which
he said, he will do; that which he promised, he will fulfill. For this reason
the Spirit directs man so that he not experience God in any other way, nor

---

[46] 1 John 4.

[47] 2 Cor. 11.

[48] Matt. 16.

[49] 1 Kgs. 15.

[50] Gal. 5.

take any other way to life, than that which is expressly commanded of God. The Spirit directs him to hold only to the pure [72] word of God.[51] Even if all is changed and modified and even if the infidels flourish, if great signs and miracles are worked,[52] and if all speak at variance with the pure commandment of God, may he not move, but may he rest firm in the word which remains eternally. The world can do what it wants, but this man will honour God as the true God and will judge as vanity and lies all that which is not proven by the holy scriptures.

It is better to know this by experience than by a book. Nonetheless this book is written [74] for the elect, so that they might passionately desire and pray that the Spirit be given them, be made into new men, and have knowledge of the things of God by his Spirit. It is written so that they might kill and destroy all the passions of the flesh and of the old man and pursue the honour and glory only of him who can do and does all, our good Father the eternal God. It is written for us in order to love him and to edify and help our neighbour with all goodness. [76]

10. Unbelief, Unfaithfulness and Scepticism

Unbelief, unfaithfulness and scepticism are to feel and believe less or otherwise than is worthy of the infinite goodness, mercy, wisdom and power of God. These persons [B vii] can in no way trust in God, but seek uncertain things or other means to have aid and help. Full of inconsistency, they fear when there is no reason to fear, they trust that which is not sure. Without a sure goal or decision, they are changeable as the moon, subject to all trickery and deception.[53] For where there is not the light of faith, that is, the clarity of the word of God, there reign the princes of darkness.[54] There men trip and fall into the ditch. We take the evil way as if it were good; we take the imagination of men as if it were pleasing to God; we take abominable and diabolical teaching as if it were God's holy ordinances. For whatever comes from this unbelief and whatever is done without faith can only be sin – despite its beautiful appearance as holiness or as a good work.[55] [78]

---

[51]   Ps. 36.
[52]   Matt. 14.
[53]   Ps. 13.
[54]   2 Thess. 2.
[55]   Rom. 14.

11. Faith

Faith is a great and extraordinary gift of God. By it we are made sons of God. Faith is a true awareness, experience and knowledge of God our Father who is good, perfect, powerful and wise.[56] It is a knowledge that for the love of himself God elected us to be his sons, saved us and redeemed us by our Saviour Jesus.

Faith, therefore, never doubts the holy promises of God or that which he spoke by his people filled with the Holy Spirit. Rather, fortified and confirmed by the word of him who cannot lie, faith condemns all human understanding and holds firm to all that which God has said. Assured by the unchangeable truth, and illuminated by true clarity, faith fears nothing and holds firm without any doubts. [B viii] Strongly armed against all its enemies over whom it gains victory, faith holds fast by the promises of him in whom it believes.[57] In fact, nothing is impossible for faith. All that for which it asks, it receives. It cannot fail, for it exists and goes forward by the word of God. Whatever is not in this faith, whatever is according to the knowledge of the world, is sin.[58] [80] Faith cannot be attracted to another besides God; it cannot stand but in God; it can only receive that which is from God. For faith, all is nothing apart from God; nothing pleases it besides God and his voice. Because it is attached only to him, it cannot be confused, but will perfectly obtain that which it believes and for which it hopes. [82]

12. Merit

'Merit' is a term full of arrogance, fully repugnant to God and all scripture, invented by the spirit of pride and error to bring to nothing the grace of our Saviour. For the damnable doctrine of merits declares that the man who turns himself to God gains merit and that he merits coming out of sin. It declares that man merits coming to confession, having his sins remitted, and coming into the state of grace. This doctrine presumes that by doing good works man can make satisfaction for his sins and acquire the kingdom of heaven and paradise. Such blasphemies could not be more self-evident.

What can a useless, good-for-nothing servant merit? Jesus, who is truth, commands us to say, even if it were possible that we could do all

---

[56]   John 1.

[57]   Mark 10 and 11.

[58]   Rom. 10.

that is commanded of us,[59] 'that we are still useless servants'.[60] Who is he that has always done that which God has commanded him?[61] It would mean being without sin, just, as holy, perfect and merciful as [C i] God, without any covetousness or evil desires.[62] If we are all evil and all our just actions are as abominable as the dirty rag soiled by the unsightly blood of a woman's menstruation, where is [84] the merit?[63] If we do not even have the capacity to think something on our own,[64] but if it all comes from God and if we can only do evil in ourselves, as we are slaves, captives, sold to sin, and if we cannot do the good that we want, but rather the evil which we do not want,[65] from where comes the pride to say: 'I will merit the kingdom of heaven by my works'?

Pride, would you go up there to heaven and say: 'I will become like the Exalted One'? Do you not understand that justification is done without merit by the grace of God, by the redemption of Jesus?[66] Do you not understand that we are saved by grace and not by ourselves? It is the gift of God and not by works, lest anyone should [86] boast. If we are justified and saved by grace, it is not by works, otherwise grace would not be grace.[67] For a salary is not given to the worker according to grace, but as a debt, as something due and merited. But to him who believes, his faith is counted for justice, without works.[68] [88]

13. Grace

Grace is the benevolent, kind, favourable and merciful regard of our very good Father. Out of love for himself and so that his plan to give life and save those whom he had ordained to life would be firm, regardless of the one to whom he gives mercy, of his works, of his origin, of where he was born, or of anything else, he forgave this poor sinner by his very dear [C ii][69] Son. This poor sinner has been held prisoner of the Devil, of sin, of

---

59   Luke 17.

60   1 Pt. 1.

61   Matt. 5.

62   Luke 6.

63   Isa. 64.

64   1 Cor. 3.

65   Rom. 8.

66   Rom. 3 and Eph. 2.

67   Rom. 11.

68   Rom. 4.

69   The first half of C ii (here, the next six lines of translated text) seems not to be present in the so-called 1525 edition used in the Hofer text of 1980.

hell and of damnation because of the evil in him and his cursed conception and birth. He is in sin by which he is made and born as a child of wrath.[70] And sin and rebellion against the law of God live and reign in him.[71] The good God and Father of mercy takes him to be his adopted son, to be his heir and coheir with Jesus Christ. He gives this sinner the strength of the Holy Spirit.[72] By this Spirit God renews him by faith, writing his holy law of life and the Spirit on the heart of this poor sinner. He draws the sinner to love him who is the true good, and to follow and love his holy will by renouncing and detesting his own will and all that is his own. He takes him under his protection and guard, fortifying him in all temptations, steadying him when he is unsteady and in his faults which come upon him by the infirmity of his flesh. God will never allow sin or death to have victory over him. Rather, by giving a living and true faith, God allows him to obtain what is true and incorruptible and to overcome and triumph over all his enemies. [90]

14. The Doctrine and Tradition of Men

Human doctrine wants to meddle in the things of God which relate to the salvation of the soul and to the adoration and service of God. Such meddling is nothing else than an abomination before God, vanity, a lie; it is diabolical doctrine, error and vain trickery.[73] By this God is served in vain and his wrath is provoked upon those who serve him in this way.[74] These are given over to a disordered conscience. They are servants of creatures and not of the Creator.[75] For we are servants of the one whose commandments we keep and that for which we work. We are its servants when we follow and hold to [C iii] its doctrine and word.[76]

The more human doctrine has the appearance and shape of holiness, the more it is dangerous.[77] This was evident in the doctrine of the Pharisees, and above all in the Antichrist. He has the shadow of being of Jesus and is more effective and capable of deceiving and tricking than any other. So much so that even the elect, if he could do it, would be deceived. The

---

70   Rom. 7.

71   Rom. 8.

72   Eph. 2.

73   Col. 2 and 1 Tim 4.

74   Matt. 15.

75   Rom. 1.

76   John 8.

77   This phrase is pointed to in the margin of the text with a small hand. Obviously then, this phrase was important for the author or editor.

pretext these men have who make laws and ordinances is that they come together [92] in the name of Jesus, so they presume to have Jesus in their midst and to be driven in an infallible manner by the Holy Spirit. They have many other such pretexts which are very dangerous. So let us, rather, examine the law of our Lord to test all their ordinances and to see what fruits the constitutions and customs made by these authors will bear. By this we will know the tree. [94]

15. Holy Scripture

Holy scripture, both Old and New Testaments, such as the books of Moses, the prophets, the holy histories of kings and judges, psalms, songs, proverbs and teachings that Solomon wrote, with the gospels and the holy doctrine of the Apostles, contain purely that which we must do, that is to say, that which we must feel and believe of God our Father.[78] By this we can serve him in Spirit and in truth with our heart. We can assure that his holy habitation, which is our body, will be always guarded in all purity and cleanliness and that it will stay away from all filth and iniquity.[79] The figures and commandments in the ceremonies of the law indicate in a hidden way and in a shadow that which Jesus Christ and his Apostles taught in a clear way. So also the sacrifices prefigure the only true and perfect sacrifice accomplished in the death of Jesus that the holy [C iv] gospel shows us. [96]

For this reason only, that doctrine contained in holy scripture is useful to teach, instruct, correct, warn and exhort.[80] Also, only that doctrine enables one to test the spirits, to know which spirit drives and leads him who speaks and to know by which spirit our own spiritual movements are brought about and whether that which we call 'good intentions' comes from God. Jesus displayed this clearly to the Tempter, he who comes against the scripture, and to Peter and the other disciples, saying that 'it is necessary that the scriptures be fulfilled'.[81]

Yet that which is not clearly and firmly founded on scripture, which cannot be destroyed,[82] should be rejected if it concerns matters of salvation and that which comes from God – spiritual and heavenly things. And all those who love Jesus must be formed by scripture, above all those who

---

[78]   John 4.

[79]   1 Cor. 3 and 6.

[80]   1 Tim. 3.

[81]   Matt. 4 and 16; Luke 24.

[82]   John 9.

announce and bear his name.[83] For scripture gives a faithful testimony of Jesus. For this reason it is given to us by God to console us so that in all our temptations and afflictions, no matter how they come upon us, or when the wicked oppress the just, we might always have our hope in God who never abandons his own.[84] [98]

It is necessary to treat and study scripture with the fear and reverence of God of whom it speaks; it is necessary to examine diligently not in pieces or parts, but in its entirety, considering what comes before and what comes after, considering for what goal it is written and for what reason that which scripture contains is said, finding other places where what is said is said more clearly or overtly, [C v] and comparing one passage of scripture with another. For it is all written from the same Spirit who speaks more clearly in one passage or another, even though all those who spoke that which scripture contains spoke by the Holy Spirit.[85] This is why one passage explains another. [100]

16. The Church

The Church of Jesus Christ is the holy congregation of the faithful who by true faith are united and incorporated into Jesus Christ, of whom they are members. And even though Jesus is the true Son of God, all his members are, by him, sons of God.[86] Jesus is the head, and true Christians are his body. He is the bridegroom; the faithful are his bride whom he has purified by his blood. His blood gave life to his body and saved his people from their sin.

This Church does not consist of hierarchies, laws, ordinances and orders given by human will, but in the true union with our Lord Jesus by faith, listening to and believing his holy voice.[87] It has no particular place, [102] but Jesus is there where two or three people are gathered in his name. Such an assembly seeks only that which brings honour to God. That which it believes by the clear word of God is that for which it seeks and asks. So it receives fully what it asks for. The small or the scorned are not found in this congregation since he who is lesser has more honour.[88] The greater serves the lesser, for the faithful members of Jesus do not serve themselves, but others. He who speaks prophecy, exhorts or admonishes,

---

83   John 5.
84   Rom. 15.
85   2 Pt. 1.
86   Eph. 4 and 5
87   John 10 and Matt. 18.
88   2 Cor. 12.

does it for the edification of others. He who interprets, puts scripture in the common language – he does this for others and not for himself. [C vi] In the same way, those who have other graces or gifts of God share them with the rest.

Nothing goes against the Church of Jesus more than scorning the simple folk and not teaching or instructing them with all diligence. For the holy Apostle said: 'A curse be on me if I do not evangelize'.[89] For if those who have a better understanding and the grace of our Lord do not teach doctrine to the ignorant, nor correct those in error, [104] nor pick up those who have fallen, they will die in their sin.[90] Their poor souls will be demanded from the hand of those to whom our Lord had given grace. On the contrary, those who, for the love of Christ, devote themselves to all will grow in virtue and will shine as the stars.[91][106]

17. The Keys of the Kingdom of Heaven

The keys of the kingdom of heaven are the knowledge of God, the word of God, the holy gospel and the nourishment of souls.[92] These cannot be given or communicated to anyone by man, but by God alone.[93] By giving his Holy Spirit, he opens the understanding of the scriptures and preaches the holy gospel.[94] To him who truly believes heaven is opened; he is released and his sins are forgiven him.[95] For by faith his heart is purged and he is saved. But for him who does not believe, heaven is closed; he is bound and his sins are not forgiven.[96] For he does not believe in the name of the Son of God and for this reason his sin remains.[97]

These keys have always been hidden by those who should have used them to instruct and teach others, to purely announce the word. But they hid them, taking out the word from the nourishment of the sheep.[98] They

---

[89] 1 Cor. 9

[90] Ez. 3.

[91] Dan. 12. At this point Farel adds four pages of new text in the 1542 edition. He writes that on earth all churches can be composed of believers and unbelievers. For this reason one ought not to separate oneself from the preaching of the word and the sacraments to found another community. It too will have unbelievers. The pastor should, nonetheless, work to drive out the overtly sinful members from the midst of the church.

[92] Luke 11; Matt. 23; John 21.

[93] Matt. 28

[94] Mark 16 and John 20.

[95] Acts 15.

[96] John 3.

[97] Matt. 23.

[98] Jer. 23.

did not enter [the kingdom of heaven], nor did they let those who wanted to enter. For nothing is more intolerable for hypocrites and wolves than [C vii] to encounter [108] pastors[99] who announce and preach purely the word of God, which is the nourishment of poor souls. This nourishment gives a poor soul knowledge, opens his understanding, gets rid of error, purifies the heart and permits him to discern and know the voice of the pastor from that of the murderer.[100] [110]

18. The Sacraments

Sacraments[101] are signs and public attestations of that which ought to be in the faithful. They serve to maintain and increase love among them.[102] For the Christian is pushed more to love those who confess and believe truly and publicly that in the death and passion of Jesus and the blood that he shed, they have the remission of their sins and are transplanted from the old man Adam into Jesus Christ.[103] They confess that they want to follow him and live for him as his disciples; they renounce all for the love of Jesus. And as a sign of this they are baptized and receive the baptism of water.[104] They confess that our Lord gave his body in dying to unite them all in one body. Because of our love for him, we love each other as he loved us.[105] We sacrifice our lives for each other and give thanks to our Lord,[106] taking the bread of blessing and drinking from his cup, reciting [112] and remembering[107] the death of our Lord until he comes again. We are pushed more to love such [confessors] than those who do not have such a confession.

For we do not know the hearts as God knows them. He alone knows what is in a person's heart. But we know only that which is outside, judging and appreciating the interior according to what we see on the exterior. We

---

[99]   Or: shepherds

[100]   Ps. 18.

[101]   This chapter is significantly revised in the 1542 edition. For example, the beginning of this chapter in the 1542 edition reads: 'The sacraments are signs, seals, confirmations and protestations of things that our Lord does and gives to his own and should be for the faithful. They serve and profit the confirmation, growth and augmentation of faith in God and also the love of each other'.

[102]   'Les sacrementz sont signes et protestations des choses qui doivent estre es fideles, servantz et proffitants à conserver, croistre, et augmenter la charité l'ung avec l'autre'.

[103]   Matt. 16.

[104]   John 11.

[105]   1 John 3.

[106]   1 Cor. 10 and 11.

[107]   'racomptans et rememorans'

are thus very often deceived and many men who partake of the sacraments are very far [C viii] from having the thing signified by them. These things are accessible to the good and the evil, as are all exterior things which are on the outside. Our salvation cannot rest in this exterior practice as if in having it we are saved and in not having it we are damned. We should not, however, slight the sacraments, but take them and use them according to the instruction of our Saviour Jesus.

For this reason, one must not believe or think that the baptism that man gives can save. For there is only one Saviour: Jesus – who saves by the power of the Father and who gives the Holy Spirit.

In the same way, we must not believe that we have forgiveness of sins and eternal life simply because we come to the holy table of our Lord. For by the sacraments we have the assurance [114] and guarantee of divine grace.[108] For our sins are only forgiven if we believe that our Lord Jesus Christ died for them.[109] We have life only by believing in him.[110] We are assured by the guarantee[111] of the Holy Spirit that is given to us who testifies in our spirit that 'we are sons of God'.[112] Scripture shows us that all dwells in the heart by the work of God and by his gift when he enlightens us with true faith.[113] [116]

19. The Mass

The mass is a teaching founded in such a way that we cannot even cite its name in holy scripture. It is clear that it was introduced to overturn the holy table of our Lord. And it does not take a great mind to know if it is of God or not. The holy table of our Lord shows us that all are one and that we must not come before others and leave behind the needy in their

---

[108]   The 1542 edition inserts here: 'if by the faith that we have in Jesus and by his Spirit who resides in us and who joins us to Jesus, we are in Christ, clothed and nourished by him, so much so that we live in him and he in us'.

[109]   Rom. 4.

[110]   Eph. 2.

[111]   'l'arre'

[112]   Rom. 8.

[113]   In his lengthy addition to the 1542 text Farel states: 'The holy sacraments are not naked signs, worthless and empty, but by the power of the Spirit of God who is their author, they are efficacious and of a great power, good, and great growth for the children of God who use them and receive them as is fitting. The others who profane their use will be led to great condemnation and judgement. For this reason pastors should diligently take care lest they contaminate a thing so holy by giving it to such dogs and swine seeing that it should only be given to the children of God'.

needs or difficulties.[114] For we who eat [D i] from one bread and drink from one cup are all one body. But on the contrary, the mass is to show the great difference between the priest and the people. For they say that the priest has the same authority as the angels, as the Virgin Mary, the mother of Jesus, and as all the saints who are resting in our Lord. For this reason, [118] it is dangerous to touch that which the priest touches and to drink that which he drinks.

By the mass the poor, the widows and orphans are destroyed.[115] For by it the Church of the Pope gains all the goods of the world. And that which should come to the poor members of Jesus is offered and employed in rich clothing and diverse methods of vestments taken both from the infidels or pagans and from Jewish ceremony. Also one must not be silent about the fact that the imitation of these pagans is against the commandment of God.[116] For they make and erect statues and ornate images of gold and silver and precious vestments before which candles and lamps are lit. In this an immeasurable amount of resources are spent, but the poor are forgotten. In the same way, the bones of the dead are superstitiously enshrined and surrounded by gold and silver and precious stones, standing in the way of the word of God: [120] 'man will return to dust'.[117] All of these abuses were introduced by the greed of Satan. God will not let these abuses go unpunished. For idols and idolaters will be confounded, but God alone will be exalted.[118]

When the holy people came to the table of our Lord, we used to read in the language that all understood a portion of the holy scripture, saying prayers understood by all, with great sorrow of heart.[119] But in the mass all is said [D ii] in a language that people do not understand, in singing and in laughing.

Even more, those who came to the table were [122] formerly urged to help the poor who could not earn enough, whose needs we know. But in the mass we are urged to give to those who are outside of this world, to get them, as the priests say, out of purgatory, which is an invention of Satan and his helpers against holy scripture. By this invention innumerable souls go to eternal perdition. And all are eaten and devoured by the lazy bellies of these priests, monks and nuns. Their money is used for things that the simple know all too well.

---

[114] 1 Cor. 10 and 11.

[115] Here again, the author or editor of the 1534 text has printed a pointing hand to emphasize this particular argument.

[116] Ex. 20.

[117] Gen. 3.

[118] Isa. 1 and 2.

[119] 1 Cor. 14.

At the table of our Lord, the faithful give thanks to God for giving us a perfect and accomplished sacrifice which need not be repeated, which replaces all those sacrifices that God commanded by Moses to obtain the sanctification of the body, all those unfinished sacrifices needing to be repeated because they could not fully sanctify the faithful.[120] In remembrance of our Lord Jesus who once was offered for us to cleanse our sins,[121] they all take and eat from one bread and drink from one cup, waiting for [124] the triumphant and marvellous coming of Jesus which will be like his ascension to Heaven, where he is presently sitting at the right hand of his Father until his enemies are put under his feet.[122] For the coming of the Saviour will not be invisible, but will be seen by all like lightning which comes from the East and is seen all the way to the West.[123]

In the mass, instead of giving thanks to God for our redemption, the priest, with his assistants, offers bread and wine for their redemption and [D iii] salvation. And this day after day, as if the sacrifice of Jesus was insufficient, without full efficacy, like those offered by Moses. The bread is not taken or eaten by all, but elevated and worshipped as if it were God. This is not done in memory of Jesus, but in memory of others, as in the *Communicantes*.[124] [126] We act as if Jesus had descended and not as if we were awaiting his coming.[125]

I leave aside the various invocations for sins and many things concerning the mass which are directly against holy scripture. For to show the iniquity and abominations which are in the mass would take a very long book. There is no one that could sufficiently show how much it is against our Lord.[126] If the world does not return and come back to the pure doctrine of Jesus, God by his rule will soon make known to the world what the mass really is and how much it displeases him. [128]

[Much more has been written about the mass in a little treatise called the Declaration Concerning the mass, its fruit, its cause, its means and why we ought to maintain it.][127]

---

[120]   Heb. 9 and 10.

[121]   1 Cor. 10 and 11.

[122]   Acts 1 and Col. 3.

[123]   Matt. 24.

[124]   This is the moment of the mass at which one venerates the memory of the Virgin Mary or some other saint by whose intercession is granted the favour of God. See Joseph-André Jungmann, *Missarum Sollemnia: Explication Génétique de la Messe Romaine*. Vol. 3 (Paris: Aubier, 1954), pp. 83–94.

[125]   This sentence does not appear in the so-called 1525 edition.

[126]   This sentence does not appear in the so-called 1525 edition.

[127]   Farel is probably speaking of the *Declaration de la Messe* published also by de Vingle in 1534, written by A. Marcourt.

20. Penance

The penance of which Jesus speaks and which he commands is a change of life, a change of goals and of heart.[128] It is as if a man who wished out of hate to put his brother to death, changed and modified his goals by true love and came to save and deliver him from the hand of those who wanted to kill him; or as if he who wished to seduce a woman by word or otherwise, would strive for and assure that she lived in holiness and would be pained to see her as something other than a faithful wife.

This penance is more necessary than any other. For we are all lovers of ourselves and of our [D iv] pleasures. We hate that which goes against our own will and the taking away or prohibition of that which we love. We must change this reality and hate ourselves and that which naturally pleases us. For since we are born and conceived in sin [130] and have an evil inclination by nature, all our desires are pulled toward evil and our will is against the will of God. That which we desire greatly also will be contrary to the will of God. We must hate that which we desire naturally and give it up along with ourselves and our will, our mind, our understanding and all that is of us. We must love God with all our heart, our soul, mind, understanding, power and strength, and submit ourselves to his holy law and commandments. We must destroy our will and uphold his – taking back our heart from all creatures here below, so that we might be entirely attached to Jesus. We must let no desire remain in us but that which is of God and for God. We must love God and our neighbours, doing good to them and helping them as God commanded us for their good. For in receiving Jesus, we receive the Father.[129] And in helping those in need, in giving food to those who believe in Jesus Christ when they are hungry and drink when they are thirsty, we honour Jesus.[130]

This penance is the re-creation of the heart, when God gives us a new heart, as the prophet demands.[131] And in this way, the works of death die and those of life [132] are raised up. Otherwise, without this change, which is done by faith when we are united with and grafted onto the good root Jesus, all is sin and abomination before God, even though it seems beautiful and good before men.[132] But after this change and penance everything profits and comes to good, [D v] because the root is good and renewed by faith. [134]

---

128   Isa. 55.

129   Matt. 10.

130   Matt. 25.

131   Ez. 36 and Ps. 1.

132   Rom. 11.

21. Good Works

Good works, even though commanded by the law, do not come from it and are not done by its strength. They are done by the strength of faith, by the power of God who lives in us, and by the Spirit when he writes the holy law in our hearts and gives us a new heart which fully follows the will of God and that which he commands.[133]

For this reason we must not think that any works are good if they are not that which God commands and that which the Spirit works in us.

This means that all that man does from his own ability, invention, knowledge, prudence, understanding, that which comes from his will, and all that which God has not commanded expressly, no matter what these imitate, cannot be a good work, but only evil and sin. And the more it seems good, the more it is pernicious and to be fled from. For having the form of holiness it pulls us from God more easily. And man returns slowly to God, thinking he does well and lives well. We perceive this with idolaters, [136] who pray, serve and worship another than God alone. With those who murmur, who do nothing but mutter the words without understanding,[134] they honour God with their lips, but serve in vain, following the doctrine and commandments of man.

With the pilgrims who look for God here and there, they do not take care of their servants or of those of whom God gave them charge.[135] By this they deny the faith and are worse than infidels.

All these people are not content with the holy law of God, but, [D vi] as if it was insufficient and imperfect for the holy life, they also take up the inventions of men. They are no longer content simply to be called 'Christians', but brothers of Saint James, of Saint Sebastian, of Our Lady of Comfort, of Our Lady of Grace, of Our Lady of Le Puy, of Our Lady of Loretto, of Our Lady of Montserrat, of the First or Second Orders of Saint Francis of Assisi, [138] or of the major orders, the minor orders and the lesser orders.[136] So it continues with all who take such offices, which we call 'spiritual'. They promise that which is not in their power, like perpetual chastity outside of holy marriage, keeping many laws, statutes, and ordinances alongside the law of God which they cannot bear alone. They believe that if they add other commandments, they could bear all more easily – as if the multiplication of laws and commandments would make them stronger and give them strength. Yet this simply loads them further and makes their situation worse, producing wrath, as pin-pricks

---

[133]   Jer. 31, Rom. 8, and Ez. 36.

[134]   '*en aux barbotteurs, qui ne font que murmerer parolles sans entendement*'

[135]   1 Tim. 6.

[136]   '*...des grandz, des mineurs, ou des minimes*'.

of sin, and making sin abound. For where there is no law, there is no transgression.[137] And yet all these kinds of people desire and work to be sanctified by transgression. [140]

22. Why Good Works Ought to be Done

One must not perform good works to obtain paradise or eternal life.[138] For these are not given because of works, but by grace, through faith, by the gift of God.[139] He gave this gift when he gave Jesus his Son to die for us and for the remission of sin. This remission is given by the blood of Jesus which was shed for us and is the only source of any good or profit which comes to us or to another. We receive it only by giving thanks [D vii] to God, in recognizing his infinite goodness, grace and mercy when he justified and saved us, and not by any of our merit. For even when we were his enemies and in sin, Jesus died for us and reconciled us to God by his death.[140]

So the Christian's heart, ardent with the love of our Father, desires only to honour and glorify him.[141] In order that God be honoured and magnified in his life and in the lives of those around him, the Christian strives to accomplish God's holy commandments.[142] He does good to all, evil to none, loves all, prays for all, and desires that all come to the knowledge of the truth. By the great desire that he has for God, as a loyal and true son towards his [142] all-good and all-wise Father, he does not take pleasure in anything besides that which serves the honour of the Father. He does not simply serve God to get his reward (even though the reward is so great that one cannot calculate the great inheritance that God gives to his children), for by this he would act as a mercenary. Nor does he serve out of fear of the punishment which will come upon those who do not do the will of God, for this would be to serve as a slave. But he seeks those good works commanded of God, not imagined by men, by true liberty of the Spirit, looking only for the glory and honour of God. For all good, salvation, grace and life are given to us by Jesus Christ and not by anything else. Let everyone examine his works to see whether they seek anything other than the honour of God. [144]

---

137   Rom. 4.

138   Eph. 2.

139   Eph. 2.

140   Rom. 5.

141   1 Cor. 10.

142   Matt. 5.

23. Fasting

The fasting which our Lord demands is to break all the ties with evil and with that with which we treat our neighbour cruelly; it is to feed him who is hungry, to house those without a home, to clothe the naked; it is [D viii] to have pity on those who are like us and share the same flesh as us – the same as all the needy.[143]

This fasting is pleasing to God and very helpful for many, actually for all.[144] But the other type of fasting is a bodily exercise, and helps only a few in comparison with the first. For the second tries to bring the flesh into servitude; it tries to mortify the flesh by taking away foods. This fasting is not in the power of any person to arrange or command of another person; he who fasts can alone judge whether he has the Spirit of God. He alone can judge when and how he is to afflict his body, not by choice and distinction neither of foods, nor of fixed times to eat, which is useful. He should not afflict nature so much so that [146] he cannot serve his neighbour. The father and mother who stay away from food to the point where they are not able to provide food normally for their children do not fast, but kill their children. In the same way, the servant or worker who does not do what he should do steals from his master. For this reason, our Lord did not give a law or time of fasting, but commanded us to live soberly in order to serve him and to help our neighbour without any distinction of foods.

Those who proclaim themselves leaders of the Church have placed a great and unbearable burden on the poor folk in order to oppress them (a burden which they themselves do not touch with their littlest finger).[145] It would be good for them to fast a day as they command, working as he who by the sweat of his brow feeds his family. They would learn not to forbid foods and not to command fasting, but only that which God commands and forbids. They would not burden the poor worker with other burdens; they would give him consolation, not [148] more [E i] affliction. For Jesus came to lighten burdens, to give rest to the weary and the exhausted. But his adversary makes the burden of the weary greater and gives more work to the weary. [150]

---

[143]   Isa. 58.

[144]   1 Tim. 4.

[145]   Matt. 23.

24. Prayer and Praying

Praying is an ardent speaking with God[146] in which man does not know what to say or ask. But the Spirit who is with the faithful prays for us with great groanings which one could not even speak.[147]

In prayer the mouth is really not required to speak, but the heart only. For our Saviour Jesus taught us that when we pray we should say 'Our Father who are in heaven, etc'.[148] This does not mean that we should only say these words with our mouth, that with these we would have what we ask, for that would be as the superstition of the enchanters. But [Jesus teaches us] this very beautiful prayer in order that in our heart we should think of God as it says: that he is our God and that in true faith and in good conscience we go to him. In it we lift our hearts to [152] heavenly things and ask only that which is contained in this very holy prayer. By it we understand that all that we ask that is not contained in this prayer is not the will of God.

This means that all the prayers of the prophets and holy ones directed by the Spirit of God were in accord with what is asked in this prayer. It is necessary, therefore, that our heart speaks to God as to our good Father, and that it prays only to him. For prayer is the true sacrifice of worship by which we give honour and glory to God, for he alone wishes to help us.[149] For this reason he wants to be honoured by this honour and does not want it to be [E ii] given to any other, as it is clear in his first commandment.[150]

It is, therefore, gross idolatry and very displeasing to God that we appeal to another besides him. For this comes from our unbelief in his infinite goodness and mercy, as if there were someone better and more merciful than he, or more powerful and wise, or as if he could not help us or did not know how to do so. To help us and extract us from this unfaithfulness and unbelief, he bought us back by himself living fully in his Son; he saved us and healed us of all our sicknesses.

And so, let us watch that our prayers not turn to sin, committing idolatry in praying to another besides God, [154] or praying before people to be seen, or muttering or multiplying many words.[151] But with great desire and few words, let us pray so that the tongue stops much sooner than the

---

[146]   The 1552 text adds: 'Praying is an ardent speaking with God from whom man asks and begs that which he has promised; that is, to aid his people, delivering them, forgiving them, saving them. In prayer, man declares God's power and magnifies his name and reign'.

[147]   Rom. 8.

[148]   Matt. 6.

[149]   Ps. 69.

[150]   Isa. 62.

[151]   Ps. 108 and Matt. 6.

heart and begins to speak much later than the heart. Let the tongue never speak in prayer if the heart is not with God. We must recognize the dignity of him to whom we are speaking and of what we say to him, for above all he hates hypocrisy. May we ask firstly for the kingdom of God, that he reign in us, that he destroy all our sin and that he put his justice in us. Then nothing will be missing for us.[152] [156]

25. Almsgiving

Almsgiving is mercy and compassion; it is to save and help another because we are inwardly moved with pity when we see his poverty and needs. When a father sees his son in great need, his heart and bowels are moved and warmed with compassion, and he goes straightaway to help and save his son.[153] Likewise, a mother's love for her child is so heated that she would pass through [E iii] fire and her enemies to save him. This also happens between brothers and between friends.

This mercy and very affectionate and ardent desire is attributed to God by scripture, in which he is called merciful Father, slow to anger, prompt to pity.[154] Could a woman ever forget her son without having pity or compassion for him? Or could a mother feed her child, whom she breast-fed and carried in her womb, and then simply forget him? God says even though she might forget her child, nonetheless I will never forget you.[155] He has shown this very well, seeing our very great misery and poverty, and having pity on us. Even when we were his enemies, according to the times, he gave his dearly beloved Son for [158] us. He brought us back to life and saved us. He fully healed us and took away our mortal sickness by his afflictions, death and suffering. He made us rich with his riches that he gave us in his Son, giving us with Jesus the inheritance of heaven and life eternal, making us his sons and inheritors, and delivering us from all our enemies, evils and sins.

For we ought to be like our celestial Father, who is so full of mercy towards those to whom he owes nothing and to whom he was not held to show such mercy and grace. He gives such great gifts to them. We ought and are restrained to have compassion and pity on all the poor by helping and saving them. We ought to help above all those of the household of the faith, sharing with them all goods, graces and gifts that God has given us – things which God gave to us to use for and to aid each other.

---

[152] Matt. 6.

[153] Luke 15.

[154] 2 Cor. 1, Ex. 34, and Isa. 49.

[155] Rom. 5.

This mercy and compassion should be so great that we ought to do good not only to our friends and neighbours, but in the same way that the Father sends rain on the just and [160] unjust, and raises up the sun to shine on the good and bad, so we [E iv] ought to do good to our friends and enemies.[156] We ought to pray to God for those who persecute us and put us to death, giving back good for evil, feeding our enemy if he is hungry and giving him drink if he is thirsty. We ought to love and have compassion on all those who are in need, no matter who they are, those poor, ignorant and imprisoned in error, who persecute that which they do not understand.

And we ought to do all this only for the honour and glory of our Father who is in heaven, without having any other motivation than to advance his honour and glory. Giving thanks to him, remembering always his grace and mercy which he showed us, conforming ourselves to him and to his holy will, fleeing the worship of this world, not seeking to be acclaimed by men, we must always give the glory to God alone. This pity and desire should serve the good and profit of our neighbour – he whom our Lord presents before us and whom we can help and serve because we know his need.[157] For God commands us to help all those whom we are able to help.

But it certainly is not almsgiving to give to those who can work, who have abandoned some or all of their belongings, have abandoned their [162] work (even though they could live without relying on anyone), and have done this to be without work and at their leisure, without the trouble that comes with living in the world, to live in laziness in a monastery or other place where they only serve to burden the poor people and poor labourers, as are the churchmen, monks and nuns, who by their rules and statues are separated from others. Rather, it is to give them a noose to hang themselves and a sword to pierce themselves by feeding their wickedness.

Whatever one does for the [E v] dead or to obtain something from God is not almsgiving, but true idolatry. For one presumes on the commandment of God and does not work for his glory and honour alone. But the aid which we give out of compassion for our neighbour who is in need and only for the honour of God, this is the true almsgiving. [164]

26. The Adoration of God

The true adoration of God, his true service, is to give one's heart entirely to him, recognizing him as the only sovereign Lord and Master, true God

---

156 Matt. 5.
157 Luke 10.

and true Father, without any other, not waiting for any other salvation, or life, or deliverance from our evil and sin than from him. It is not looking for him here or there, in the mountains, in Jerusalem or in any other place, but in Spirit and Truth.[158] For one must not seek [him] in or ask [him] of any other creature, whether corporeal or visible thing, but in and of those who are spiritual, who worship God in Spirit and truth, in ourselves, in our hearts.[159] For the kingdom of God is within us when we have a solid faith in him. He is not in any religious observance. For there is no way to have or find God merely by acting, nor by being in a certain place. For God does not reside or have his habitation in things made by men's hands, nor in things visible, but in us who are made spiritual, renewed, united and conjoined by true faith to our head Jesus Christ.[160] [166] He is the mercy seat on which rests all the divinity, where are all the treasures of knowledge and wisdom.[161]

We ought, then, in all things and everywhere to address in all our needs our Father, always falling back on his help – he who continually helps those who love him. [168] [E vi]

27. The Adoration and Worship of the Saints

The worship, adoration and prayers done for saints, and for all others who are out of this world, is a thing done without faith, against the word of God. In this God is dishonoured, because his honour is given to the creature. In fact, one also dishonours saints, because one appeals to them despite that which they did, said and taught. For the saints do not want us to trust in them, but in God.[162] They forbid this false worship according to the word of God. All images which man made to honour or bow before, all these offerings, candles, vows, novenas,[163] and all these ways to act with which the world is presently full were not commanded by our Lord, but condemned.[164] All these inventions are condemned so much so that he wants those who invented these things to be cursed, even if they were to be angels of heaven.[165] For he does not want us to change or take away

---

158   John 4.
159   Luke 17.
160   Acts 7.
161   Rom. 3.
162   Acts 3 and 14.
163   'neufvaines' A traditional Roman Catholic devotion consisting of prayer said (most typically) on nine successive days, asking to obtain special graces.
164   Ex. 20 and 1 Cor. 5 and 10.
165   Gal. 1.

from his word, according to which we must be governed; otherwise, it is sin.[166] He also forbids us to do that which seems good to us: we must rather do only that which he commands us, without changing or reducing it. And since we are servants and sons of God, the Lord and Father so very wise and so very [170] good, we must walk and act according to his holy commandments and will, and not according to our or another's imagination.

Those blaspheme who say that the saints are our intercessors, advocates and mediators between God and us, the way, the life and the hope. Their treatment of the saints is outrageous and they dishonour our Lord Jesus who alone is mediator, who intercedes for us with the Father.[167] He is our advocate, who speaks for [E vii] us, the only way, life and truth, and no other.[168] Our hope is in God alone: he who puts his trust in him is happy; he who puts his trust in another is cursed.[169]

Miracles and other things which have happened to us should absolutely not shake us, pull us out of the word of God, or allow us to entertain another faith or belief than that which is according to the word of God. For the heavens and earth will pass away, but the word of God will not pass away – it will remain eternally.[170] Nothing that is written in the holy word will pass away until it is all fulfilled. Our good master Jesus warned us enough about the miracles which would be done in the time of the Anti-Christ. This Anti-Christ has changed and destroyed everything [172], so much so that nothing pure remains on earth. And this comes to pass by false prophets, false teachers and lying doctors who instead of edifying others by truth have destroyed them by lies, false signs and miracles for the seduction of those who have not believed the truth.[171] For he who looks closely at these things would find no true miracle, but only trickery and deception to gain money. Has not God demonstrated and revealed in many places the falsity of miracles and of their inventors so that his own people would come back and return to the light and truth and so that the unbelieving would be condemned? The unbelieving introduced and contrived miracles, the worship of saints and all such seduction by their greediness. Has not the falsity of these miracles and their inventors been shown in Paris with Saint Regnault and revealed in the temple with

---

166   Deut. 4 and 12.

167   1 Tim. 2 and Rom. 8.

168   1 John 2 and John 14.

169   Ps. 90 and Jer. 17.

170   Matt. 5 and 24.

171   1 Thess. 2.

the image of Lancelle, and in many other places?[172] In this we know the judgement of God and his vengeance on idolaters who have been warned of this trickery, but want nonetheless to continue in their iniquity and not return to the true God. [E viii]

Christians, give honour to God and serve him alone, as all the saints and blessed who [174] have gone before to the kingdom of heaven.[173] By this you will not be judged and condemned with those who have honoured creatures and the work of their hands.[174]

We should all pray for each other for as long as we are here, where we can make known our needs to each other. We should correct and exhort each other, rejoice in the goodness, grace and lifting up of our neighbour, and be sad for his hurt, error, downfall and poverty. Holy scripture is full of these many requests for each other in which we help each other by our prayers. Do not doubt in this the goodness of God.[175] Rather let love be conserved and grow as we invite each other to pray and let thanks be given to God by many when he gives that which many have asked for in their prayers. By this God will be more greatly praised and honoured.

But for those who are outside of this world, and who sleep and rest, let us not ask them to pray for us, for this is a vain thing and contrived without scripture. For that is what the princes and leaders of the blind say, the university doctors, that the saints have such love for us, that they are moved to pray to God for us [176] when we pray to them and call upon them. I ask myself who told them that the saints know and realize our situation, that they see our hearts and the desires for which we call upon them, and that they pray when they hear our thoughts. If this is really the truth, that the saints pray as truly as when they were in this world and more fervently show love to us, why do they not do the other works of charity which are as necessary as prayer, as our Saviour taught us clearly, like [F i] preaching the holy gospel, disciplining and admonishing? Would it not be much more necessary now than ever for Saint Andrew and Saint Thomas and the other Apostles to preach, seeing that the world does not know what it ought to do?

For to believe in the Pope, in what he does and commands, would be to follow one who does nothing according to God. For the Pope has, as he says, paradise and hell for sale. Jesus, however, gives to the poor the kingdom of heaven. But the pope gives his pardons, indulgences and

---

172   In the 1542 edition Farel gives several more examples: 'Has not the falsity been shown ... in Paris with Saint Regnault, and in the temple the image that we say is of Notre Dame of Laurette, of Saint Cosme, of Saint Francois de Paul, and the crucifix at Muret....'

173   Matt. 4.

174   Isa. 2.

175   2 Cor. 1.

remissions to those who have money.[176] The poor do not receive anything. The Pope gives also to those who have great foundations; by this the poor gain nothing. Nor is it possible to believe in universities, for we see only meanness, [178] error and garbage – pride so great that they want us to believe them without scripture. They want us to believe them on their authority, by the nod of their head or the wave of their hand. Of this Jesus never made use. They take away from the people all the judgement of that with which they are confronted, not permitting them to read or hear anything but that which pleases them, promoting only their name and their universities. They make use of their decrees and judgements [177] against that which does not please them, so that we believe in them and adore them in receiving that which they say without contradiction, holding all that they say as an article of faith. Those who know them cannot bear this. Everyone sees that their case is not well founded, because [180] they defend themselves by authority and force of fire and sword. Who would believe in a priesthood which is all wicked or in orders which only create disorder?

The poor people are not able to believe those who have borne and do bear the truth because darkness has reigned for such a long time and the Anti-Christ reigned so greatly over the people, princes, [F ii] kings and nations, persecuting and putting to death all those who spoke for the truth. For this reason the unknowing people cannot believe that it can be the truth. It is like the crowd who asked for Jesus to be put to death when they could not believe that he was the Son of God, seeing that all the great persons and the council of those thought to be wise had condemned him to death.

If the saints, therefore, pray for us as they did in the past, why do they not in their great love clearly show the way we ought to go and do the other deeds they did in this world for our instruction? Let us leave behind these opinions and fantasies that men have dreamed up and hold purely to that which is clearly commanded. Let us serve God alone, and call upon him by our only mediator and advocate our Lord Jesus, who promised us that all that we would ask of the Father in his name we would receive.[178] Therefore, let us hold firm in his word and no other. [184]

---

[176]   Matt. 5.

[177]   'determination et sentences': Farel himself was the object of a determination of the Faculty of Theology of the University of Paris. See Rodolphe Peter, 'Recherches sur l'imprimeur de la Determinatio attribué à Guillaume Farel', in: Actes du Colloque Guillaume Farel, pp. 221–30.

[178]   John 14.

28. Feast Days

Our Lord commanded us to rest on the seventh day.[179] He wanted us to sanctify this day without doing servile labour, like the labour of the land or similar such work. This does not mean that working on this day would be to do evil or he would never have commanded to work and earn a living by the sweat of one's brow.[180] But he commanded it so that we would protect charity, having compassion for workers and servants, not oppressing them by continual labour and work – giving them one day of rest after they had laboured six days. He clarified this command when he said 'the seventh day is the rest of the Lord God. You will do no work, you, your son, your daughter, your male servant, your maid servant, your cow [F iii], your donkey, and all your animals, and the stranger who is within your gates, so that your male servant and your maid servant can rest as you. Remember that you were slaves in Egypt'.[181] [186] The Lord created the heavens and earth in six days and rested the Saturday which is the seventh day.[182] This shows us the great rest that our Lord Jesus announced to us is the command to cease our works of sin.[183]

The Christian should not make a distinction of days or times or years, as if one was more worthy than another, more holy or better than another.[184] Properly speaking the faithful man counts only one day for all his life, on which, by the movement of the Holy Spirit, he works out his sanctification in all purity of heart, destroying sin, living justly, doing the work and labour that is for the honour of God and for the profit of his neighbour.

---

[179]   Ex. 20.

[180]   Gen. 3.

[181]   Deut. 5.

[182]   Heb. 4.

[183]   1542 text: 'For all our days are equal and we ought to employ ourselves everyday for that which the day of rest represents. We ought to think of God, of his great, high and excellent works, of his word, and do our work out of love. But in respect to our coming together to hear the word of God, to take the holy sacraments, and to give rest to the workers and servants, so that it be without confusion the Church has the liberty to set aside certain days, no matter which ones, or a part of a day when we cease manual labour. This ought to be done without superstition and in guarding good peace and unity with other Churches. It ought to be done without superstitious conformity or a scandalous, anger-provoking diversity, but with great love and edification. When the day has been decided, no one is allowed to violate it or trouble the order which it establishes, not because of the day, but for the word which is preached on it, for the sacraments which are administered, and for the honour we ought to give to the Church, the bride of Christ'.

[184]   Gal. 4. For more on 'feast days' in early Reformed thought see: Lambert, 'Preaching, Praying, and Policing', pp. 188–95 and Marianne Carbonnier-Burkard, 'Jours de fêtes dans les églises réformées de France au XVIIe siècle', *Études théologiques et religieuses* Vol. 68, No. 3 (1993), pp. 347–58.

These works are to help those who are in need, to witness to his faith, to come together with the faithful to hear the word of God, to take the bread of thanksgiving, to come to the table of our Lord with his brothers, and to give rest to his own inasmuch as love requires it. The works are not to observe days, not simply to honour them, for this is a remnant of the idolatry of the pagans and of the superstition of the Jews from which the Anti-Christ has composed his laws and customs. Rather, the Christian does all to honour God and to maintain love with his neighbour. [188]

The multitude of feast days that those in the church of the wicked have invented to have masses, offerings and such like things, is all self-conceit against the word of God. When he can do it without scandalizing the simple who have not yet heard the truth, the Christian should not leave his work [F iv] by commandment of the Pope or his bishops. But if he cannot do it without scandalizing the poor – those ignorant by innocence – he should not do his work before them but wait for them to come to the knowledge of the truth, bearing the tyranny until the light of the Son of God, the holy gospel, will break down the horns of the Anti-Christ, destroying him by the breath of his mouth. This is already greatly begun.

Yet, all those who love the Lord should lift their heads. For salvation is coming. Such a one should work even more when he rests his body to employ his spirit for the things of God, thinking and meditating on his holy law, attaching himself to his holy word, looking at the holy gospel, and fleeing all superstitions that are kept until the present by all idolatry, blasphemy, debauchery and iniquity. [190]

It would be better if everyone did that which was done in the early Church: after hearing the word of God and taking the bread of benediction all together at the table of our Lord, all went to work. Alas! Think how much wickedness, filth and sin we would have avoided. But it was necessary for the Anti-Christ to have his reign, so that Jesus would triumph over him as over all those who come against him. He has stretched his mighty hand over those who oppose him and will not pull it back until he has accomplished all of his plans. [192]

29. Confession to God, Reconciliation with our Neighbour and Confession to a Priest

Confession in scripture is to give glory to God, to magnify and exalt him, confessing his goodness, power and wisdom.[185] [F v] By this confession man looks at himself and his misdeeds and condemns himself; he judges himself to be altogether different than God. He gives honour to God who is good

---

[185] Matt. 11.

and just and knows that man is evil, unjust and sinful. Being humbled for his sin by such confession, he seeks and returns to the infinite goodness of God. Hating great and elevated things, he gives grace to the humble and lowly by Jesus Christ who has forgiven him. In this way the holy prophet Daniel confessed to God his sin and that of the people.[186] Scripture is full of this sort of confession which admits that there is nothing pure or clean but God. [184]

There is also brotherly reconciliation, used when we have offended our neighbour and have displeased him. For this we come to ask forgiveness from each other. For this reason our Lord, forbidding hate and rancour, commanded us to ask for such when our flesh overpowers our spirit. By this we are taught that we are all brothers, having one spiritual Father.[187] When our brother sins against us and he repents of it, we ought to forgive him. So that we do not forget to forgive, he wills that in prayer we ask forgiveness of our Father and that we also might truly forgive.[188] For as we do, so will it be done to us. He commanded us above all to love and to be prompt to forgive, so much so that we ought to drop everything to reconcile ourselves with our brother – as he told us concerning him who offers his gift on the altar.[189] For in the time when Jesus began to preach in Jerusalem and the surrounding area, the people did not appreciate each other, but only gave an offering at the Temple.[190] For this reason the entirely stingy doctrine of the Pharisees became popular which cried 'Corban, Corban, gift, gift', meaning that one took away aid for father and mother to give it to the temple.[191] Such a gift did not consider that our Lord wants goodness and mercy and not sacrifice, [F vi] and the knowledge of God more than an offering.[192] For this reason Jesus said: 'when you must do the important work, as it was told you and you have learned, of the gift that you [196] offer at the altar, leave it there and go reconcile yourself to your brother, and return there in love and charity with him'.[193] For the end of the law is love.[194] He who loves his neighbour has accomplished the law.[195] He who forgives, has forgiveness.[196]

---

[186] Dan. 9.
[187] Luke 18.
[188] Matt. 6.
[189] Matt. 5.
[190] Matt. 15.
[191] Mark 7.
[192] Hos. 6.
[193] Matt. 5.
[194] 1 Tim. 1.
[195] Rom. 13.
[196] Matt. 6.

The confession that we make in the ear of the priest was invented and commanded by the Pope and his cohorts.[197] It has greatly served him to know the secrets of kings and princes and to trouble the world, so that in troubled water he could fish for countries and kingdoms. By such confession he can better act in his own interest, so that the princes among whom he creates dissension combat each other. By this confession invented without scripture, the Pope changed a great deal and found many subtle ways of pillaging the world. For priests, monks, nuns and all sorts of these people, hearing these confessions, became aware of all sorts of trickery, deception and all wickedness, and subsequently used it. By this method, the people were taught all kinds of error. By his cohorts, the Pope made everyone believe that which he wanted and heard about all that was against him, so that he could oppress and destroy them. [198]

Who could tell of or number the great multitude of souls which have been seduced by this confession and pulled into Hell? How many poor women have been drawn to impropriety? How many virgins corrupted, widows devoured, orphans destroyed, princes imprisoned, countries ravaged, powers and houses brought to nothing, great bordellos of men and women established sumptuously and kept up?

The miserable people were so blind that in receiving this damnable institution they did not think [F vii] of the great burden it would be and how impossibly unbearable it was to confess once a year to one's own priest all the sins that we thought, said and did. It is clear that no creature, no matter what it is, can understand its sin or, even less, be able to recite its sins.[198] But this was invented so that the prophecy could be fulfilled in these men which said 'they have afflicted consciences with vain error without giving them any rest or assurance of the grace and mercy of God'.[199] The Scotsman[200] can speak and say [200] what he wishes. All his scribbling is not enough to unburden the conscience. In another way, the Thomists, against Scotus, will never leave man in peace by their doctrine.[201]

Christians, pull yourselves away from the cruel tyranny of him who has put on your backs and shoulders unbearable burdens which he does not touch with even one finger. Come to him who took our burden and put it

---

[197]   Here again, the author or editor has printed a pointing hand to emphasize this particular argument.

[198]   Ps. 18.

[199]   Rev. 9.

[200]   'Lescot': *The Scot*, *Scotus*. John Duns Scotus (1270–1308).

[201]   Thomists: theologians following Thomas Aquinas (1225–74). On Scotus' and Thomas' doctrine see: Alister McGrath, *Iustitia Dei: A History of the Christian Doctrine of Justification*, 3rd ed. (Cambridge: Cambridge University Press, 1998), pp. 117ff.; Thomas N. Tentler, *Sin and Confession on the Eve of the Reformation* (Princeton: Princeton University Press, 1977).

on his shoulders and carries it.[202] Trust in and be assured by him. Come to him alone and no other – neither priest nor Pope. He will give you rest and peace in your consciences as you bear his light burden.[203] Have confidence in him and not in your confessions. Call upon him and not upon these cruel tyrants full of all pride and iniquity. For the good Jesus is humble and good natured.[204] He will save you from all your sin and by him you will have all grace and blessing.[205] [202]

Contrition[206]

Contrition of heart and a contrite heart are not a cold distaste or a simulated pain as displayed by those who are papistical and over-devoted, but a great troubling and emotion of the heart afflicted from all sides, so much so that it is totally broken, shattered and torn apart, as [F viii] the word signifies: there is nothing whole in the heart.

This shattering happens to a heart knowing and feeling the judgement, wrath and indignation of God that it merits because of its sin and transgression. This man knows that he has no refuge, no aid, no help from any place below, seeing the law of God which condemns him to perdition is just and holy. He knows that no creature in heaven or earth can deliver him. For it is necessary that all that is written should come to pass and that all the threats and curses fall upon the transgressors of the law.[207] For the heavens and the earth would pass away before one single word of the law would not come to pass.[208] God does not play around with or treat lightly that which he has said. [204] Being in this anguish and tormented on all sides, the heart only has refuge in the infinite mercy of God, falling back on him as the Father of all mercy.

The very merciful God does not despise this heart so broken and torn, but receives it with grace and pardon.[209] For a broken heart is more pleasing than anything else man can present. By this, by the curse that Jesus Christ bore, he takes away from this poor man the curse of the law.[210] By the

---

[202]   Isa. 53.

[203]   Matt. 11.

[204]   Matt. 1 and John 1.

[205]   Gal. 3.

[206]   No chapter number in the 1534 edition, but Chapter 35 in the 1542 edition.

[207]   Lev. 26 and Deut. 28

[208]   Matt. 5

[209]   Ps. 1

[210]   Gal. 3

death that Jesus endured, the Father gives grace and forgives him, so that he will live.[211]

The heart sorry and afflicted because of the wrath and indignation that it feels by its sin receives from Jesus Christ a total consolation, peace and joy. By faith, it feels in itself that it is delivered and absolved by Jesus. And not only absolved, but incorporated and united by true faith in Jesus, it receives from him the gifts and graces, goods and eternal inheritance which are freely and without his meriting them given and granted to him by the eternal Father, by Jesus Christ. Bitterness and sadness are [G i] changed to great joy, which will be fully revealed at the coming of the Saviour. At his coming we will be raised again and made like unto him.[212] [206]

30. The Forgiveness and Remission of Sin

The forgiveness and remission of sin is given by God alone.[213] For he alone can erase our sins for the love of himself. That which is said to the Apostles and to those who bear the word of God, 'those to whom you remit sin, they will be remitted; and those whom you do not pardon, will not be pardoned',[214] was explained before in the article concerning 'the keys of the kingdom'. The 'keys' are nothing else than to announce the remission of sins in the name of Jesus.[215] Those who believe in this pardon will obtain it; those who do not believe remain in their sins.

Indulgences and the forgiveness of popes can well take away money, extracting it from the misled, but cannot take away sins. It can only make them worse and greater, because one believes by money to have the gift of God which is the remission of sins.[216] The absolution that priests give is given by mumbling and putting his hands on the head. It is pure fantasy to believe that by trusting in this word 'I absolve you' said by the priest, one has the remission of sins. Where is the scripture, that in believing this we have remission of sins? Where is the promise? [208]

But when it was announced to all that the Father had such a great charity and love for the world that he gave his only and very loved Son to save the world, that he shed his precious blood to forgive our sins and

---

[211]   The 1542 text adds: 'For this forgiveness, God does not look at the great amount of pain in the heart, nor to anything that is in man, but to himself, to what he has given for the salvation of the poor sinner, to JESUS'.

[212]   John 3.

[213]   Isa. 43.

[214]   John 20.

[215]   Luke 24.

[216]   Acts 7.

to purge us of all our faults, and that he is the lamb of God who bore the sins of the world, our hearts, in believing this by [G ii] true faith, are most certainly purified and our souls are brought to life. He who does not have this faith, but seeks something else and trusts his works, indulgences, confessions, supplications, or some other thing no matter what, rests in death, for he does not believe in the only Son of God. For if we could be absolved by some other thing than by Jesus Christ, he would have died for nothing.[217] If we could be cleansed of our sins and protected from evil in another way, Christ would have shed his blood and suffered so many plagues for nothing.[218] In these matters we clearly see the fulfillment of scripture concerning those who reject and who cause others to reject him who bought us back – our Saviour Jesus, true power and strength of God, perfect and sufficient to save us.[219] When we seek in any other than in him the remission of sins and forgiveness, [210] whether in pilgrimages, indulgences and other invented things, of which there is no promise at all in scripture, we reject Jesus and force him to be rejected by others. For there is no other thing under heaven by which we can be saved, but in the name of Jesus. [212]

31. Satisfaction

Satisfaction for sins given by things that man can do is a very great self-conceit and very foolish, full of pride, encroaching upon God and his holy word. Being nothing but ashes and dust, this self-conceit presumes and is proud of what it cannot have and is not able to have – the satisfaction of the infinite justice of God. By this pride it rejects the power and efficacy of the death and suffering of Jesus and esteems the shedding of his precious blood insufficient to appease and satisfy our Father and to turn away his wrath. It rejects them as if Jesus did not bear our sins on the cross, bearing our punishment and weakness, but [G iii] as if all that he bore was of no power or efficacy and that we should appease the wrath of God by bearing our own sins.[220] We could never ridicule and condemn such blasphemy enough as it comes fully from the Anti-Christ. [214]

Every Christian should know that he cannot stand before God, nor flee and avoid his wrath, without Jesus, who is our mediator between God and us. He must know that he cannot be freed or discharged from his sins, or

---

217   John 3.
218   Gal. 2.
219   2 Pet. 2 and I John 4.
220   Isa. 53.

avoid the punishments due to him without Jesus alone. He has no other way.

It is necessary to believe that Jesus purged us and bore our sins and the punishment that we should bear.[221] For this reason all that we do and ought to do should not be for our sins, but only for the honour and glory of God who is fully content with what Jesus suffered for us. He requires nothing else but that we believe firmly that our salvation is accomplished by his grace, gift and mercy in Jesus; he requires that we love him, that we give thanks to him, that we rescue and help our neighbour by our love for him; he requires that we give him all honour and glory for he alone justifies us, saves us and sanctifies us. We can credit nothing to our works, virtues or powers. [216]

32. Excommunication[222]

Excommuning or excommunication[223] is barring from the table of our Lord him who is in sin and who has not pulled back from it after the admonition of one, two or three, and after that of the whole congregation of our Lord, that is, all those who love him and believe in his word.[224] This is done so that by his shame and sadness, he will come back for the better, leaving his sin.[225] [G iv] Excommunication is not given for us to hate him who is excommunicated, but so that we can love and correct him as a brother, desiring his salvation. All those who no longer take the bread of thanksgiving with him should pray to God for his salvation.[226] It is a loving correction and full of charity, to pull the poor sinners out of their sins.

Regarding the method of excommunication of the Pope and bishops, it is as far from the evangelical excommunication as they are far from God, their doctrine far from that of God, and their lives from those of the Apostles. Above all they show their stupidity when they excommunicate in general him who has done something which nonetheless remains [218] unknown. How can I avoid this man at the table of our Lord if I do not

---

[221]   Isa. 53

[222]   The 1542 edition places Chapters 32–36 after Chapter 17. Hence, the material on excommunication and the good pastor is placed after the material on the keys to the kingdom of heaven and before that of the sacraments.

[223]   The 1542 edition adds more than ten pages of explanation to this chapter. Largely the additional material is a more thorough apologetic for the necessity of excommunication. Farel thinks that a correct use of excommunication, based on the Biblical witness, is for the good order of the Church and a true amendment of life of the excommunicated.

[224]   1 Cor. 5; See Epistola 31 in *Calvini Epistolae*, Vol. 1, p. 158.

[225]   2 Cor. 2.

[226]   2 Thess. 3.

even know him – let alone you, Pope or bishop, since you do not even know his name?!

By excommunication the faithful are prohibited from taking the bread of the Lord with the excommunicated. Our Lord said it in this way: 'If your brother has sinned against you, correct him among yourselves alone. If he listens to you, you have gained your brother. But if he does not listen to you, take two or three brothers with you, so that by the mouth of two or three all will be spoken. And if he does not listen to these, declare it before the assembly, to the whole parish. And if he does not listen, he should be for you as an infidel and publican'.[227] There our Lord commands that if we know a brother has fallen, we should admonish him in private. If he accepts our admonition, he is won to our Lord. Otherwise, to better attract him to God, [220] we ought to take with us two or three good people who can gently correct and admonish him of his fault. If he does not want to amend himself, then all those of the [G v] parish, for the honour of God, should pray and admonish him to return and leave his sin. If after all this he does not want to do anything, then we ought not to converse with him, but only as an unbeliever with whom you would not want to come to the table of our Lord, nor converse with, nor approve his life or his faith. For the rest, however, you can drink and eat with him to win him and pull him back. So must one converse with the excommunicated in all charity.

The papists and all the church of the Pope do not practice any of this. For this reason their excommunication is as much to be feared as a leaf which falls from a tree. That [222] we feared it so much was to accomplish that which was prophesied: 'The fall and movement of the leaf will frighten you as the sword and you will flee before it as before the rapier'. So one fears the movement of a leaf of paper or piece of parchment with a little bit of wax or lead as death. But where there is faith the adversary can do nothing with his letters and fulminations. [224]

33. False Pastors

False pastors, as the Saviour said, come under the appearance and clothing of sheep, but inside are ravaging wolves.[228] No matter how much they simulate serving God, they only serve their bellies and by soft words seduce and pillage the simple.[229]

These wolves do not preach the pure word of God, but only their fantasies and inventions, mixing the straw with the wheat. They mix the

---

[227]   Matt. 18.

[228]   Matt. 7.

[229]   Rom. 16 and Jer. 25.

teaching of man (which is called diabolical) with the teaching of our Lord – inventions full of new [G vi] tricks designed to seduce the people for a morsel of bread, promising life to those who are dead in sin, judging as dead those who have true faith.[230]

Above all their doctrine says: 'Here, here is Christ', as if they held him in their hands. Or they say he is in the hands of another or he is in [226] a secret place hidden inside a box. They want to confirm their word by false signs and miracles by which many are deceived, looking here below for that which one must look for above at the right hand of God, not on earth.[231]

These false pastors feed themselves, not their sheep.[232] For they devour all the milk, that is, the work of the poor, in so many ways that one cannot imagine them all. If there is any rich person, he is devoured by force to contribute to religious foundations. But there is no chance that the word of God be fed to people, so it must be forbidden by fire and rapier that it might not come to the fore. [228]

Christians, good Jesus said that 'by their fruits you will know them'.[233] Look at their pride, envy, stinginess and heart's debauchery. If you cannot otherwise understand, realize by that which the Holy Spirit prophesied that 'they have renounced the faith'. Their teaching is diabolical, for they forbid holy marriage, so much so that it is not honourable to marry, but only at the times when it pleases them, even though God never forbids this.[234] Also they forbid meat, as if meat made us worse in relation to God at one time than at another and as if that which entered the mouth dirtied the man.[235] They pretend that the creature that God gave to be used and eaten was not good and that we ought to reject it, even though the word of God states the opposite of their teaching.[236] [G vii] [230]

34. The Good Pastor

The good, true and faithful pastor above all is our Saviour Jesus who gave his life for his sheep, leaving his food to feed the starving – indeed, the drippings of his word.[237] For the meat that he desires above all is to do the

---

[230]   Ez. 13.

[231]   Jer. 23 and Matt. 24.

[232]   Ez. 34.

[233]   Matt. 7.

[234]   1 Tim. 4.

[235]   Matt. 15.

[236]   1 Tim. 3.

[237]   John 10 and 4.

will of God his Father. In feeding the sheep, he does not talk of himself or do anything of himself, but his Father speaks in him and works in him.

His teaching is the teaching of his Father.[238] He does not break either the law or the prophets, but keeps them and fulfills them; he did not go against scripture, but held that it was necessary that it be fulfilled. He taught his sheep and disciples about this fulfillment, working in them its knowledge. By his model and actions as the good pastor, we can know other pastors. For insofar as one follows Jesus, one will be a good pastor; insofar as we pull away from him, so far will we be closer to [232] the Anti-Christ.

For this reason the good pastor and faithful minister will lead and serve the sheep for the love of God, ardently desiring life and salvation for these poor souls.[239] By his holy teaching and good example of life, the good pastor will forget himself in order to feed them with the word, to seek that which is from Jesus and not himself, and to direct all sheep everywhere to live according to the holy and good will of God. He will invent nothing of himself, nor propose anything invented by another, even if it were an angel of heaven who found it. Rather, he will only propose to the sheep that which he believes perfectly and that which is firm and approved by holy scripture.[240] [G viii] He will not tolerate his sheep who were liberated by our Lord Jesus to be put again in subjection to tradition or human ordinance.[241] Take, for example, vestments, meats and other things that are external: the faithful can use them for the honour and glory of God, in all good, so long as they make no distinction or give scandal to the weak of faith. For all is open and free for a Christian who is a son of God; that which is of God is given to him to use in a holy manner.[242]

The good pastor will show and teach that true justice is in the heart – a heart which, having true and full faith, fully loves God and his neighbour for the love of God. In this way the good [234] pastor announces the word of God purely, without mixing anything with it, and is diligent with holy scripture. He examines scripture to exhort, reprove, admonish, correct and teach, so that his whole congregation can serve the Lord with their whole hearts according to his holy commandments.[243]

In honouring the holy state of marriage he will be husband of one wife, sober and moderate, careful and diligent with the sheep, full of good manners. He will readily lodge and receive guests with friendliness in his

---

238   Matt. 5.
239   1 Cor. 10.
240   Ps. 115 and Gal. 5.
241   Acts 15 and Col. 2.
242   1 Cor. 10.
243   1 Tim. 4.

house. He will be able to teach and instruct; not a drunkard, not a detractor, not given to dishonesty and vile gain, but of good conscience and just, not a murderer, nor a fighter, without stinginess, knowing how to govern his house well, having obedient children in all honesty, not being a novice or without experience, as holy scripture shows us.[244] [236] By the example of the pastor, all the faithful should learn to know who God is and what is against God. That which is commanded of God is different than what we have seen until the present time. Pastors [H i] should serve the sheep and not be served by them.[245] They should be the least of all and let the sheep, as the greatest, be seated while they themselves stand.[246] [238]

35. The Power of Pastors

The entire power of pastors is to edify in what is good, to instruct and teach the people by the pure and simple word of God.[247] Apart from this they are not able to act as pastors, but have turned into ravaging wolves and false prophets, which God permits because of the sins of the people.

When true pastors purely evangelize, God speaks in them with such great power that believers have life eternal and nonbelievers are silenced.[248] A messenger of God or a true evangelist will never be defeated. For God, as he has promised, gives to his own words of wisdom against which no one can resist.[249]

Since the world cannot resist the holy teaching of God, it takes out its displeasure on the bodies of those who bear the word, forasmuch as they are seen to be at fault. Hence, they put to death true evangelists, as was done to the prophets and to our Lord Jesus with his Apostles. By this we can know more fully that the power of the truth that the servants of God announce is unbearable to the world and completely contrary to it. [240]

Do we not see the books which speak of our Lord being burned and their possession and reading forbidden upon great penalty? In this we see clearly that the foundation of those who forbid them is very poorly built and very weak.

The true Christian who is founded on the true rock can read and hear anything. I could read an endless stack of books [H ii] talking of miracles, of signs, and of the things that the superstitious people now worship,

---

244   1 Tim. 3 and Tit. 1.
245   1 Cor. 3.
246   Luke 22.
247   1 Cor. 10.
248   Matt. 10.
249   Luke 21.

before I would believe that there is more than one God or would serve and call upon another god than him.

Do you want to hear of even greater foolishness and madness? See how we freely tolerate plays full of mockeries, villainies and obscenities; dishonest and foolish songs, books full of all vanity, refuse, lies, blasphemy, stinking evil, disorderly words for the perdition and corruption of all society! By these books the wrath of God arises and is provoked on all. Yet it is not permitted to read [242] the holy scripture to the simple people to whom it was given. There the New Testament containing the death and suffering of Jesus, the doctrine which each Christian should hold and believe, is forbidden.

O God, why such horror? O sun, can you shine your light on such a country? O earth, can you bear such people and give fruit to such people who so despise and scorn your creator? And you, Lord God, are you so merciful and so slow to anger and vengeance against such great outrage done against you? Have you not commanded your Son to be King over us? Should his holy ordinances that you commanded him to teach us be forbidden as sinful, evil and hurtful to those who read them? Is the holy gospel like the law of Mohammed, which no one dares read, or speak about, [244] except a few people? Is the New Testament like the books of the enchanters or sorcerers which all dare not read? The ceremonies of Moses and what he wrote, are they more holy, better and more useful than all that which Jesus clearly taught, seeing as they have never been forbidden as has your holy gospel? The Pharisees, [H iii] the Jewish people and the Samaritans, are they more important than the poor people who bear the name of your Son, called Christians, who have actually read and heard a little of your holy scripture – not they who simply wear the name 'Christian'? Did you not, Lord, command that all should have your holy law written in their houses, that they should think on it every evening and morning, that the fathers should teach the law to their children and servants, and that all should know your ceremonies and statutes?[250] Should your holy gospel have such little [246] reverence that we ought not speak of it, look at it or read it? Why did you command that it should be preached by all people to all creatures and that all creatures should have it and know it, if it is not permitted for each person to read it?[251]

O sinful judges, because the scripture condemns you, as Jesus is for you a rock of scandal and his odour for you the odour of death, do you want to bring down the elect and those for whom Jesus is true Jesus and Saviour – he who by his holy gospel has destroyed your head the Anti-Christ? Do you do this dishonour to God that his work should be hidden from his

---

[250]   Deut. 6.

[251]   Mark 16.

children as harmful and mortal? Do you say that 'good is evil' or that 'light is darkness' to condemn it? From where do you get this audacity and evil courage but from your father and master the Devil, who, as he did from the beginning, promotes himself to block the word of God from reigning and having its way?[252] You do this not without cause: for it is the only thing needed for coming into the eternal kingdom,[253] for illuminating the hearts of the poor sinners sitting in the darkness of death, and for letting them know and hear the great abuses [H iv] in which they have been stuck for so long.[254] We wish that these poor ones would change their opinions about this way of hypocrisy which now seems beautiful and pleasant in [248] its ceremony, pomp and circumstance, and that they would be converted to the true way which is that of the holy gospel of Jesus Christ leading to eternal life. His reign will be without end. He will have dominion over all of you his enemies and you will one day be humiliated and put under his feet. It would be much better for you to have never been born if you keep permitting all these hucksters and books to have free rein, and not those announcing the gospel or the books which contain it, by which the simple are instructed.

Rise up, O Lord, show that it is your desire that your Son be honoured, that the ordinances of his kingdom be published, known and kept by all! May all know you by your Son, from the greatest to the least.[255] Make the trumpet of the holy gospel heard from one end of the earth to the other. Give power to the true evangelists. Destroy all the sowers of error, so that the whole world might serve you, call upon you, worship you and honour you. [250]

36. Our Obligation to True Pastors and What Obedience and Honour We Owe Them

Those who hear good pastors should test and judge that which they say and seek diligently to know if it is of the word of God.[256] Once they have tested it, they should hold to it and believe it, not because of the pastor who bears it, but because it is the word of God.

If they find that the pastor bears something other than the word of God, they ought to guard themselves not to trust in it or believe it. Even if [H v] one of the greatest Apostles of God or an angel of heaven came to teach

---

[252] Gen. 3.

[253] Luke 11.

[254] Luke 1.

[255] Jer. 31.

[256] 1 Cor. 14 and 1 Thess. 5.

something else than the pure word of God, we should not hold to any of it or believe it. For, we ought not to have other nourishment than the pure word of God. Scripture clearly testifies that whatever is not clearly proven by scripture should not be received. God has not brought about anything on earth that he has not prophesied by his servants the prophets.[257]

When, therefore, the word is brought purely according to holy scripture, we must obey it, for we obey God and receive our Lord in receiving it. [252] We should feed him who brings us the doctrine of life.[258] For God commanded that he who evangelizes and preaches the gospel ought to live from the gospel.[259] For this reason those who are taught and comforted by the word of God should share all goods with him who serves them in the word. We ought neither to pay him an enormous amount, as we have fed the pompous in rubbish until now, nor leave him a pauper, but feed him and clothe him in such a way that he can duly perform his office. Without being puffed up by the abundance of riches, nor constrained by need to do otherwise than he should, he ought to have sufficient means to live. These are the two honours we ought to give to the elder, to the minister of the word who serves in the gospel.[260] [254]

37. The Sword and the Power of Justice and Corporal Superiority

We are composed of two things which conflict greatly with each other: soul and body. The soul and the spirit having knowledge of God by faith, are delivered out of slavery and transferred from death [H vi] to life, from sin to justice, from wrath to the adoption of the children of God.[261] According to the Spirit, it flows from this that there is only one Father, God and only one Lord, Jesus. There is neither man nor woman, male nor female, servant nor lord, slave nor free, nor any distinction of superiority, nor of subjection, for all are one in our Lord.[262]

Yet according to the body, which is still subject to corruption and in which we await the redemption, there is a great difference. A father and mother have power over a child and the child is subject to them.[263] The husband is the lord and head of the woman and the woman is subject and

---

257   Amos 3.
258   1 Cor. 9.
259   Gal. 6.
260   1 Tim. 5.
261   John 8, Rom. 6 and 8, Eph. 1 and 2, and Matt. 23.
262   Gal. 3, 1 Cor. 15 and Rom. 8.
263   Eph. 6.

submissive to his power.[264] The relationships of master and servant, free and slave, and princes and subjects remain.[265]

All these relationships which accord with the ordinance of God rest unchanged so that property might be preserved.[266] These relationships allow us not to [256] harm others in body or property. For the punishment of the evil ones and those who do wrong to those around them, God has established the power of the sword – kings, princes and lords, and all those who have the administration of justice.[267] So that they can better exercise their office and have a fortified hand, they watch and guard that we do no wrong to any other, keep all in peace where they have authority, and collect tributes, taxes and other things as they command.[268]

It is true that if everyone had a true and perfect knowledge of God and if charity were firmly rooted in the hearts of everyone, so much so that we kept the commandments of God, not doing to others what we would not want done to us, there would not be need for the sword to defend property, for no one would harm anyone else and there would not even be any evil ones to punish. But because Jesus reigns in the middle of his enemies, all property has been and will always be surrounded by evil ones.[269] [H vii] It cannot be otherwise so long as our bodies will live.[270]

For this reason, the sword and justice are necessary. Everyone must obey and be subject to this [258] power in those things which are under the sword, whether body or property, whether the judgement is good or bad, in all things that are not against the commandments of God.[271] For in this we must obey God and not men.

When, therefore, justice orders us to pay a tribute or commands us to leave the country, even if we have built a building or something similar, we must obey.[272] But if it is demanded of us to worship another god, to commit perjury, to do evil or to steal, we must obey God alone and not men. Yet in all [260] the service we owe that will not offend God – whether payments, portions, tributes or taxes – we must obey with honour.[273]

Those who have superiority and the sword should consider well and think clearly about how they will employ this authority and power,

---

264   1 Cor. 6.

265   Eph. 5.

266   Rom. 13.

267   1 Pt. 2.

268   Rom. 13.

269   Ps. 109.

270   Matt. 13.

271   1 Pt. 2.

272   Acts 5, Jer. 24, Ex. 1.

273   'rentes, censives, tributz et impostz'

knowing that up above is he who has power over all. He has placed them as agents to deal with and direct their subjects, as a good father is careful with his children.[274] They ought to give to each that which is his due, without making any distinction between poor or rich, or small or great, or of any standing, exemption or non-exemption (which have been invented against God and his holy power). Those in power must guard themselves against selling justice or receiving presents.[275] For the more they are elevated and called 'gods', having such an honour to be called sons of the Most-High, the more the judgement will be severe on them, if they do not fulfill their office and fulfill with sanctity the power that God has given them.[276] [262]

Subjects also must take [H viii] caution not to rise up and rebel against lords and to fight them, for he who fights against the power of the sword fights against the ordinance of God.[277] Faith and the renewing of life do not take away this subjection, and even less does baptism. We must not say that he who is baptized, even if he is a slave or was in bodily servitude at one time, should now be free as the Pope has written. Rather, by the confession and profession that he made at baptism, promising to keep the law of our Lord, he is bound to serve his lord as before.[278] He must serve him in all faithfulness and not only with the eye, no matter how unfaithful his master. By this the name and teaching of God will not be blasphemed as wicked, nor will that which belongs to the lord be taken away from [264] him.[279] With an even better heart the faithful slave should serve that master who is faithful as one who is an inheritor of the kingdom with him.

This means clearly enough that the faithful can have temporal lordship, have slaves, bear the sword and administer due justice. When God gives them grace to be able to help their country, elected officials should do it as charity requires, defending the good and punishing the evil. They should help their neighbour and use the grace that God gave them to deliver the widows and orphans from the hand of the oppressors for the honour of God, to announce his glory, to take away all that which is against the good and which inhibits the simple people. All good kings and judges did this.[280] For if the Christian cannot exercise the office of justice or bear the sword by the ordinance of God and the power given to him from on high, he ought neither to have servants nor children, to have [I i] power and

---

274   Ex. 10.
275   Ex. 22 and Ps. 8.
276   John 18 and Eccl. 5.
277   Rom. 13.
278   Col. 3.
279   1 Tim. 6.
280   2 Ch. 18 and Jud. 6.

authority over them or over their bodies, nor should he correct them nor punish their faults. But such a thing is against the scripture. [266]

When it is a question of the things of the soul and the spirit, these things must serve that which they must serve, as it was said above. But the body serves that which speaks to the body. Let us not change or mix the one with the other, mixing and confusing all: the freedom of the spirit should not be confused with the body or the feeding and schedule of nourishment of the soul with that of the body. Rather let us assign and distribute to each that which belongs to it. As such we will avoid confusion.

Those who hold the sword know that the power they have is from God. For this reason without fearing anyone, without making or permitting any exemption, they hold it over all those who are in the place where God has given them power. For no one, no matter his social standing or position, should be exempt. Privilege, prerogative, dignity or other exemption does not serve them, for the [268] word of God says: 'Every person should be subject to the sovereign powers, which do not bear the sword in vain, but are ministers of God'.[281]

38. Marriage

It is in the nature of the adversary of our Lord that he must despise, bring low, dishonour and make contemptible everything that God has honoured and magnified. In the beginning of scripture we read of the true, holy and pure commandment that we ought to hold and fear; if we ever ate of the fruit of the tree of knowledge of good and evil, we would die.[282] But the serpent mocked this commandment, saying that we would not die, but that great good would come in the eating of it and [I ii] that we would be made like unto God. We see this mockery in our times against the things that God wanted to be honoured like the holy power of the sword, which by priests has been brought so low that it cannot perform its duties, being in subjection to those who themselves ought to be subjects of the sword. By a bit of tonsure or oil, priests hold under their feet this holy and very necessary power.

In the same way the holy and worthy state of matrimony is dishonoured. This state was worthily instituted above all by our Lord before the sin of man and honoured by the presence of our Saviour when he began to show the power of the Lord his Father, changing water into wine, wanting holy marriage to be a mystery, sign and [272] representation of our salvation,

---

281 Rom. 13.

282 Gen. 3.

of our good and of our triumph.[283] By marriage the husband and the wife become only one body, one flesh, as Christians are one thing[284] with Jesus – the bridegroom of the holy congregation of the faithful, which he had richly adorned and clothed.[285]

But if you look at those for whom holy marriage is forbidden, it is a quite an honour for marriage! For they are such that I do not know if I ought to call them 'men', for they have nothing about them that is human. Rather, they are 'devils', except that devils have given more honour to Jesus and his word than these poor and pitiful murderers of souls, these crazy wolves, dirty, vile and more villainous than Sodom and Gomorrah. These ought not to be in a state as noble as holy marriage, but as swine always in their muck and filth, far from this holy state. It was ordained to protect the holy temples of God from all pollution – the habitation of the Holy Spirit, that is the members of our Lord Jesus – to the end that they not be polluted with adultery [I iii] [274]. [286] This holy, pure and clean state is ordained by God himself. God made the woman to help the man in holy marriage in performing true and perfect charity, which is the fulfillment of the law.[287]

When marriage is purely guarded, the two are but one body in true charity and love. Notice also what care mother and father have for their children who come of a loyal marriage. In such a family the father knows that his children are his and the mother never loved another or ever abandoned herself to anyone else, but was always loyal to her husband. What offices or works of true charity are there not in this holy state? If we increase in the good, what joy is not there because of the good and the prompting to always do better when inconvenience arrives? What compassion and sadness over evil? In the holy state of marriage the works of charity are practiced visibly and there is no manner of living where charity has so many occasions to flourish at all times and at every hour. For He who is charity established this state, honoured it and [276] commanded it. And he who is the devil, being full of hatred, ruined it, dishonoured it and forbade it as much as he could.

God wills that he who cannot be continent without lusting should be married and that a man should marry a wife to avoid fornication.[288] He wants the woman to have her own husband, living together in all sanctity with him so as to flee the temptation of incontinence.

---

283   John 2.

284   'chose'.

285   Matt. 19 and Eph. 5.

286   1 Cor. 7.

287   Rom. 8 and Gen. 2.

288   1 Cor. 7.

God did not give any exemption of time or persons, but only when it is a relative (and only the most ignorant would not understand that marriage with a relative should not happen).[289] God wishes that marriage, done with the consent of fathers and mothers if the man and woman are still under their charge and correction, should come to pass [I vi] and [the two] never be divided. But the critics of God, putting themselves higher than him and over-ruling his commands, have found that there was a certain time so holy that this evil and polluted state of marriage should not be consummated, nor the husband be joined with his wife. By this they imply that the [278] time of innocence when Adam and Eve were married was not holy!

They have also found that there are people of such great holiness, purity and dignity that they can never be in this vile filth, as they say, of marriage. If ever these people, without looking at the great dignity and nobility they gain by their double sack and tonsure, got married, they would have to live separately. They have made up a whole series of degrees of relation, conditions and obstacles which make marriage untenable and an obstacle – unless gold and money can make it unstuck and strengthened. If these holy and worthy men are corrupt, adulterers, villainous monks, committing enormous crimes, we would say 'there is a bit of sin', especially if we perceived something which brings dishonour or damage to the state of the priesthood. Yet it is not nothing compared to the priest who gets married – for then he receives the punishment of fire and death. What would some men abused by friar[290] or priest say [280] if, under the pretence of I do not know what kind of holiness, they had to stay away from their wives at certain times and certain days so that their wives could commit adultery with these holy teachers?

O holy state of marriage, how you are dirtied and dishonoured! O world brutal and destitute of all sense and understanding, are you without eyes? Are you so blind that you grope around in full daylight as if you were in darkness? Did you think that at some time this holy state would be forbidden, that the accomplishing of the command of God would be sin, or that going clearly against the pure and express commandment of God [I v] would be a lesser and smaller sin than to follow the commandment of God?

Alas, Christians, return and do not neglect that which Jesus Christ your Saviour honoured. Children of God, hold as good that which your Father

---

[289]   Lev. 18.

[290]   *Litt.*: 'Cordelier'. Friars of the Franciscan Order (*Ordo Fratrum Minorum*) took on the name 'Cordelier' in France. The name referred to the cord which they wore around their waist as part of their habit.

ordained and do not let yourselves be seduced by these false anti-Christs, enemies of Jesus.

You kings, princes, lords, judges and others to whom our Lord has given authority over his people, do you not see the great scandals that the priests, friars and monks do in your countries and realms, ravaging and seducing girls and wives?[291] Do you not see that they openly commit vile and base adultery and fornication, by which we see poor girls by the thousands seduced and lost and an uncountable number of marriages wasted and broken – from which many murders come? For the honour of God, of whom you are ministers, be virtuous and careful to correct and punish [282] these abominable crimes which everyone is infected by and full of today.[292]

Do not be held up by the exemptions and privileges claimed by these vile swine, for they are not properly founded, as I said above, speaking of 'the sword and power of justice'. To ward off such scandals and wickedness, holy marriage must be honoured according to the institution and command of God. Otherwise you will be found guilty before God as accomplices of their stinking lives and perdition, for which a horrible judgement will come upon you.[293]

Husbands, love your wives and live with them to avoid fornication.[294] Be grounded in the word of God and not in the murmurings and dreams of monks and priests. Understand the dignity of your state; in it lived all the holy patriarchs, prophets and apostles [I vi] of which scripture speaks. You must acknowledge and respect marriage and not some vain dreams.

Wives, obey your husbands and be subject to them in all as to our Lord, for the husband is the head and the wife is under his power.[295] Take caution when you are separate from each other so that you do not fall into incontinence. Keep faithfulness and loyalty, for every wife who breaks her marriage must be condemned to die with the wicked.[296] The thief should not even be punished as [284] greatly as the adulterer, for to break a state so noble and holy is a crime which we cannot punish enough. If you manage to avoid the hands of men or bodily death, fear the hand of God and eternal death, which we cannot flee if we disobey him.[297] Understand that in holy marriage you are called together by the virtue of God and not

---

[291]   Matt. 7.
[292]   Rom. 12.
[293]   Eccl. 6.
[294]   Eph. 5.
[295]   Eph. 5.
[296]   Lev. 20.
[297]   Matt. 9.

that of man. For this reason fear him who joined you together, who chose your body to be his holy temple and dwelling.

All of you who do not have the special gift (given only to a few) to control your heart, action and will, take up this holy and honourable state.[298] Enter into it in all fear of God. Use his holy institution for his honour and glory, and for the edification of your neighbour. Persevere in this state, fleeing all the separations that men have invented. For as long as the wife is his wife and the husband her husband, the marriage cannot be broken or separated, except for the reason of adultery alone when the wife breaks faithfulness and loyalty promised to her husband.[299] [286]

Such is holy marriage that if one of the partners is a believer, she can live with the partner who is not a believer, as the unbeliever can remain with his believing partner.[300] This does not block the good of marriage; it is still according to God and [I vii] the children are also holy and good as if both parents were believers. But all this has been trampled under foot to slander and dishonour holy marriage, which our Lord wants to put back in its rightful place and to honour as he instituted it.[301] [288]

39. The Instruction of Children

Those who truly love the honour and glory of God have a great desire to have descendants and children who will honour and serve God, magnifying his name and his glory after they have left this world.[302] For this reason the first and principal thing in the instruction of children is to teach them to fear and love God.[303] They ought to teach them the holy commandments of God purely,[304] showing them the works of God, how he has punished the wicked and brought low the proud. Parents must teach children that all those who trust in their own power, virtue, wisdom, parents, friends

---

[298] Heb. 13.

[299] Matt. 5 and 19.

[300] 1 Cor. 7.

[301] In the 1542 edition, Farel continues here with several pages of instruction for husbands and wives to live in peace and holiness.

[302] Gen. 15 and 25.

[303] Eph. 6.

[304] In the 1542 edition Farel adds: 'how to speak to God and pray to him, how and what to pray to him, how to confess and give thanks, the holy ordinances of Jesus. They ought to describe and demonstrate to them the power and effectiveness of these ordinances. By the grace of God an excellent instruction booklet has been made for this by Calvin – a book that should be praised and used by all children so that they will have a sufficient understanding of that which every faithful Christian ought to know and a willingness to flee what is evil and pursue what is good'.

or in any creature that exists, will be found to be confused, as Pharaoh and all those who worshipped idols or as the children of Israel who had confidence in their temple, sacrifices and the observance of the law.[305] On the other hand, parents should help them understand how God kept his own who were not haughty and did not trust any other creature, but followed his holy will and believed in him. Such were Noah, Abraham, David and Ezekiel. [290] The knowledge of the holy stories serves greatly – equally from the Old as from the New Testament. Holy scripture is very useful for those who wish to teach and instruct well.[306]

For this reason the father and mother should make an effort that their children, both sons and daughters, have knowledge of the scripture and that which is contained in [I viii] it. For scripture serves all and is profitable to all. It is not like fables or lies, or like the evil arts, or like the *Koran* of Mohammed, which we ought to forbid for Christians, but it is very holy and very worthy that all in every time, era and state should have knowledge. For nothing serves more to fear and honour God, no matter what we see or hear, than that which holy scripture contains.

With this scripture, father and mother, by action and word, should give an example to their children in how to love, fear and honour God. They must keep watch over themselves, no matter how young the children are and even if they seem to know and understand nothing, not to say a vile thing in their presence which would scandalize them. For it would be better that we [292] tie a millstone around the neck of those that give a bad example to children and they be thrown into the deepest part of the sea.[307]

We must also teach a child not to be over-dependent on anyone, not to be lazy, but to be a profit and help for his neighbour. So taught, their lives will be to the honour and praise of God, for the profit of their neighbour, and very active. The teaching therefore will instruct them to work in that for which they will be best suited, whether a trade or a worker of the land. According to the ability of the parents and the capacity of the children, they should learn the principal languages, like Latin, Greek and Hebrew so that if God gives them the grace to be able to teach and bear his word, they can drink directly from the fountain and read scripture in the original language in which it was written, as the Old Testament was written in Hebrew and the New in Greek. To see how God is wonderful in his works [K i] and how men are changeable, they can also see what is written in the nature of animals, trees, plants and other things which God created [294] to serve man, [and what is written] about the diversity of people

---

[305]   Ex. 14 and Jer. 12.

[306]   2 Tim. 3.

[307]   Matt. 18.

and countries, reading the histories that show the great changes in cities, countries and kingdoms.[308] They can study also what has been written for the good administration of the public domain, such as good laws and ordinances to keep the people in peace.[309] For from all of this the faithful heart can profit and be served for the honour of God and the profit of its neighbour. [310]

In whatever social state he is, the child should have knowledge and understanding of holy scripture, so that he will not be led like the blind. This is the holy will of God that his scripture be read and heard by all. For presently it has been translated into more languages and multiplied in more books than ever, so much does our Lord desire that all be full of his holy scripture. [296] In the same way, in reading the history and customs of the pagans one can see where sin is in the customs that Churches keep at present, customs that so many people find so amazing in how they were introduced, seeing that scripture is so far away.

Fathers, because our Lord gave you his name, wanting that you be called fathers, make sure that your children have good and faithful teachers or teach them yourselves in the fear and teaching of our Lord.

And you children, obey your fathers and mothers in true charity, goodness and gentleness as our Lord showed us. [K ii] [298]

40. The Preparation for Death

The preparation for death and for dying well is a true life in entire and perfect faith, not fake, but lived in charity. It is not necessary to speak about this much with a believer, for it would be like wanting to give a great deal of instruction and warnings on how to prepare oneself for rest to him who has worked with great toil the whole day, not allowing him to have the rest he so desires. Who does not rest willingly after great work and toil?

From this it comes that the Christian heart is assured of the good will of God our Father, by the Holy Spirit who witnesses to the elect.[311] The Spirit was given to the elect, guaranteeing that by faith they are sons of

---

[308]   The margin states: 'Example of Moses' [see Acts 7:22].

[309]   Acts 7.

[310]   The 1542 edition continues: 'To be able to judge that which they read or hear, and to be able to point out its faults, they should also have knowledge of dialectic. And to formulate that which they have to say they should be instructed in rhetoric – without setting aside the other liberal arts like arithmetic, geometry, music and astronomy. Certainly these sciences are gifts of God. We ought not to disdain them simply because they are misused, nor should we use them too much'.

[311]   Rom. 8.

God. They have, then, a firm faith that our Lord paid everything and satisfied what the believer owed for his sins, and that where Jesus is, the believer will be. He does not fear to go there; rather, he has a very strong desire, want and wish to be delivered from this mortal body and to be with him.[312] The Christian does not look at his good works or any prayer, but with a true faith he trusts entirely in the infinite goodness of God.

Let every one watch well (if he is wise) that he not follow the poor foolish people full of all fables who counsel that man must consider his good [300] works and that in them he gather his assurance. In Jesus alone ought to be all our assurance, in his justice which is divine, his purity, innocence and holiness, as the true might and power of the Father to save us.[313]

The true believer, feeling that his time to pass from this world is near, so much so that his body is worn out and that his bodily powers and strength are [K iii] failing, gives thanks to the good and ever-merciful Father who does all according to his good will.[314] Being strengthened and having his spirit sustained by God, the believer prepares himself for the wedding, for the beautiful feast of our Lord, in whose hand he puts everything, as in the hand of him who is able to do everything – whether life, death, health or sickness. Above all he commits his spirit to God to receive after his pilgrimage in this valley of misery, without considering his sin, faults, demerits, neglects, nor entering in judgement with this poor servant. Rather, for the love of him who never committed any evil, perfectly kept the law of God, accomplished his holy will and bore our sin, he wishes to be received in mercy.[315] God is so great in his gift of grace and mercy that he gives him full grace and a full remission of sins. In believing firmly that this is granted of the Father, the Christian does not rest his heart in another but in God alone, not asking any other for help but God, the very good and ever-merciful Father. [302]

Concerning those whom our Lord put in his care, the Christian will leave the charge and responsibility to God, without anguishing too much in his heart. For God is good, powerful and wise enough to do everything well. In any case, as he ought to have done all his life, in the end he ought to compel and admonish them to persevere in the holy Faith and the

---

[312]   John 12 and Phil. 1.

[313]   In the 1542 edition Farel writes several extra paragraphs here giving general guidance for a faithful funeral ceremony. He gives guidance to those who have a minister and those who are without. Farel writes: 'If there is no faithful pastor and one cannot have the consolation that God has given to his people by true ministers, let him be consoled in our Lord by reciting, if he can, some passages of holy scripture like 'For God so loved the world that he gave his one and only Son', 'Come to me all you who are burdened', etc'.

[314]   2 Cor. 4, 5 and 12.

[315]   Isa. 53.

teaching of God, to follow his holy word, his holy gospel, to keep his commandments, and to keep himself from going against the will of our Lord – and to consider any other subject he will see to be useful for their salvation.[316] As to the distribution of that which God put in his hands, he will give it out to his own, urging them to peace and all friendliness and charity [K iv] together. If he has a good, faithful and prudent friend who would be able to help his family by good counsel or otherwise, he will recommend them to him. He will not command anyone to take up another state than the only rule of our Lord. He will not run here nor there, but will encourage each to do his work by which he can gain a living according to God and not otherwise. He will not command that his children give anything out of their love for him, for he does not want to usurp [304] God's honour.[317] For God's honour alone must we give to those in need, as he commanded.

So giving over everything to our Lord, armed with the justice of Jesus Christ by true faith, by which Jesus is all ours, in joy of spirit, the Christian takes his rest. He praises and thanks this good Father that it pleased him to make an end to his miseries, to take him out of this body of death, so much so that he will never sin again. He will now rest, waiting for the resurrection of his body, when his life, which is [at present] hidden in our Lord Jesus, will be fully manifested.[318] [306]

41. The Resurrection

The Father, full of mercy, who has done all for the love of himself, bore and suffered in great patience and tolerance the children of wrath ordained to death. He bore all to show the very great richness of his goodness, mercy and gentleness toward the children of mercy.[319] These he elected and ordained to life before the foundation of the world, ordained that all will rise in their own bodies, for the great confusion and incredible horror of the reprobate and nonbelievers and for the marvellous joy, glory, triumph and happiness of the faithful whom he chose.[320] Because the unfaithful are always breaking the law of God, wanting to break down and destroy [K v] that which God has done and ordained, they must receive their due reward with the prince of iniquity.

---

[316]   John 14 and 15.

[317]   Farel is likely opposing bequeathments for prayers for one's soul after one's decease.

[318]   Col. 3.

[319]   Prov. 16 and Rom. 9.

[320]   Eph. 1.

It is necessary that the death for which they served and bore fruit be made manifest in their bodies, no longer a bodily death, but eternal. So the true and faithful Father, according to his promise, will declare the life that he gave to his own, making them like his Son. For as he was raised up from death to life immortal and incorruptibility, so all his members who by true faith are united in him will rise in incorruptibility and immortality, [308] in great glory.[321] For as death could not overcome Jesus to prevent his resurrection, so too it is not able to prevent all his members, the true believers, from coming back and living in their own bodies in immortality.

However, all true Christians know that from ourselves and from all that comes out of us we would be as pitiful as the reprobate. We know that by the grace of our Father and not at all from ourselves we are separated from the lost and miserable and counted among the sons. For this reason all true Christians do not fear using this body for the honour of our Father or using this corruptible life for his holy gospel. For in truth he will give it back to us so much more noble and excellent, such a life greater than we could even imagine.

O true champions and warriors of the word of God, have courage: the victory is close at hand, the [310] triumph ordained with the great captain Jesus. Do not turn your backs in this mighty battle! Enter forcefully into it for the honour of such a good Father and great king who looks upon us to see what the battle is and who battles in us. He leads us and directs us by his Spirit so that all will be well. [K vi] Give to him alone the glory. Do not rest with visible and present things, but with the invisible and with those things which are promised to us! [312]

42. The Day of Judgement

The full revelation of the glory of the elect, of their good, salvation and life, and the consummation of everything, after which every creature longs in anticipation, will be at the triumphant and fully victorious coming of our Saviour and Redeemer.[322] At the moment when all his enemies will be put under his feet and all will be made subject to him, the elect will come before our Lord in the air. The very great glory and power of our Lord Jesus will be seen there.[323]

What anguish and distress will there be for those who persecuted him, who hated him unto death and did not want to bear him! Enraged with

---

[321]   1 Cor. 15.
[322]   Rom. 8.
[323]   1 Thess. 4.

envy and strife, they put him to death by a wicked will. They acted thus
in the beginning towards righteous Abel, then towards others, then in the
very person of Jesus, and shall finally do so with the last righteous and
elect person. For all that which is done to the elect is done to the body
of Jesus – for they are his body, flesh of his flesh, and bone of his bone.[324]
Who can speak of his anguish? Let us leave this awful thought to the
murderers who shed the blood of the faithful, unless in thinking on this we
would have the opportunity to give thanks to our good Father who set us
apart and [316] separated us from among them to be his own, not because
of our works or merits, but by his grace and infinite goodness.

So the elect, whose names were written and numbered in the book
of life before the world was made, the true children of God by adoption
and grace, separated from the wicked and put at the right hand on high
and with dignity, will hear the voice full [K vii] of gentleness, grace and
mercy: 'Come blessed, blessed of God my Father, to whom by me he gave
his blessing as he promised. Receive as inheritance the kingdom which is
prepared for you from the beginning of the world'.[325]

Here you will see all those who come to Jesus and are holy inheritors
of God with him who have the blessing of the Father. He promised to
Abraham that by his seed (which is Jesus) they would be blessed. The
kingdom of heaven was prepared for these from the beginning of the
world.

You should realize by this that these are the only sons of our Lord, to
whom he gave his blessing by Jesus, unifying them to him. For from the
fullness of grace which is in Jesus all those who receive him by faith, who
are his members and are united to him, were ordained to life from the
beginning of the world.[326] For before the world was created, God foresaw
and elected his own. Yet he does not say: 'Come circumcized and baptized,
or numbered with my apostles and disciples, or named Jew or Christian,
or who were such and such'. Rather, to all languages and nations he
says 'Come, you to whom my Father gave his blessing and for whom he
prepared the kingdom from the beginning of the world'. For nothing can
block the election of God and his unchanging purpose, even if the one
whom he ordained to life was born and raised in Turkey, or died [316] in
the womb of his mother. Because he has ordained him to life, he is loved by
God in the womb of his mother as Jacob was.[327] The decree of God is firm.
For the election and grace of God and his Spirit, by whom he sanctifies his
own in Jesus, are not bound by any time, place, person or ways of doing

---

[324] Eph. 5.
[325] Matt. 25, Gen. 22, and Gal. 3.
[326] John 1.
[327] Rom. 9.

things. God gives freely, without regard to parents, [K viii] people, places, or the life of the person to whom it is given.

On the other hand, it profits nothing for the nonbelievers and reprobate to be the children of Abraham or Isaac according to the flesh. They are struck with all the sanctification that one can have corporally such as baptisms and purifications that man can administer. They could have been taught by the most holy of prophets and apostles, by the mouth of Jesus himself, so much so that they understand and teach that which they learned; they could have much virtue, do great miracles, have great appearance of holiness, but have it all serve for nothing.

Look at Esau crying on his brother, receiving him lovingly, being born of the same womb.[328] Look at Judas an apostle, preaching that which he learned from Jesus, doing all sorts of miracles, but being in the end nothing. For this reason those who have prophesied and done miracles but are not part of the elect will be rejected.[329] By this the world is greatly abused, not having knowledge of the ordinance of God. These things are not possible to judge, for it is impossible to judge any being holy because of miracles or other things before the coming of our Lord. For by miracles or similar things we are not made holy. I do not even need to speak of miracles which are simply invented. For miracles are performed also by the reprobate. But those whom God loved greatly, like many prophets and John the Baptist, never performed any. [318]

Therefore, give all the glory to God and not to creatures, ceremonies, sacraments or anything else that man can administer.[330] For God alone saves and gives life to his elect as he has planned. Ask that his holy will be done both in your life and in your death. But only the sons who desire that the will of their Father be done will want this. [L i]

Consider that when the opportunity arises and as our Lord works in them, his elect show themselves to be children of God, but not through hypocrisy, papistry, muttering, distinction of days, meats, clothing or places. The Spirit of God is not manifested in these – the Spirit who tugs at the hearts of the elect and enables them to love and honour God. He compels them to put their trust in God. He who is elect manifests himself by true charity towards his neighbour whom he helps for the honour of God, with the same desire as if he was doing it for God. In himself God does not have need of us, our things, of drink, of food, of a house or of clothing, but he wants to be served in our neighbour, so much so that what we do for our neighbour we do for God.[331] For this reason he will say on

---

[328]   Gen. 33.
[329]   Matt. 7.
[330]   John 10.
[331]   Ps. 49.

the day of judgment: 'I was hungry and you gave me something to eat, thirsty and you gave me something to drink, was homeless and you took me in, naked and you clothed me, sick and you visited me, in prison and you came to me'.[332] By this he makes us understand that we must help our brother in all his needs and in all his difficulties. For if God sends us to help those who are in need, we ought truly to help and rescue them.

Know and learn that this spirit of error keeps and possesses entirely those who, instead of giving that which they ought to their needy and poor children, give it for pardons, masses and relics to indulgence peddlers and priests. [320] These also see the poor that cannot work, dying of hunger, thirst and cold, and leave them or give them only a little. They make, rather, great religious foundations, masses for the dead, churches, chapels, altars, images, convents and cloisters. They feed lazy men, sound and in good health, who [L ii] would be able easily to make a living. Such are these beggars and other swine.

Many also have at their door their sick neighbour and many afflicted people, to whom they could give solace and help, but they leave the service of them that God has commanded and run here and there, from place to place, on voyages created by their imaginations.

Know that God does not demand this of any, but only that which he has commanded. You will soon realize how much you are spending on that and on everything. For nothing is yours to keep. God put money in your hands to accomplish his will, not your own. For our Lord did not say, 'I was on the mountain or in Jerusalem, in Rome, or at saint James and you came to me', but 'I was sick and in prison'.

Spend that which God has given to you to help your poor children, to console and help the sick, the prisoners and the needy. By this you will do the [322] works that God asks of you. This is the will of him who alone gives the plenary remission of penalty and culpability, and forgives all for the love of himself by our Lord Jesus.

I will not mention the judgement of the wicked. They will read it, if they want, and give themselves more grace than the others for whom they have forbidden the holy scripture. Let them know, however, that if they are not penitent the gentle Jesus who awaits them with mercy will greatly avenge the injury they do to him in scorning his holy word and putting to death his servants who bear and announce it.[333] Sooner than they think they will descend with the devils in eternal penalty and torment. And despite them, the just whom they treat so poorly, will go with their King Jesus,

---

[332]   Matt. 25.
[333]   Rom. 2, Lev. 32, Job 21.

after these brief miseries and tribulations, to possess glory and the eternal kingdom.[334] [L iii] [324]

[Conclusion]

We have written this book so that all honour and glory be given to God alone and to no other. We pray that all those who read it will not have the rashness to judge quickly, but to ask for the grace of the Father full of mercy and his Holy Spirit to consult scripture in examining this document with care. As much as they find it to be approved by scripture, so much ought they to hold and support it according to the rule of faith. They ought not to look at the length or brevity of the presentation, at the great or small number of its supporters, at its kind of holiness, or to the opinion of knowledge. Rather, by pure eye [326] and simple heart, they ought to test what we propose, and this according to the word of God. It is much better to hold to the truth like Elijah and worship one God alone, than with the innumerable idolaters to come against his holy commandment, no matter how many people of great renown have lived in such a way for such a long a time. For nothing can break down the law of God or his word. There is no limitation against it. For by it the whole world will be judged by our Lord Jesus and those that are with him. May his holy kingdom be pushed forward and spread through the world, so that all the earth would adore and worship one only God, fearing him, loving and honouring him by our Lord Jesus Christ who directs and governs us by his Holy Spirit. Amen.[335]

---

[334]   Matt. 25.

[335]   On the following page of the 1534 *Summaire* is added a treatise on purgatory written by an anonymous author. For an extended discussion see Gabrielle Berthoud, 'Farel, Auteur du Traité de Purgatoire', in *Actes du Colloque Guillaume Farel*, pp. 241–52.

CHAPTER 7

'The Reason for which This Work was Written and Had to be Revised and Why it Was Lengthened' (appended to 1542 *Summaire*)'[1]

Translation and notes by Jason Zuidema

Grace, peace and salvation be given to all those who love Jesus and desire that he reign over all

By his holy grace, the Lord God himself makes us know how to please him. He makes light come upon his own and gives grace and blessings to them according to his good pleasure and in great goodness and mercy.

It is true, beloved in our Lord Jesus, that already about 13 or 14 years ago, the good and faithful servant of God, doctor and pastor of the Church, Johannes Oecolampadius,[2] by request of some good people, admonished me to give some instruction in my native language to those who do not know Latin. The work was to touch briefly on a few points in which the world was not well taught, so that all those of the French language could have a better knowledge and understanding of Jesus – who is purely known and served by so few. It was to be written so that those in the very great shadows of error, in which so many are ensnared, could be pulled out and leave, and so that we could [220] have a certain help to better understand that which we read in the holy scriptures. Yet seeing my littleness, I did not dare try or propose to write anything – as I also did not dare to preach, waiting for our Lord by his grace to send people more appropriate and more sufficient than myself.

Yet when this holy man ordained of God and legitimately placed in the Church of God told me to preach, he started with the invocation of the name of God. I did not think it would be lawful for me to resist

---

1   This appendix was attached to the 1542 and 1552 editions of the *Summaire*, both published by Jean Girard in Geneva.

2   Oecolampadius (1482–1531) was a reformer in Basel. For Farel's relationship with Oecolampadius see Henri Strohl, *Guillaume Farel: Biographie Nouvelle*, pp. 117ff.

and according to God I obeyed. Being asked for and demanded by the people and having the consent of the Prince who had an understanding of the gospel, I took up the charge of preaching. Also, confronted by his admonition to write, I could not refuse, and I worked diligently to do as I was exhorted by such a great pastor. In the most brief time that was then possible, I put out this little book, striving to pull back the people from the abuses of the Pope and his schools, which are greater and more numerous than anything else. For this reason, I greatly desired that those who read this little book would carefully examine what I wrote it against and what I said against the horrible abuses of the Antichrist, who above all worked to abolish and destroy the power of Jesus, grace, the [221] faith, and all evangelical doctrine. He wishes to hide the name of Jesus, taking everything – the word of the gospel, the sacraments and the use of the keys – otherwise than they ought to be taken.[3] He wants to make one thing mean another.

Hence, it seemed to me that it was fitting at this time briefly and lightly to speak of the reason why I rewrote the work now. I touched on the main points without a fine declaration of the things which were treated. I leave the work of more clearly treating the subjects presented to men more capable than myself. Even though this little book is produced by the least of those who have written, it has not been without fruit. As I have become aware, many have been edified by it, and in hearing the seductions of Satan, have pulled themselves back to Jesus. They have taken heart to study and consider more diligently holy scripture. The kingdom of Satan which tries to rob God of his glory, has been abolished and diminished, and the power of Jesus has been more greatly manifested and increased among many. This enemy has worked to arm himself with what is contained in this little book, leading his own to take what is written here in the opposite sense than was my understanding. For this reason I was greatly astounded in seeing such evil and cursedness – that one would so pervert and turn over the meaning of that which another has written and use all to serve a contrary purpose than that for which it [222] was ordained.

Yet, knowing the depravity of Satan and those whom he leads and directs, such perversion does not surprise me at all; for he is so utterly foolish in working to make the holy gospel serve superstition. He leads his own to make blind followers and to recite the liturgy in a language they do not even understand. They have become like the enchanters who take words which are not common and make them serve their charms and enchantments. Also, those seduced and led by Satan take the gospel in like manner and murmur it without being heard, as if it was commanded to drive out sickness and to avoid all sorts of evils by the power of recited

---

[3]   See Matt. 16:18-19.

words by such a person in such a way. So, those seduced by Satan bring in all damnable idolatry and pull away the poor, ignorant people from faith in Jesus. Such faith comes only by the hearing of the pure preaching of the gospel, which ought to be recited and written according to what the evangelists left – so that we can hear it, and in hearing it we believe in Jesus, and in believing have salvation. By thwarting a salvific hearing the damned enemy of our salvation and the great adversary of God works to change the good of God into very dangerous and even deadly poison and venom, of which he is totally full. Satan compels and draws his own to [223] overturn the truth of God to lies, and to take that which serves for the maintenance and approbation of the truth to prove and support lies.

For who wrote more clearly or so evidently among all the evangelists as Saint John when he wrote on the divinity, eternity and power of Jesus? Even though Jesus took our nature and was made true man as we are, in everything like unto us, first in the nature and the substance of our flesh, but also in the poverty with which we are surrounded, he was without sin. Yet he is the divine word and truly God, by whom all things were made and created and without whom nothing that was made was created. He is of the one and same essence with the Father and the Holy Spirit; he is eternally begotten of the Father of whom he has all that which he has and with whom, according to his divinity, he is equal. He is of one same essence and power, as this holy evangelist clearly shows when he openly holds up the two natures in Jesus: the divine and the human.

Despite this clear truth, Satan continues to attack as he showed by the abominable Arians, who in their heresy held that Jesus was purely a creature with a beginning and not the true and eternal Creator. They held that he was God only by a participation of grace and not [224] by nature, and that he was not of the same essence with the Father, nor equal to him. All this is as if there was in the Holy Trinity inequality and diversity of essence, nature and power – where in fact the three persons are in no way distinguished or different in substance. Really there are only personal distinctions, by which the Father eternally gives being to the Son, who has his being from the Father, from whom he is eternally begotten. The Father has his being from no one, being of himself. The Holy Spirit proceeds from the Father and the Son, as the holy scripture witnesses, and as good faithful servants of God showed and proved. Those who are of the Church of Jesus believed and still believe these truths.

Yet, these miserable, problem-filled messengers of Satan tried to arm themselves with Saint John and, by him, tried to prove their very abominable heresy. In this same way most of the other heretics worked to enliven their errors by the holy scriptures – just as Saint Peter wrote was happening with the letters of Paul. We ought not to be too shocked if because of this little work Satan exerts himself to rise up against that which I have done. Yet, it would be marvellous to have some good come from it – especially if it were for the honour of God and for the profit of the [225] children of our Lord – if Satan does not work to pervert it.

For my whole life Satan has tried to reverse all that I have done, rather, that which our Lord wished to do by his grace in me and by me. While I was preaching and writing, Satan prepared to battle with me on his own so that he could overturn and destroy the holy ordinances of Jesus and mix up everything. Not only did he work against me and my ministry, but he also dared to rise up against the doctrine which was taught, preached and written by the good servants of God and my outstanding brothers in our Lord who preach Jesus with me. These brothers surpass my littleness by the very great grace and goodness of God and the excellent gifts which God gave them, both in gifts of preaching and of writing. These gifts are clearly evident when they write and by their work – as any who have heard them can testify.

This mean adversary of truth spoke to my listeners and by his brazenness attacked me. In my presence he troubled their spirits and tried to persuade them and lead them astray to believe that I was of diverse and contrary argument, faith and understanding than such [226] good and faithful servants of God with whom, so much as they will persevere so, I desire to live and die with them. But God knows how such spirits, who have risen up against me and my brothers, tried to bring down the order of the Church, not those of Babylon who are mixed up and out of order by the Pope, but Christian Churches, ordered by the holy gospel. They declared such an opinion based on the holy ordinances of Jesus, speaking of baptism and of the Holy Supper of our Lord. Among these are found some who wanted to reject the children of Christians in the Church and to deny that baptism belongs to them and should be administered. They believed that I was of such an opinion, even though before I had put a hand to this booklet I had testified in practice and in writing that baptism belongs to little children. I baptized children, taking them from the pomp and presumption of the Pope, and wrote the prayers of exhortation, demands and promises that we should keep when children are presented to be baptized.[4] My opponents ought to have great fear and shame in attributing this teaching to the holy gospel which, in fact, declares the grace of Jesus on children and the place they have [227] in the kingdom of heaven.

Yet this was not enough. For their own glory or otherwise they tried to unbalance good and holy persons as if they were not healthy in the faith

---

[4]   Farel is here probably referring to his *Maniere et fasson*. This first version (probably hand-written), now lost, was written at the behest of the Bernese authorities for use in Farel's missionary activities in 1528 or 1529. A second edition was published as *La Maniere et fasson qu'on tient en baillant le sainct baptesme* (Neuchâtel: P. de Vingle, 1533).

or not feeling correct before God. They wanted me to treat all subjects fully, yet in the brief nature of this booklet nothing is treated as fully or as precisely as it could be and as other good and upright servants of God have done. Most people know that there is a difference between a little entry or introduction and an entire and full declaration, yet they did not want to take this into consideration, for hate and ambition block off too much of the understanding of those who, only looking for an occasion, no matter what it is, take it, even where there is none. By this they do not understand to what this book points – holy scripture – nor to the fact that I treated summarily the things proposed, seeing as our understanding was different than that of those holding the opinion of the Pope. In a work so brief and summary, it is not proper to put forward all that we could or all that we know, but rather to show things in passing and to give a little taste. Our goal was not to treat everything exactly or to chew everything thoroughly.

And above all [228] when touching the being of God and the divinity, I only wanted to speak in the simplest way possible for me, without leading the readers to consider God in his naked being, which is completely incomprehensible.[5] Rather, I wanted the beginnings, so that the spirit of the simple folk would not be burdened by grappling with the very great mystery of the Trinity or the distinction of the three persons. I stuck to speaking of God and presenting him as he declared himself in the things that he did. I showed the great love which the Father showed us, in giving his Son for us – in that the eternal Son was made man and endured so much for us – and in the effect or operation of the Holy Spirit in our hearts. When the simple folk would hear this, without being too greatly compelled from the beginning, they could proceed farther ahead. For a man does well what he does little by little. According to the capacity of his spirit, he will advance and does not need him who writes to put all that he does and knows everywhere and in all that he writes.

For this reason such men have judged only by the poverty of their hearts and have tried to persuade all people that I meant the opposite of what I wanted and meant, turning over its meaning by their malice. Others were no less unreasonable, being so presumptuous as to want to bind [229] the servants of God – wanting to constrain me not to speak and not to treat more fully or to treat differently that which is in this book. It would have been a very great foolishness on my part to presume to write in the way that they argue. It is even greater foolishness and twisting to want, against my intention and against necessity, to bind all not to say anything more, nor otherwise than that which is declared in this booklet,

---

5 '...*sans mener les lecteurs à considerer Dieu en son Essence nue, qui est à tous incomprehensible*'.

not tolerating any other words or more ample explanation. By this Satan has shown himself greatly enraged through his disciples, yet I am still alive, daring to play with what I wrote. I am confronted by people who are totally ignorant, but really opinionated and stuck in their foolishness and by others who show clearly to whom they belong and try to give (to me and those who know me well) an explanation to each other regarding what I wrote – as if they understand my work better than I do myself! Yet, their effort is in vain, for, by the grace of God, I understand better the contents and reasoning behind what I wrote than all those that Satan has seduced. As I resisted such troublers verbally and publicly, so also the good people with me [230] resisted these disturbers of the peace and concord of the Church. They hinder the building up of the Church, for they cannot bear fruit for its edification, nor can they tolerate others that can bear such fruit.

In writing I was able to confront their poor arguments. By the grace of God I could fight all adversaries who rose up to destroy the holy word that I bear. Our Lord has triumphed in me until this day and his adversaries have been defeated. I was able to confound their machinations for the last five or six years. By bringing back and augmenting this little booklet, I was able to try to treat more fully what was so briefly stated [in the first edition], to shut the mouths of those poor spirits.

Yet the ever merciful God and all kind Father accomplished my desire to send persons so full of his gifts and grace, not only to help me and follow up in that which the good God had done by me, but to go ahead of me, flowing in great grace. In preaching and writing, they have received great graces and holy affection to be used for the honour of God, as they faithfully are doing. Because of all the energy it [231] takes to fight against such persons, I have devoted myself for all this time to pray to God that he preserve his servants and multiply their number, as is greatly necessary for the restoration of the Churches. Among others, I pray for my good and full brother Jean Calvin. He participates in the cross of Jesus with the faithful servants of the Lord and walks straightforwardly in the work of the gospel. In all, he comes in only by the door of his very holy and certain calling and goes out by the command of God. According to the grace that God has given him, Calvin, in his *Institutes* dedicated to the King of France, treated so amply all the points which belong to the preservation and understanding of the doctrine of Jesus (that I have treated in this little book and others) and confounded all that which his adversaries could bring forth. By the great grace of God, he clearly surpassed my actual and possible treatment of the subjects and has, therefore, taken away the need and desire for myself and others to write more complete and greater works. Because of his book I do not think that anything else is necessary than to send all interested to such an excellent work. I pray that any who have read my little booklet and desire a more [232] ample declaration than what they have seen here in summary will go and study the *Institutes*. After reading that book they will no longer need my little contribution or make an effort to read this little booklet. Drawing from the greater abundance of heavenly water in these *Institutes*, than in my very tiny drops of water, as it pleases the Lord, one would there be drawn to the sea of all doctrine in the holy scriptures. The scriptures are for us the pure source of all truth – as said Moses, the Prophets and others of the Old Testament, and the Evangelists and Apostles of the New Testament. In reading and studying we must always look purely for the honour and glory of God and the edification and peace of the Churches – for this reason scripture was given. We ought therefore to read these beautiful *Institutes*, so that we can have a greater knowledge of Jesus and of the faith which is in him and of his holy ordinances. By it we will know what we ought to follow or flee and how and to what end we can have more consolation and fruit in the holy scriptures. This book will help make scripture's effect even greater and make it serve the glory of God and the edification of others.

I thought quite a bit about and was hesitant to make this [232] thing public, for above all there are those much more capable of writing than myself. I take more pleasure in seeing the works of others than my own. Yet I saw that this little booklet was asked for by many and was even printed without my approval many times. I feared also that because of its brevity many would pass over it who would not want to study the excellent work of Calvin. Even more, I feared that they would only read this little treatise and not draw from the pure fountain of the holy scripture, in which, above all, I pray that all remain. For I would rather have all my work spoiled and abolished, than to cause one to refrain from reading the holy scriptures because of my work.

So, therefore, let no one do evil for his own benefit and let no evil spirits presume so imprudently to overturn that which I believed and presently believe. According to this belief I speak and write, then as now. Let them not try to make this booklet serve anything I do not intend or their own pitiful ideas or the maintenance of their errors. For before God and his Church, I protest that I did not do or say, nor wanted to do or say, willingly or conscientiously, anything which could serve any heretic or person who contests the truth. My intention, rather, is to serve the truth simply and purely. [234] I wish to serve those who teach it and fight for it, and all the true, faithful Christians who walk and try to walk according to the pure rule, ordinance and word of Jesus. To serve the truth and silence lies, I have set out this little booklet. For a second time I have treated and adjusted that which I could understand so that I could take away the opportunity of perversion from those who pervert everything.

Because Calvin has already amply grasped everything that I desire to teach, I have not made a lengthy treatment. For certainly his work so greatly pleases me in our Lord that willingly, if it was in my power, I would withdraw this little booklet as worthy to be read and set it aside so that I could give place to such an excellent work which, by the grace of God, has taken its place. That book ought rightly be seen and read. I pray, therefore, that all those who read this little treatise or any other work, and above all those who read the holy scripture, to pray and invoke with an open heart our good God and Father from whom is all good and every good and perfect gift, that by his very holy grace and infinite goodness he would wish to assist us all by his Holy Spirit to take and receive whatever comes from him purely and [235] rightly – as he wants it to be taken, received, kept and understood. We ought not to permit in any manner that things which are good and holy, ordained for our instruction, correction and consolation, be used otherwise than to give all honour and glory to God's holy name or be used to hinder us in any way from putting all our trust in him or falling back on his help.

For our own sakes we ought not to do evil. By our evil and perverted intelligence; by our human understanding and foolish reasoning; and by the affections that we have for ourselves, for our honour, glory, fame, advancement, profit, help and rest; and by the affections we have for our own pleasure and for that which we love or hold dear – no matter what it is – we honour and love something else besides God and that which is good. By this we change the good into our evil, and change the holy thing totally dedicated to God to filth and profane use, making it serve something other than God or in another way than that which God wills. By this perversion the doctrine of light is changed into the dark error of sin and iniquity. We must not allow that which serves us by taking us back from evil and perdition, to be twisted and conformed to us so that we be eternally ruined, lost and confounded. Man ought not [236] to estimate himself in his own or another human's eyes more than in God's. When he makes holy scripture serve another meaning and end than that which the Holy Spirit revealed, he foolishly contaminates a thing so holy and divine.

Certainly all manner of curses follow and come upon the pitiful man who abuses holy scripture; he is like the man who kills himself and starves with good bread and good wine by taking it in another manner than it ought to be taken. Even more, he is like the man who mixes venom with good bread – he wastes the bread which is very good and will sustain life, by mixing it with venom, thereby making it deadly. In another way, the man who gives up eating bread wastes himself and shrivels up, dying of hunger. Hence, the man who is not fed with that which is contained in holy scripture dies of hunger and is lost and he who mixes the venom of his understanding (of which all the sons of Adam are poisoned) with and among the holy scriptures poisons himself and others. For this reason, therefore, let us all with ardent prayers pray to our good God and Father who is so peaceful and merciful that we might not mistreat his holy scripture in this way, but that we treat it well and in very great reverence and fear of God. We ought to pray in great dejection of ourselves and for the honour [237] and glory of God alone. We cannot presume anything of ourselves, but wait for everything from God, assured that he has not said anything, or commanded anything that is not entirely good and does not profit greatly. The good Lord makes us understand, believe, hold, follow and keep his word because all that he has said and commanded is true and good. He gives us grace to reject all that is done, said or commanded contrary to him, no matter how good it seems or appears, so that we not be turned away from the holy truth by anything that exists in heaven or on earth.

The good God touches the heart of all, so that in all humility, fear and reverence of his holy name, all would approach him in the name of Jesus. We will read, hear and study holy scripture in his name. We will admit all our faults and ignorance, never having shame to confess that we are humans – pitiful, ignorant and entirely full of sin. We will not fear our bellies, so that we can tell the truth without being spoiled. Nor should we fear for our lives for the truth of God says we must lose them. Above all, pride must not lead us into putting ourselves above all others. All these like attitudes lead to our ruin.

Certainly many are silent concerning the good that they know because they fear [238] the loss of their benefices or their lives. Others, having a little understanding, imagine[6] that they are unable to know everything, yet in great arrogance and disdain of everyone speak of the scriptures and pervert it, making their interpretation serve their own foolishness. Hence, rather than building up souls they leave them aside or beat them down. With clamour and great dissension they raise themselves up against each other and everything is confused. Often those who have the same opinion cannot agree with each other and fight each other with words. They become so heated with each other that their friendship is lost and in its place hatred grows. Instead of asking for the honour and glory of God and the salvation and edification of each other, each looks for his own glory and the ruin of his neighbour. When such a miserable affection gains a hold and leads men, it is as if they look out of a red-tinted window thereby

---

[6]   'cuident', cuider 'imagination': an important word in Calvin and Farel's polemic against the libertins. See Jean Calvin, 'Contre les libertins spirituelz, epistre contre un Cordelier, response a un certain holandois', Series IV, *Scripta didacta et polemica*, ed. Mirjam Van Veen (Geneva: Droz, 2005), pp. 21, 84 n. 4.

making everything seem as if it were red. Through this perspective we judge everything that we see and hear otherwise than it ought to be judged. So radical is this perspective that a man governed by evil affections has no other care or desire and strives for nothing else but to maintain and keep up that for which he has affection and to destroy that which is contrary to his affection. This has been so clearly seen and [239] experienced until the present time. Even great persons, who have great gifts and graces of God, who diverged from each other on a very few points, took the issues far differently than they ought to have, and behaved in such a way that they have truly demonstrated that they are mean-spirited. Our Lord suffered also in such a way, and so these men and all others ought to humble and renounce themselves and diligently seek and pray to our Lord. They need to better understand that which he wants and follow that which pleases him in holiness and true love.

Knowing, therefore, that our poverty is so great and seeing so many examples before us and not trusting in ourselves or in that which we do, but having trust only in God, we pray to him with all our heart that of his grace he would illuminate us with his Holy Spirit which he has promised to give us. Because of his infinite goodness and very great grace, he has given us the great treasure of holy scripture, allowing it to be published for all to read. By the power of his Holy Spirit we receive this good thing which is so great and excellent. To understand scripture the good Father gives us a right and healthy understanding to be used in holiness. Because this understanding has been revealed by the power and inspiration of the Holy Spirit [sic] and not [240] by human will or affection, it will be by God's power that scripture is interpreted in purity and holiness.

By the power of the Spirit scripture will be received and understood according to the good will of God. This will is declared for us in scripture so that we can comprehend it. It needs to be entirely kept, purely observed and fully accomplished. All our desires and affections need to be driven by that which God wants and commands – not looking to any other but him, not seeking any other than the honour and glory of our good God, not being drawn by any other affection than that of him. For growth in the Christian faith and for the good and salvation of all, for the peace, union and concord of all the Churches, we will be led and governed by the Holy Spirit to gain all true knowledge from Jesus. So much will the Holy Spirit dominate, that all people everywhere will live according to the pure and holy ordinance of God by a true and lively faith, working by charity for God's honour and glory like true children. In the end, as heirs they will possess the kingdom to which Christ has called us to live and reign eternally with him. The End.

CHAPTER 8

Liturgical Practices and Forms (1533)

*Translation and Introduction
by Theodore Van Raalte*

Introduction

History

Maniere et fasson was not entirely original to Farel but derives in large part from the Bernese liturgy of 1529. Bruno Bürki writes that it is an 'adaptation of the Bernese liturgy of 1529. But it equally calls to mind the liturgies of the other cities that Farel had visited'.[1] We may add that it certainly exhibits Farel's style, for instance, in its frequent exhortations to the Church. The vital importance of the document lies in its being the first Reformed liturgy for the French speaking churches.

Based on what Farel writes in his explanation for the *Summaire* it appears that he had first written copies of all or some of these forms as early as 1528/9. Kaltenrieder points out that in June and mid-August 1530 delegations from Bienne sought and later received from Farel 'the books on Lord's Supper and the Baptism of children' and in return gave Farel Biennese citizenship.[2] Just what the state of these 'books' was remains unclear, but it does make sense that Farel would be the man to consult for liturgical forms since he was the leading French speaking Reformed pastor at the time in this area, and had begun to establish churches with office bearers and official worship services. For instance, in 1528 Farel obtained and appointed four pastors in Aigle.[3]

---

[1]   Bruno Bürki, 'La Saincte Cène selon l'ordre de Guillaume Farel 1533', *Coena Domini I: die Abendmahlsliturgie der Reformationskirchen im 16./17. Jahrhundert*, ed. Irmgared Pahl (Schweiz: Universitätsverlag Freiburg, 1983), p. 339.

[2]   Andre Emile Kaltenrieder, 'The Liturgies of Guillaume Farel: Their Meaning and Relevance', (Ph. D. diss., Rhodes University, 1980), p. 49. See also pp. 10, 44.

[3]   Kaltenrieder, 'The Liturgies of Farel', p. 48.

Style, themes and use

Farel's prolific scripture referencing in this document suggests that he wanted people to have confidence that the forms rested on the authority of scripture. This would have been important for teaching the young Reformed pastors who Farel was in the business of recruiting in the Pays de Vaud and for helping them in apologetics and evangelization. This teaching function also comes to the fore where the document becomes more a directive to pastors than the actual form they might read in worship.

One also should notice how often the Lord's Prayer and the Apostles' Creed appear in the forms. The forms for baptism, the Lord's Supper, and the directory for worship all contain the prayer and the creed. Maintaining these nurtured continuity with the past and helped the people learn them. Another common liturgical motif comes from Psalm 124:8, 'May our help be in the name of God who made heaven and earth. Amen'.

Some themes recur throughout the forms. First, the preface opens with a summary of the gospel of forgiveness, and this central message appears repeatedly thereafter. Law and gospel show the need and the gift of forgiveness, respectively. Second, the stark contrast between truth and lie, the Devil and the Spirit, etcetera is maintained. Third, in line with the previous theme, we repeatedly encounter the view that whatever God has forbidden in scripture ought to be rejected in his Church and whatever he has commanded ought to be observed – the regulative principle of worship. Fourth, concern to pray for those in authority occurs repeatedly. Farel often refers to their office – both here and elsewhere – under the term 'the ordained power of God'. Intercessions for those who remain in the Roman Catholic Church also occur, asking God to show them mercy. Fifth, doctrinal themes recur, such as God forgiving sins out of self-love, unconditional divine election, and the Church as the body of true believers. Sixth, predictably, the pair 'visible–invisible' play an important role with respect to the sacraments and true faith. Finally, concerns for the development of a common Church polity, for practical things like baptism and marriage registers, and announcement of banns occur. The common Church polity, carried out 'with the consent of the congregation', for the sake of peace and unity, should 'attract the ignorant'. It is clear in these documents too, that Farel never lost sight of winning souls.

Farel's important role in transmitting the ancient *sursum corda* to the French speaking Reformed Churches and tying it to the teaching that Christ's true body is in heaven has been highlighted by a number of authors.[4] The form for the Lord's Supper thus includes a blessing in the

---

[4]   See Chapter 1 of this volume.

paragraph that follows the *sursum corda* which highlights that one's union with Christ is the mystical union, affected by the Holy Spirit.

How did these early forms fare among the French? Farel's form for marriage was retained in the *La forme des prieres* of 1542 in Geneva, and subsequent editions of the same. His form for visitation to the sick – original to Farel but dependent on a priest's manual – was also retained in summary form.[5] Contrary to Oecolampadius, he excluded the Lord's Supper and private confession from the liturgy for visitation to the sick.[6] In line with this Farel specifies that baptism be performed, 'in the full congregation of the faithful'. His form for visitation to the sick exhibits a robust outward spirituality – the sick should be given bread, wine or fruits if the preacher has any – and reflects also his concern that 'the true Sun of justice should always shine in that church' where the people are 'true and living images' of God, full of love for their neighbour.[7]

As to the use of these forms in Geneva, Farel preached in the Church of the Rive in Geneva in 1534, and on Easter Sunday that year he administered the Lord's Supper to more than 400 persons in the Convent of Rive. He followed his own liturgy, administering the Lord's Supper and baptism. Shortly thereafter he solemnized the first marriage according to the new rites.[8]

Translation

In this translation the original page numbers are inserted in square brackets, but numbered by recto only, as in the original. The original text marked the pages of each quire only up to the fourth folio. I have added page markings for the unmarked folios that follow (v–viii).

Two earlier independent English translations of these liturgical forms exist. The first, by Andre Emile Kaltenrieder, was appended to his dissertation but never published elsewhere.[9] Unfortunately, the dissertation itself has never been noticed by Farel scholars. Kaltenrieder's translation is careful but wooden. In the footnotes he takes into account the changes introduced in the 1538 edition of the forms, but he does not reproduce Farel's marginalia which include a plethora of scripture references. Here

---

[5]   *La forme des prieres et chants ecclesiastique, Genève, 1542, avec une notice par Pierre Pidoux* (Kassel: Barenreiter, 1959), p. 7. Kaltenrieder, 'The Liturgies of Guillaume Farel', pp. 133–4.

[6]   Amy Nelson Burnett, *Teaching the Reformation: Ministers and Their Message in Basel, 1529–1629* (Oxford: Oxford University Press, 2006), pp. 51–2.

[7]   Farel, *Forme d'oraison*, pp. 49–50. See also Malachi 4:2.

[8]   Hubert Wyrill, *Réforme et Contre-Réforme en Savoie, 1536–1679: de Guillaume Farel à François de Sales* (Lyon: Réveil Publications, 2001), p. 48.

[9]   Kaltenrieder, 'The Liturgies of Guillaume Farel', pp. 159–213.

and there this translation draws inspiration from Kaltenrieder's for difficult French expressions. However, the present work is a completely fresh effort. The second translation, undertaken by Blair Reynolds, appears to be a self-published effort, and suffers from numerous false cognates, grammatical misunderstandings, and unintelligible receptor language formulations.[10]

Besides breaking up long sentences, adding paragraph breaks and introducing some subtitles in the following translation, I have also made several changes to the marginal notations of the 1533 publication:

- First, notations from the outside margins have been moved to the bottom of the page.
- Second, the original scripture references listed chapters by Arabic numerals, but did not cite verses because they followed Lefevre's 1530 *La Saincte Bible en francoys* in which divisions within chapter were indicated by marginal letters ranging from a to g. I consulted Lefevre's Bible to establish which modern verse or set of verses would correspond to the sections indicated.
- Third, given the nature of footnotes, it is necessary to insert the footnote somewhere: this can be misleading given the original references were marginal without any indication that they were to be tied to one particular word over another. However, each line in the original contains only five to eight words, so the insertion point of the footnote in this translation cannot stray far from the author's original placement. Where a list of references substantiates a single idea, I have kept them together in one note.
- Fourth, scripture references are for the modern English Bible; where this varies from Farel's – for instance, in the numbering of the Psalms or the naming of the book of Nehemiah – the original has been indicated in square brackets.

---

[10]   Guillaume Farel, *Manner and Method: First Liturgy of the Reformed Churches of France*, 1533; *Summary and Brief Declaration: Promises Very Necessary for Each Christian to Trust in God and to Aid his Neighbor*, trans. Blair Reynolds (Bristol, IN: Wyndam Hall Press, 1985).

Liturgical Practices and Forms

These are the practices and forms we observe when administering holy baptism in the holy congregation of God; when uniting those who come for holy marriage; and when celebrating the holy supper of our Lord in those places which God has visited with his grace.

Whatever God has forbidden ought to be rejected in his Church and whatever he has commanded ought to be observed, in accordance with his holy word.

Included here are the manner in which public worship begins, continues and ends, together with the prayers and exhortations made by all and for all; and guidelines for the visitation of the sick.

O Christians, for the honour of God our all-good Father, do not pay attention to customs,[11] times and years,[12] people, crowds, and the appearances that everything can have – whether in knowledge, power, doctrine, holiness or authority, even if this were an angel from heaven[13] – but think about, pay attention to, and examine diligently only what the good Saviour Jesus ordained and commanded. Of him the Father said:

> This is my well-loved Son, listen to him (Matt. 17:5).
> Give glory to your Name, O Lord (Ps. 113:2).
> Test the spirits to see whether they are from God (1 John 4:1).

Preface[A ii]

When, in the time of his humility,[14] our Saviour and Redeemer visibly communed in this world,[15] he came to complete the work of his Father[16] just as he had been commanded,[17] comforting the poor,[18] healing the sick,[19] and preaching the year of favour and forgiveness.[20] He preached how the

---

[11]   Lev. 18:3.

[12]   Gal. 4:10.

[13]   Gal. 1:8.

[14]   Phil. 2:5–8.

[15]   1 John 1:1–2.

[16]   John 4:34.

[17]   Heb. 5:4–6.

[18]   Matt. 4:23.

[19]   Luke 6:6–10.

[20]   Luke 4:18.

Father, moved by the greatness of his love, had given his only Son to save the world, so that all who believe in him might have eternal life.[21]

The murderer, liar, adversary[22] – the Devil – strongly resisted[23] this good Saviour by means of his own over whom he had power and dominion,[24] accusing and slandering him. They accused him of being a glutton, a drunkard, a friend of tax collectors and sinners,[25] a Samaritan,[26] a heretic, possessed by the devil, doing his work by the power of Beelzebub,[27] a sinner who transgressed the law of God.[28]

The Saviour warned his own that these things would come when he said that just as he had been persecuted so they would be persecuted, and that people would lie about them as they had about him.[29]

Today we see this being fulfilled just like it happened formerly to the apostles and other servants of God.[30] We see the afflictions, the deaths, the heavy persecutions on those who wish to follow the gospel purely. Wherever the successors to the scribes and Pharisees,[31] destitute [A iii] of the truth and wisdom of God, have power and can direct the ordained power of God according to their will, they use the sword. This sword's task is to defend good persons and punish evil ones,[32] but how they rage after the blood of the righteous![33] They desire only their death,[34] indeed, some among them even have the task of executioners. Horribly do they torment the poor whom they are able to keep in their hands, as if by force and torments one must draw people to Jesus and to the faith. Our Saviour commands gentleness and benevolence.[35] Both he and the apostles wished to draw sinners through sweetness and all benevolence,[36] without drawing any other sword than that of the word – which is the sword of the Spirit.[37]

---

[21]   John 3:16.

[22]   John 8:44.

[23]   1 Pet. 5:8.

[24]   Eph. 2:2.

[25]   Matt. 11:19.

[26]   John 8:48.

[27]   Matt. 12:24.

[28]   John 9:16.

[29]   John 15:18–20.

[30]   Acts 4:12–21; 5:18; 7:51–60; 8:1; 12:1–5; 13:50; 16:20–40; Heb. 11:32–40.

[31]   Matt. 15:8–14; 27:11–21.

[32]   Rom. 13:1–4.

[33]   John 18:30–19:6.

[34]   Acts 22:22.

[35]   Matt. 11:28–30; Luke 19:41–2.

[36]   Acts 2:14–21; 2 Tim. 2:20.

[37]   Eph. 6:17.

But wherever these persecutors are unable to carry out their will to murder and to kill, they use bald-faced lies as they defile and manage to defame the holy teaching of our Lord and of those who keep it. Do they not cry out that these cursed dogs who want to maintain this new faith are heretics, living as beasts, renouncing everything, maintaining neither faith nor law, renouncing all the sacraments, not wanting to baptize, keeping nothing of the holy table of our Lord, despising the Virgin Mary and the saints – both male and female – and rejecting marriage?

Who would want and who would be able to recount [A iiij] all that these poor people say? May our Lord show mercy to them and give them understanding, particularly those who sin through ignorance. May he do so in order that all may be able to see the truth and have a full understanding of how things proceed, and thus recognize those who lie so boldly. They talk and speak against what we openly do and say in the churches – the churches which God by his grace has visited and made blessed in the reformation of the holy gospel – condemning and reviling them without cause and wrongfully, contrary to God and reason.

To the end that we might keep watch and prevent them from deceiving and from giving out their lies as truth, here is presented for all the faithful the form and practice that we observe and the exhortations and prayers that we make when baptizing. The same is found for holy marriage and for the most holy supper and table of our Lord. Everything is written in the language common to the people who are present, as upheld by the holy teaching of God, which is our source.[38] Each believer can perceive and understand the matter without paying attention to how the ancients – or rather the modernists[39] – practised it, since they presumed to change and transform[40] the holy ordinances of Jesus, mixing their flour[41] with the holy teaching and institution of our Saviour.

For the Lord God commands us not to walk[42] [A v] in the commandments of our fathers, nor to keep their ordinances, nor to be polluted by their idols, seeing that he is God. Therefore we must walk in his commandments, keep them and do them. Thus no one will find here the entreaties and invocations of the priests by which they entreat the devil as if he possessed the children and they were demoniacs. This cannot be, seeing that the Son of God did not receive them in this manner. We ought to understand the same about the entreated and enchanted water upon which the priests blow, saying that the Holy Spirit descends in the fountain of this water.

---

[38]   1 Cor. 14:6–16.

[39]   Jer. 23:16–34.

[40]   1 Tim. 4:1–3.

[41]   Matt. 24:4–5.

[42]   Ezek. 20:18–19.

For the Holy Spirit does not have his place or dwelling in water but in the heart of the believer.[43]

Salt, spit and oil are not here. Rather, after holy prayer and teaching, we baptize with pure, clear water just as the Saviour was baptized[44] and as the apostles performed it.[45]

In holy marriage we do and maintain likewise – we reject all this riff-raff of robes and other doings which are not taken from holy scripture.

In the holy table of our Lord whatever is offensive to the word has been removed. Nevertheless we are concerned as much as possible to conform to the lowliness of the weak, so that they not be offended by anything.[46]

And I believe there is no one who loves and fears our Lord who [A vi] will not take pleasure from seeing and hearing how this serves the glory of our Lord and the edification of his Church. All this our Lord in grace cleanses anew of all the flour of Egypt and the leaven of the Pharisees,[47] bringing it back to the purity and simplicity of the gospel, to the end that all of this might be said and done according to the pure word of God.

Explanation of Holy Baptism

The baptism we administer is the one which our Lord needed to undergo to fulfil all righteousness,[48] just like he needed to be circumcised.[49] He commanded that his disciples and apostles should baptize.[50] This baptism is visible and physical; it does not make the person good or evil.[51] For both good and evil persons can receive it, as it appears in scripture from the case of Simon Magus and of Saint Paul.[52] One must not attribute to this baptism that it gives grace *virtute operis operati*[53] as the doctors of the universities say and muse in their sentences. For only the baptism that Jesus gives saves, purges and cleanses, being of the water of life, the Holy Spirit and fire.[54] Thus Saint John said that he would baptize with water for

---

[43]   1 Cor. 3:16.
[44]   Matt. 3:16.
[45]   Acts 8:36–8; 10:47–8.
[46]   Rom. 14:1–3.
[47]   Matt. 16:6.
[48]   Matt. 3:15.
[49]   Luke 2:21.
[50]   Matt. 28:18–20; Acts 8:36–8; 10:47–8.
[51]   1 Pet. 3:21.
[52]   Acts 8:13; 9:18.
[53]   That is, by virtue of performing the ceremony.
[54]   Ezek. 36:25.

repentance of life, but that one who would come after him would baptize with the Holy Spirit [A vii] and with fire.[55] Saint Peter speaks similarly of those who have been baptized with the Holy Spirit: Can anyone prevent these here who have received the Holy Spirit as we have from being baptized with water?[56]

The holy baptism of Jesus is invisible, internal and in the soul when the Holy Spirit is given.[57] It is not bound to ceremonies, persons or times, but to the sole pleasure of God who gives grace, faith and salvation.[58] But the baptism by which we are visibly received into the Church and among Christians is visible. Yet we should not receive it without seeking the invisible, which comes from the Spirit,[59] so that just as we are received among Christians visibly we might also by grace be true children of God. Time and place are not determined for those who need baptism; let love and the edification of the assembled Church be the rule in this matter. We perform baptism in the full congregation of the faithful,[60] to the end that the one who is baptized might be received and accounted by all as a brother and a Christian, and that all might pray that he might be as much a Christian from the heart as he is accounted externally. For it is not fitting that something done in the name of all should be done almost by no one – as it most often happens that an exceedingly small number are present at baptism.

Let being present at holy baptism not be considered scornful! [A viij] For each and everyone is admonished[61] and can understand what the baptized one is bound to and how he must live. Then we will ask for the grace of God to do and to maintain that to which we are bound. So we come to present our children, which those most closely associated with the children must do, those to whom our Lord gave this office. Thus, when their closest ones come with affectionate love to present them to the servant of the people in the word, he begins in this manner:

May our help be in the name of God who made heaven and earth. Amen.[62]

Then he says:

---

[55]   John 1:31–3; Matt. 3:11.

[56]   Acts 10:47.

[57]   Luke 17:12–14.

[58]   Col. 2:13–14.

[59]   2 Cor. 4:13–14.

[60]   Acts 2:38–41.

[61]   Rom. 6:1–4.

[62]   The author or editor has printed a hand in the right margin pointing to these words as rubrics for the minister, to emphasize that here begins the form proper.

Do you present this child to God and his holy church and congregation, asking that he be baptized?

Respondent: Yes.

The Servant:

The Holy Spirit by the mouth of Saint Paul admonishes and commands us to pray for all because this pleases God who wants all to be saved and to come to the knowledge of the truth.[63] For this reason he gave his Son to redeem our souls;[64] thus we all are bound to pray for each other. We shall therefore pray for this child that God would grant him a true and living faith and that the visible, external baptism might be for him [B i] a true sign of the invisible, internal baptism which God is pleased, out of his grace and by his Holy Spirit, to give him. We shall therefore say humbly, from the heart:

Our Father who are in heaven, hallowed be your name, your kingdom come, your will be done on earth as in heaven. Give us today our daily bread, and forgive us our offenses as we forgive those who offend us. And lead us not into temptation, but deliver us from evil. Amen.[65]

God almighty, eternal Father, full of all mercy! In your goodness you promised us that you would be God[66] to us and our children, just as you were to Abraham and his own. We humbly pray and entreat you that you give this child your Holy Spirit, receiving him in the covenant of your mercy according to the ordinance of your unchangeable purpose.[67] We pray that in the time ordained by you he may know you as his God, praising and serving you alone, living and dying in you, so that this baptism and reception into your holy assembly which we have performed may not be in vain. Rather, may he be truly baptized into the death of your Son[68] in renewal of life,[69] pleasing you and being acceptable through Jesus Christ your Son our Saviour. Amen.

[B ii] Listen to the holy gospel tell us how we shall present the children to our Lord.

---

63 2 Tim. 2:1–4. Note the prominence of this text throughout the forms.

64 John 3:16; Rom. 3:7–14 [*sic.* 3:23–6?]; 8:28–34.

65 Matt. 6:9–13; Luke 11:2–4.

66 Gen. 17:1–2; Rom. 3:29; Eph. 3:1–6.

67 Jer. 31:31–4; Isa. 46:10–13.

68 Rom. 6:1–4.

69 Eph. 1:5–7.

After this they presented some children to him that he might lay his hands on them and pray for them. But the disciples rebuked them. And Jesus said, 'Permit the children, and do not prevent them from coming to me, for to such belongs the kingdom of heaven'.[70] And he put his hands on them and blessed them.[71]

You have heard that our Lord wants the children to be presented to him like this, for he is as well the Father and Saviour of children as of adults. Therefore as much as it is in us, we shall present to him this child, receiving it by baptism into his Church and communion, praying that he, by his grace, would grant his holy blessing. Amen.

Do you therefore bring this child to be baptized?

Respondent: Yes.

The Servant:

It is certain that our God is the true God and that he desires to be served in spirit and in truth.[72] Do you therefore promise before God and his congregation that you will commit yourself and take pains to instruct and teach this child in the holy doctrine of our Lord, in his holy law and faith, teaching him the commandments that God has given for us to keep when he said:[73]

I am the Lord God who brought you out of the land of Egypt, out of the house of slavery. [B iij] You shall have no other gods before me. You shall not make any image or likeness of the things which are in heaven above or on the earth below or in the water under the earth. You shall not bow down to them nor serve them, for I am your Lord God, highly jealous, visiting the iniquity of the fathers upon the children to the third and fourth generation of those who hate me, and being merciful to a thousand generations of those who love me and keep my commandments. You shall not take the name of your Lord God in vain, for God will not hold innocent him who takes his name in vain. Remember the day of rest to hallow it. Six days you shall labour and do all your work; the seventh is the rest of your Lord God. You shall not do any work, neither you, nor your son, nor your daughter, nor your servant, nor your chambermaid, nor your animals, nor the stranger who is within your gates, for in six days God made heaven and earth, the sea and all that is in it, and he rested on the seventh day. Therefore he blessed the day of rest and hallowed it.

---

70   Matt. 19:14–15; Mark 10:13–16; Luke 18:15–16.

71   Mark 10:16.

72   John 4:24.

73   Exo. 20:1.

Honour your father and your mother that your days may be prolonged on the land which your Lord God gave you. You shall not kill. You shall not commit adultery. You shall not steal. You shall not speak false testimony [B iiij] against your neighbour. You shall not covet your neighbour's house. You shall not covet your neighbour's wife, nor his servant, nor his chambermaid, nor his ox, nor his donkey, nor anything else that belongs to him.

And also you shall teach him the faith and belief of true Christians and the confession which believers make when they say:

I believe in God the Father almighty,[74] *Creator of heaven and earth.*[75] *And in Jesus Christ his only Son*[76] *our Lord,*[77] *who was conceived by the Holy Spirit,*[78] *born of the Virgin Mary.*[79] *He suffered under Pontius Pilate,*[80] *was crucified*[81] *dead, and buried, he descended into Hell. The third day he arose from the dead,*[82] *ascended into heaven,*[83] *he sits at the right hand of God the Father almighty;*[84] *from there he will come to judge the living and the dead. I believe in the Holy Spirit,*[85] *the holy universal Church,*[86] *the communion of saints,*[87] *the forgiveness of sins,*[88] *the resurrection of the body,*[89] *the life everlasting. Amen.*

You shall teach him also to put all his trust in God, to praise him and to serve him alone,[90] to love him with all his heart, mind, strength and understanding, and his neighbour as himself.[91] Teach him as a true Christian to deny himself, letting everything go to follow Jesus, carrying his cross,[92] that is to say, the

---

[74] John 14:2.

[75] Gen. 1:1.

[76] John 1:14; 3:13–17.

[77] 1 Cor. 8:6.

[78] Luke 1.

[79] Matt. 1:22–3.

[80] Matt. 27:27–37.

[81] John 19:13–16.

[82] Matt. 28:1–6; John 20:8–9; Mark 16:19; Luke 24:22–24.

[83] Acts 1:9.

[84] Matt. 16:27.

[85] Rom. 8:9–11.

[86] Eph. 4:3–6.

[87] Luke 24:52–3.

[88] 1 John 2:1–4.

[89] 1 Cor. 15:51–8; 1 Thess. 4:14–17.

[90] Matt. 4:8–10.

[91] Matt. 22:37–40.

[92] Matt. 16:24–6.

tribulations and afflictions that our Lord sends him,[93] so that all his life might be to the honour of [B v] God and the edification of everyone.[94] And therefore you shall exhort and admonish him, correcting him where he fails so that each one is sustained by his Christian brother in such a way that he is nourished and instructed in the holy doctrine of God.[95] Do you promise to do this?

Respondent: Yes.

The Servant: Do you ask then that this child be baptized?

Respondent: Yes.

The Servant: Name him.

N..., I baptize you in the name of the Father, and of the Son, and of the Holy Spirit. Amen.[96]

After he has put pure and clean water on his head with his hand (omitting salt, oil and spit), he speaks in this manner:

Our Lord God, by his grace and goodness, make this child – whom he created and formed in his image and likeness – to be a true member of Jesus Christ his Son, bearing fruit fit for a child of God. Amen.

Go in peace. Our Lord be with you. Take good care of the child.

Explanation of Holy Marriage

From the beginning holy marriage was instituted and ordained by God.[97] It is a good, holy and honourable thing when properly maintained in all purity, when the husband who is the head of his [B vi] wife loves, looks after and maintains her sincerely, keeping faith and loyalty with her,[98] while the wife, who was made as a helper for the husband, is subject and obedient in

---

93   Matt. 5:38–48.
94   1 Cor. 10:31–3; Rom. 14:20–21.
95   Matt. 18:8–10, 15–17; 1 Thess. 4:11.
96   Matt. 28:19.
97   Gen. 2:21–5; Heb. 13:4.
98   1 Cor. 11:3; Eph. 5:25–8; Col. 3:19; 1 Pet. 3:7.

everything, just as God commands.[99] She must honour her husband, have care of her household,[100] keep herself not only from evil, but also from every sort of evil, and maintain true fidelity and loyalty. Both of them must persevere in what is good, in accordance with the teaching of God, taking pains to live honestly without causing harm to anyone.[101] They must teach the children which God gives them in the fear and doctrine of our Lord,[102] living as God commanded.

Marriage must not be performed in the degrees which God has forbidden,[103] but we do not need to concern ourselves with the degrees forbidden by the Pope, even though one might have given gold or silver to gain a dispensation, for this is not needed to do something God never forbade.[104] The loving covenant and promise of holy marriage should not be made without the consent of the parents of the two parties,[105] for the son belongs to his father and mother and it belongs to them to give him. The same applies to the daughter, provided the parents have not passed away. In this way we can prevent fraud in this holy state and keep some good son of respectable people from being misled, terribly deceived and beguiled without the knowledge of his parents, and made to take some roguish woman with whom he [B vii] would always be rather vexed. We can also prevent some good daughter of respectable people from being overtaken by any scoundrel who gives her some forlorn child without the consent of her parents.

To take precautions against all such frauds we announce the coming marriage in the hearing of the whole church, congregation or parish for two or three Sundays. This ensures that we may be informed of all obstacles (if there be any) and that this beautiful, holy marriage may be performed only in a fitting way. When we have made the proclamation to the entire holy assembly and no obstacle is found or allegation raised in the assembly to this marriage, then they are married as follows:

May our help be in the Name of God who made heaven and earth. Amen.[106]

---

[99]   Gen. 2:21–5; Eph. 5:22–4; Col. 3:18; 1 Tim. 2:12–15; 1 Pet. 3:1–6.

[100]   1 Tim. 5:4.

[101]   1 Pet. 3:1–7.

[102]   Eph. 6:4.

[103]   Lev. 18:7–16.

[104]   Deut. 12:31–2; Gal. 1:8–9.

[105]   Gen. 24:47–51; Exo. 22:16–17.

[106]   The author or editor has printed a hand in the right margin pointing to these words as rubrics for the minister, to emphasize that here begins the form proper.

God our Father, after he created heaven and earth and all that is in them,[107] created and formed man in his image and likeness so that he might have dominion and lordship over all the beasts of the earth, the fish of the sea, the birds of the air. After he had created man he said, 'It is not good that the man be alone. Let us make him a helper fitting for him'. And our Lord made a deep sleep fall upon Adam, and while Adam slept God took one of his ribs and formed Eve from it, leading us to understand that the man and his wife are one body, one flesh and one blood.[108] [B viij] Therefore the man leaves his father and mother and is joined to his wife.

He must love her as Jesus loves his church[109] – that is to say, the true believers and Christians for whom he died and whom he washed, purged and cleansed by his shed blood[110] to make them without spot, blemish or stain for himself.[111] The woman must serve and obey her husband in all holiness and integrity because she is subject to him and in his power as long as she lives with him.[112]

And this holy marriage, this honourable institution of God is of such power that through it the husband does not have power over his own body, but the wife; likewise, the wife does not have power over her own body, but the husband.[113] Therefore, what God has joined together no one can separate[114] unless it be by mutual consent for a certain time, to attend to fasting and prayer.[115] They must keep careful watch that they not be tempted to unfaithfulness by Satan. For this reason they must also come back together; indeed, to avoid immorality each man should have his own wife and each woman her own husband. This means that those who lack self-control are obligated by God's command to get married[116] so that this holy temple of God – that is to say, our bodies – may not be violated or corrupted.

Seeing then that our bodies [C i] are members of Jesus Christ, we are strictly forbidden to make them members of a prostitute. We must maintain them in all holiness, for if anyone violates the temple of God, God will destroy him.[117]

---

[107] Gen. 1:1; 2:1.

[108] Matt. 19:4–6.

[109] Eph. 5:25–7.

[110] Rev. 1:5.

[111] 1 John 1:7; Eph. 5:2.

[112] Col. 3:18; 1 Tim. 2:11–15; 1 Pet. 3:1–5; Gen. 3:16.

[113] Heb. 13:4; Gen. 2:23–5; 1 Cor. 7:3–5.

[114] Matt. 19:6.

[115] 1 Cor. 7:5.

[116] 1 Cor. 3:16–17; 6:19–20.

[117] 1 Cor. 3:16–17.

This is especially true of the holy state of marriage, as our Lord clearly showed when he commanded that a woman who breaks her marriage should surely die, she and the adulterer.[118]

You therefore (naming the groom and bride), N... and N... – knowing that God has ordained things in this way – do you desire to live in this holy state of marriage that God has so highly honoured? Is this your intention even as you give witness here before his holy assembly, asking that it be approved?

Respondent: Yes.

The Servant:

I charge all of you who are present here as witnesses, entreating you to remember this event. And if anyone knows of any impediment – something forbidden by God,[119] or one of them being married to another, please speak in good love.

(If no one speaks against it the minister will continue as follows)

Seeing that no one has spoken against this marriage and there are no impediments, may our Lord God confirm this holy purpose which he has [C ii] given you, and may from the outset your help be in the name of God who made heaven and earth. Amen.

(The minister now speaks to the groom, as follows)

Do you, N..., confess here before God and his holy congregation that you have taken and are taking as your wife and spouse, N..., here present? Do you promise to keep loving and faithfully supporting her just as a true and faithful husband must do for his wife? Will you live with her in a holy way, keeping faith and loyalty in everything in accordance with the holy word of God and his holy Church?

Respondent: Yes.

(Then speaking to the bride, he says)

Do you, N..., confess here before God and his holy assembly, that you have taken and are taking N... to be your lawful husband? Do you promise to obey, serve and be subject to him? Will you live with him in a holy way, keeping

---

[118]   Lev. 20:10.
[119]   Lev. 18:7–16.

faith and loyalty in everything just as a faithful and loyal bride should to her husband in accordance with the word of God and the holy gospel?

Respondent: Yes.

(Then the minister says)

May the Father of all mercy who out of his grace has called you to this holy state of marriage for the love of Jesus Christ his Son – who by his holy presence sanctified marriage, making it the first sign before the apostles[120] – give you his Holy Spirit to [C iij] perfect his holy will in this noble state. Amen.

Hear how our Lord wishes holy marriage to be guarded and how it is firm and indissoluble in accordance with what is written in Saint Matthew Chapter 19:

The Pharisees approached him to test him, saying, 'Is it lawful for a man to divorce his wife for any and every reason?' And he answered them, 'Have you not read that he who made man in the beginning made him male and female, and said, 'For this reason a man will leave his father and mother and be united to his wife, and the two shall be one flesh'? Therefore they are not two but one flesh. What therefore God has joined together let no man separate'.

Believe these holy words that our Lord Jesus pronounced, just as the holy Gospel has declared them, and be certain that our Lord God has joined you in this holy state of marriage. Because of this, live together in a holy way in all peace and unity, maintaining true love, faith and loyalty to each other in accordance with the holy word of God. May our Lord grant you his grace for this.

Let us all pray now to our Father, with one heart:

Almighty God, full of goodness and wisdom! From the beginning you foresaw that it would not be good [C iiij] for the man to be alone[121] and so you created for him a helper fitting for him and ordained that the two should be one. We humbly pray and ask you that just as it has pleased you to call these here to the holy state of marriage, so you would give them your grace and goodness and send your Holy Spirit. Grant that they may then live in the holy state of marriage with a true and firm faith in accordance with your good will, overcoming all evil affections, living purely and edifying each other in all honesty and chastity. Grant them your blessing, just as you did to your faithful servants Abraham, Isaac and Jacob, so that having holy descendants they may

---

120   John 2:1–11.
121   Gen. 2:18.

praise and serve you, teaching and nourishing them in your praise and glory, to the service of their neighbour, for the advancement and exaltation of your holy gospel. Lend us your ear, O Father of mercy through our Lord Jesus Christ your beloved Son.[122] Amen.

May our Lord fill you with all grace and with all his goodness grant that you live a long and holy life together. Go in peace. God be with you always. Amen.

(For several reasons which can come up, it would be good to write the names of those whom one baptizes and the day of their baptism, as well as the names of those whom one marries, together with the date, in a little booklet)

A Brief Explanation of the Holy Supper of Our Lord Jesus Christ [C v]

As much as the baptism we perform is a visible reception among Christian believers,[123] and much like an enrolment which bears in itself an open declaration and profession to follow Jesus Christ and to hold his holy ordinances and to live according to the holy gospel,[124] so also the holy supper – the holy table of our Lord, the breaking of the bread of thanksgiving – is a visible communion with the members of Jesus Christ.[125]

It signifies that those who take and break the one bread are one body,[126] that is, the body of Jesus Christ, and members of one another, grafted and planted into him. They declare and promise him to persevere until the end and not be separated from the faith of the gospel and the union that they all have in God through Jesus Christ.

Therefore, just as all the members are nourished from one and the same food, so all the faithful visibly take from one and the same bread and drink from one and the same cup, without any distinction. This signifies that all must be nourished invisibly from one and the same spiritual bread, from the holy word of life, from the gospel of salvation,[127] all living from one and the same Spirit, out of one [C vi] and the same faith.[128]

Whoever looks carefully at the things given to the fathers while they awaited the coming of Jesus Christ would find much agreement. For

---

[122]   John 16:23–4.

[123]   Acts 2:41–7.

[124]   Rom. 6:3–4.

[125]   1 Cor. 10:16–17; 12:12–14.

[126]   Rom. 12:4–5.

[127]   Matt. 4:4; John 6:32–5.

[128]   Eph. 4:3–6.

did not circumcision signify that one belonged to the covenant which our Lord had made with his people?[129] Each one received circumcision precisely because he belonged to the number of the people of God. The other customs – such as first-fruits,[130] offerings and sacrifices of praise – were shadows and figures of the things to come[131] which Jesus Christ, who brought everything to completion, perfected and made void.[132] They were ordained to give thanks to God as a declaration that the believer desired to persevere in the law of God and to belong to his people.

Let us examine carefully for what purpose baptism and the holy table were ordained, and we will see their agreement. Ignorance of this – especially regarding our Lord's table – has caused many to err in the past and still today. For everything is now done and said in accordance with the tradition, ordinance and pleasure of men while that which God said by his word and Jesus instituted is tread upon. Where are those who ponder and consider what is signified by the bread of thanksgiving which we break and the cup from which we drink?[133] Where are those who test themselves to see whether they are in Jesus, whether the Spirit of God is in [C vii] them?[134] There are enough people who run to the priests and not to their own heart to examine it and to test whether they have a true and living faith by which they would be true sons of God,[135] grafted into Jesus Christ as his members.[136] The heart of many does not get beyond the bread and the cup which are presented to them. All their thoughts abide there, adoring them, for thus they were taught.

The memory of him who died for us and who now is seated at the right hand of the Father is forgotten, as is the neighbour. Is it not easy to understand that he ordained the holy table principally for these things, since there we must come together and be one with the neighbour?[137] For, to go to Jesus I have neither to make anyone wait, nor to be in religious orders, nor to transcend myself, seeing that the kingdom of God is within me.[138] I also cannot have Jesus with me unless I can receive him worthily,

---

[129]   Gen. 17:10–13.

[130]   Deut. 26:10.

[131]   Heb. 10:1–4.

[132]   John 19:35–7.

[133]   1 Cor. 11:17–34.

[134]   2 Cor. 13:5–6.

[135]   John 1:12–13.

[136]   John 15:1–5; Rom. 11:17–21.

[137]   1 Cor. 11:17–22; 10:23–33.

[138]   Luke 17:21.

unto salvation and life. For wherever he comes, he makes the unworthy worthy, the dead alive, the unrighteous sinners just and holy.[139]

But it is not like this with baptism or the holy table of our Lord. The deceptive person who makes others think he believes what he does not, takes baptism as a hypocrite. He takes his condemnation. So also whoever comes to the table of our Lord having no regard for his neighbour[140] – despising the faithful who belong to the Church of our [C viij] Lord, preventing the others, taking the bread of our Lord by himself and not with the holy congregation, eating and getting drunk while his neighbour is dying from hunger, not exercising charity: he comes into his own condemnation.

For how can the faith which works through love and the love of God itself be in one who sees his own brother in need and does not help him?[141] How also does he dare to presume – he who lives in sin and iniquity, a companion of unbelievers in their idolatries,[142] promiscuities, thefts, malice and other abominations! How dare he mix himself in with and draw near to the faithful who are the body of Christ,[143] making no distinction between the body of Christ and of the Antichrist, of Christians and of unbelievers, of light and darkness![144] He should pay careful attention to Chapters 8 through 13 and even 14 of 1 Corinthians. Similarly, he should examine what Saint John declares – what the Saviour said after he had administered his supper as he spoke to his apostles in Chapters 13, 14, 15 and 16, as well as what is said in Chapter 17. He will then have a fuller understanding of what was said above – how the one who comes to the table of our Lord must have a firm faith in our Lord God and in our Saviour Jesus, love towards his neighbour, and separate himself from unbelievers and their vices. He will also understand how and why he must break the bread of our Lord.

The times and the frequency with which we must [D I] celebrate the Lord's Supper and take the bread are not written for us; thus, this is left in the freedom of the Church of our Lord, just like the time of baptism. Yet it is well-shown how we must come there. The exhortations to follow will also show us this. Therefore the servant of the holy congregation who preaches the word will pay attention to the edification of the people, yes, of everyone, also as much as he can for the ignorant and unbelieving.

---

[139]   Matt. 18:10–11; Luke 19:10; 1 Tim. 1:12–16.

[140]   1 Cor. 11:18–22.

[141]   1 John 3:16–18.

[142]   1 Cor. 10:7–8.

[143]   1 Cor. 12:12.

[144]   1 Cor. 11:26–9.

Doing everything in good order,[145] with the consent of the congregation, he will pay attention to the time most suitable and convenient, conforming it also to the other churches. He will do so without superstition, to keep peace and unity with all and, as much as possible, to attract the ignorant who do not yet know the truth, without going against the teaching of the truth.

He will announce in advance the day when the holy Supper will be celebrated, admonishing them to pray to our Lord to ask for his grace that they may attend in a holy and worthy manner. On the day the Lord's Supper is celebrated he will exhort the people as follows.

The Supper of Our Lord

Our God and ever-merciful Father,[146] thinking thoughts of peace and grace and forgiveness, and not of affliction,[147] that is to say, of punishment, has desired to erase our sins for the sake of his own self-love[148] – not for the sake of our good works [D ii] or righteous deeds. He wishes to be gracious toward us, to fulfil his holy promises of giving us clean water and his Holy Spirit,[149] to cleanse us of all our impurities and blemishes, and to give us a new heart by writing his holy law within our hearts. When the fullness of time came he sent his beloved Son,[150] showing the very great love and delight which he had toward us, not sparing his only and deeply-loved Son our Lord Jesus Christ, but giving him for us.[151] Thus this good Saviour, according to the good will of his Father to reconcile us to himself, offered himself once to his Father for our redemption,[152] dying to bring together all of us who were scattered, to make us all one and the same body just as he and the Father are one.[153]

By all this our Father has shown the great treasures of his kindness and mercy more than we could say. He desired that his Son would die for us who were dead in sin and his enemies,[154] to give us life and to make us children acceptable

---

[145]   1 Cor. 14:40.

[146]   The author or editor has printed a hand in the left margin pointing to these words as rubrics for the minister, to emphasize that here begins the form proper.

[147]   Jer. 29:10–14.

[148]   Isa. 43:25.

[149]   Ezek. 36:25–7.

[150]   Gal. 4:4–5.

[151]   Rom. 5:6–8; 8:31–2.

[152]   Heb. 7:27; 9:26–8; 10:14; John 11:49–51.

[153]   John 10:27–30; 17:20–23.

[154]   Rom. 5:8–10; 1 Pet. 3:18.

to this good Father. Similarly our good Saviour vividly showed his very great love, laying down his life for us,[155] washing and purging us with his blood.[156] Therefore, in the last meal he had in this mortal life, which he said [D iij] he deeply desired before he would suffer,[157] he instituted his holy supper. He willed that in remembrance of his very great love by which he gave his body for us on the cross and poured out his blood for the forgiveness of our sins, we might take and eat from the one bread, and drink from the one cup without any distinction, just as he died for all without distinction, and as he directed all to take, eat and drink in this Supper.[158]

Therefore, let all true Christian believers who firmly believe by a true faith that our Lord Jesus Christ died for us[159] come to this holy table, all of them thanking God together for the great goodness which he has shown us.[160] Let them testify of their faith, as they believe that by the death of the unblemished Lamb we are delivered from the enemy.[161] In this way let them give thanks to this good Saviour Jesus who out of his good pleasure died for us through the very deep love which he had toward us.[162] Let us all, imitating and following him out of a perfect love, love one another just as our sweet and kind Saviour Jesus loved us, laying down and giving his life for us.

Let each one examine and test himself whether he has true faith in our Lord Jesus Christ[163] – whether he believes perfectly that by the death and suffering of Jesus [D iiij] peace was made between God and us and that God is favourable and his wrath appeased through the blessed Saviour Jesus.[164] Further, that by him we are made sons and heirs of God, co-heirs with Jesus Christ,[165] through the blood by which we are purged and entirely cleansed, and our sins erased and fully forgiven.[166] In short, that Jesus our Saviour has done everything.[167]

On the other hand, let all those who do not have true faith not presume to come to the holy table to make a show of it and bear false witness among the

---

155   John 15:9–14; 1 John 3:16.
156   Heb. 9:12–14; 1 John 1:9; Rev. 1:5–7.
157   Luke 22:15–16.
158   Matt. 26:26–9; Luke 22:17–20; Mark 14:22–4; 1 Cor. 11:23–5.
159   Rom. 4:23–5.
160   Matt. 10:9–14; John 1:20–26.
161   Col. 2:13–15; Rev. 5:8–10.
162   1 John 3:16.
163   1 Cor. 11:27–34; 2 Cor. 13:5–6.
164   Eph. 1:5–7; 2:6–10; Col. 1:18–20; 2:13–15.
165   Gal. 3:26–9; Rom. 8:15–17; Heb. 9:15.
166   1 John 1:9.
167   2 Pet. 2:15–22 [sic. 1 Pet. 2:21–5?]

body of Christ to which they do not belong.[168] The same goes for all idolaters who worship and serve another besides the only God,[169] all perjurers, lazy people who never serve or benefit anyone in anything however much they could do so,[170] all those who are disobedient to their father and mother and to whomever God has put over us for good[171] (so long as those in authority do not break God's commandments). Let all brawlers – contentious people who unjustly beat and strike their neighbours in hatred; all promiscuous people – drunkards who live dissolute lives, drinking and eating, all robbers who do wrong and injury to their neighbour, and all who falsely give testimony and charge others with offenses not come. Briefly, let all those who wickedly live contrary to the holy commandments of God, who do not want to follow the holy law of God and live in accordance with his word, following the holy gospel as true children of God not come. Let them not [D v] presume to come to this holy table to which only those should come who truly belong to the body of Christ, united to and rooted in him by a true and living faith which works itself out in love.

For if they come there it will be to their judgement and condemnation.[172] As traitors, yes, successors of Judas, they will be rejected. Yet how true it is that we are all poor sinners for as long as we traverse through this world enclosed in this body of death and sin![173] We cannot say that we are without sin before we come to this holy table,[174] holding in memory our Saviour who died for our sins and rose for our justification.[175]

Humble-hearted and contrite, acknowledging our faults, we will present ourselves and cast ourselves before the high majesty of our God through our Saviour and Redeemer Jesus in full confidence and true faith. We will ask God for grace, confessing before him that we have offended him most grievously and greatly, disobeyed his holy law, not worshipped him purely in Spirit and in truth, nor served him alone. We will confess that we have not loved him above all by honouring his holy name without taking it in vain, nor lived in a holy way to his honour and to the help and relief of our neighbour, nor taken the true and holy rest from evil speaking, doing and thinking. We have not honoured those [D vi] who have authority over us, nor shunned all adultery, robbery, lying and everything that contravenes the love of God and of our neighbour. We have done to others what we would not want done to ourselves,

---

[168]   2 Cor. 6:14–17.

[169]   1 Cor. 5:11–13; 6:9–11.

[170]   1 Thess. 3:12.

[171]   1 Tim. 1:4–10.

[172]   1 Cor. 11:29–34.

[173]   John 13:8–9; Eccl. 7:20; Rom. 7:16–25.

[174]   1 John 1:8.

[175]   Rom. 4:25.

thus transgressing the holy law of our good Father. We have all sinned greatly and, because of our deep ingratitude and our actions against his holy will, deserve the wrath and indignation of our God more than we can express or say.

Nevertheless, in spite of all our faults and sins – more than we can count because they are so many[176] – let us with humble and contrite hearts ask for compassion and mercy from our ever-good Father. Let us pray him that he not look upon our faults, ignorance and iniquities, but that he look to the righteousness, holiness, purity and innocence of his most dear Son our Lord Jesus who died for us.

God forgave us all our sins and misdeeds for love of himself, keeps us from falling further into sin, magnifies his own great name in us, rules in us, perfects his holy will in us, and gives us what the gentle Saviour taught us to ask for by saying:

Our Father who are in heaven, hallowed be your name, etc.[177]

We will pray to our Father that he give us a firm, living and perfect faith, enlarging and [D vij] increasing it in us, so that by it we might be able to conquer all the evil of our enemy.[178] We desire to live by this faith, making confession of it by saying:

I believe in God the Father almighty, Creator of heaven, etc.

My most dear brothers and sisters! You know how our ever-good Father does not desire the death of sinners, but that they repent and live.[179] For from the fullness of his goodness and mercy he loved the world with such a great love that he gave his only Son to save the world.[180] His Son openly said that he had come to save that which was lost,[181] indeed, this is a most certain saying, namely, that Jesus Christ came to save sinners.[182] This good Saviour also promised us that whatever we will ask in his name we will obtain.[183] He promised that if we forgive others their sins then our own sins will be forgiven by the Father.[184]

---

176   Ps. 18; Heb. 16 [*sic*].
177   Matt. 6:9–13; Luke 11:2–4.
178   1 John 5:4–5.
179   Ezek. 18:23.
180   John 3:16.
181   Matt. 18:11; Luke 19:10.
182   1 Tim. 1:15.
183   John 14:13; 16:23–6.
184   Matt. 6:14.

Believe therefore that when we seek mercy from God in the name of our Lord Jesus and each of us forgives his neighbour from the heart, then our Lord forgives us. Believe that through the faith we have in Jesus Christ our hearts are cleansed.[185]

Hear from 1 Corinthians 11 how our Lord Jesus Christ instituted his holy supper:

The Lord Jesus, on the night when [D viij] he was betrayed,[186] took the bread, gave thanks, and broke it, saying, 'Take, eat, this is my body which is given for you. Do this in remembrance of me'. In the same way after supper he took the cup, saying, 'The cup is the new covenant in my blood. Do this every time that you drink it in remembrance of me. For every time you eat the bread and drink from the cup you proclaim the death of the Lord until he comes'.

Let all of you notice here the institution of the holy table of our Lord as it was ordained by the only Saviour! No one should rebuke him, think himself better than he, nor desire to teach or do otherwise than he commanded.[187] He breaks the bread with his disciples and gives it to them, showing us that whoever comes to the table must be among his disciples, denying themselves and following Jesus Christ in true love.[188] He commands that eating and drinking be done at his table in remembrance of him, that is, as often as we take the bread and drink from the cup, we announce the death of our Lord Jesus Christ[189] – how he died for us, presenting his body under the sign of the bread and poured out his blood for us, as the cup signifies.

Therefore lift up your hearts on high, seeking the things that are above in heaven where Jesus Christ is seated at the right hand [E I] of the Father.[190] Do not let yourselves be held back by visible things which become corrupt through use.[191] Let all of you come with joyful heart in brotherly unity to take from the table of our Lord, returning thanks to him for the very great love which he has shown us. Have the death of this good Saviour written in your hearts as an eternal memory so that your heart will be inflamed and you will also move others to the love of God by following his holy word.

---

[185]   Acts 15:8–9.

[186]   Matt. 26:23–9; Luke 22:17–20; Mark 14:22–4; 1 Cor. 11:23–5.

[187]   John 8:46–7.

[188]   Matt. 16:24–7.

[189]   Luke 22:19–20; 1 Cor. 11:23–6.

[190]   Col. 3:1–4; Matt. 6:19–20.

[191]   2 Cor. 4:18; Col. 2:21–3.

(When giving the bread – which should be without the help of images – do not permit anyone to worship it.[192] Give it to all of them in their hand, so that they take it and eat it. The minister can say the following):

> May Jesus, the true Saviour of the world, who died for us and ascended in glory to the right hand of the Father, live in your hearts by his Holy Spirit, causing all of you to be alive in him through a living faith and perfect love. Amen.

(After all have partaken):

> Beloved brothers and sisters in our Lord Jesus! Now that you have come to the holy table of our Lord, give thanks to him for the wonderful things he has done for us. Let us pray the Father who is full of all mercy for all those who are on the earth, for all kings, princes, lords, and all who are established with authority,[193] to whom he gave the sword and the governing [E ii] of the people to defend good persons and punish evil ones.[194] Let us pray that the good God give to all his grace and be merciful to all. Let us entreat him that from his very great goodness and kindness he might fill us with his Holy Spirit, causing all of us to be united truly in one body through a living and true faith.[195] May it please him to increase it in us, so that just as we have given testimony outwardly at the holy table that we belong to the disciples of Jesus, he may give us the grace truly to be such. May he grant that we persevere in his holy teaching, separated from all unfaithfulness and from the world,[196] all of us living in true love, assisting each other in every good thing from the heart, both in word and in deed.[197]

> Labour and work hard at this for the love of him who so greatly loved us. Since you are participants at the table of our Lord as members of Jesus, do not be participants with unbelievers in their unfaithfulness. Do not be conformed to the world, but go your way in all purity, holiness and innocence. Live soberly and worthily as children of God.[198] Be merciful and loving to all, first of all

---

[192]   In Farel's summary of the Dispute of Rive before the Geneva council in 1535 he speaks three times against the practice of the priest making the sign of the cross on the bread and the cup. See Théophile Dufour, 'Un opuscule inédit de Farel. Le résumé des actes de la Dispute de Rive (1535)', *Mémoires et documents publiés par la Société de l'histoire et d'archéologie de Genève* (Geneva: J. Jullien, 1886), pp. 227–8.

[193]   1 Tim. 2:1–4.

[194]   Rom. 13:1–4; 1 Pet. 2:17.

[195]   1 Cor. 10:5–8 [*sic.* See instead 1 Cor. 10:17]; Acts 4:34–7; Eph. 4:1–4.

[196]   2 Cor. 6:14–17.

[197]   Rom. 12:1–4.

[198]   Eph. 5:1–2.

to believers.[199] Do not let anyone become poor, but give assistance to all.[200] In this way all your life and conduct may be in accordance with God and his holy word,[201] to the edification of all and the [E iij] advancement of the holy gospel, the gospel that our Lord appointed us all to live by. May the grace, peace and blessing of God be with you all. Amen.

The Order that We Observe in Public Worship when the People are Assembled to Hear the Word of God

The servant of the people in the word[202] exhorts everyone to return to God our ever-merciful Father, praying him that he send his Holy Spirit on us and that it please him to have pity on all kings, princes, lords, and all who are established in honour and authority.[203] We ask God to do so by giving them the sword to punish evil people and to defend the good ones, by showing mercy to them out of his goodness, and by giving them his Holy Spirit[204] so that they carry out their office to the honour and glory of our Lord and to the benefit and well-being of their subjects.

We pray for all who are assembled to hear the word of truth,[205] namely, that our Lord forgives all faults and sins, giving his grace and his Spirit through whom we have full understanding of all truth.[206] We pray this so that we might be able to look into, explain, declare, hear, understand, receive and keep his holy word in a pure and holy way,[207] [E iiij] fulfilling the will of this good Father by asking him for everything in the name of his only Son Jesus, just as he taught us, saying:

Our Father who are in heaven, hallowed be your name, etc.

After the prayer the preacher begins to take some text from holy scripture which he reads fully,[208] just as our Lord did in Nazareth.[209] After the

---

[199] Gal. 6:10.
[200] Acts 4:34–7; Deut. 15:4.
[201] 1 Thess. 5:11–14.
[202] 1 Cor. 4:1–2.
[203] 1 Tim. 2:1–4.
[204] Num. 11:29; Deut. 34:9–10.
[205] Neh. 9:2–4 [orig. 2 Esdras 9,a.].
[206] John 14:26; 16:25–30.
[207] Ps. 118.
[208] Neh. 8:1–5 [orig. 2 Esdras 8,a.].
[209] Luke 4:16–19.

reading he explains the passage word by word without skipping any, also leading the congregation to scripture passages which serve the explanation of the passage he is expounding. He does not go outside of holy scripture lest the pure word of God be confounded with human rubbish.[210] He must faithfully bring the word and speak nothing but the word of God.

After having expounded his text in as simple a way as possible, without casting about outside of scripture, then – as much as God gives him the grace for it – he exhorts and admonishes the listeners according to what the text conveys:[211] to depart from all sin, error, superstition and vanity;[212] to return completely to God,[213] having a full and perfect faith and trust in him,[214] setting all one's heart in God,[215] loving him above everything;[216] and to love our neighbour as ourselves,[217] living honestly without doing wrong to anyone, nor hindering anyone by offending them.[218]

He tries to edify and draw everyone to our [E v] Lord and to obeying their lords and princes[219] – whether good or bad, in everything that is not against God[220] – giving and paying all that is ordained for and belongs to them. He exhorts them to this not only out of fear of the sword[221] which the rulers have from God and fear of being punished and troubled, but also for conscience's sake. For whoever offers resistance to the authorities, resists the ordinance of God, seeing that there is no authority which was not ordained and disposed by God. This is true whether God shows mercy by giving good princes who have the fear of God before their eyes and follow the word of God,[222] having at heart the advancement and honour of God and the benefit of their subjects, or whether in wrath for the sins of the people he gives impious tyrants[223] who do not have any care except to do their own will and whatever pleases them. Of whatever sort they may be, they must be obeyed and we must desire their good and peace as

---

[210]   Deut. 4:2; Jer. 23:16–26; 1 Pet. 4:11.

[211]   Titus 2:7–8.

[212]   Jer. 25:5–6; Acts 14:15; Prov. 23:19–23.

[213]   Ezek. 18:14–17; Joel 2:12–14.

[214]   Ps. 62 [orig. Ps. 61].

[215]   Isa. 26:1–4; Prov. 3:5–12.

[216]   Deut. 6:1–5; 30:6–9.

[217]   Deut. 10:18–19; 1 John 3:10–15; Matt. 22:37–41.

[218]   Ps. 55 [orig. Ps. 54]; 1 Pet. 5:5–9.

[219]   Rom. 13:1–4; 1 Pet. 2:17.

[220]   Acts 4:19–20.

[221]   Rom. 13:3.

[222]   Gen. 45:5–9; Exo. 3:3–10; Judith 2:14–18.

[223]   Hos. 13:11; Job 34:19–24.

our Lord commands.[224] He raises up princes and brings them down, and reassigns kingdoms according to his good pleasure.[225]

And so he must exhort the Christians not to seek carnal liberty and freedom, but freedom of the spirit and the soul.[226] For if our King Jesus was subject to and paid to Caesar what he received from others,[227] so also must all true Christian believers. Every preacher [E vi] of truth should teach this, admonishing even (if appropriate) the princes who are in power to do their duties and to regard their subjects as brothers and children,[228] knowing that God is over all princes and that he will judge all according to what they deserve.

Similarly he admonishes all to keep the holy commandments of God, praying our Lord that he give the grace to observe them. He declares the law of God and his holy commandments as they are written in Exodus 20 and laid out above in the baptism form. And afterward he stirs up everyone to ask for God's mercy by confessing their sins, as is stated in the form for the Lord's Supper. Then, saying the prayer of our Lord, he exhorts them and asks our Lord for grace to be firm in the faith which everyone then confesses by saying the Apostles' Creed.

I believe in God the Father, etc.

Then he gives the charge to all, making prayer for all the ignorant,[229] that God inspire them by his grace and lead them to the knowledge of the truth. He prays that God give grace to those who have the sword, that they be able to use it in a sanctified way. He prays that God comfort all who grieve, and especially that he help and strengthen those who suffer for the faith of our Lord Jesus and for his holy gospel[230] – that God by his grace make them persevere in the confession of his name. Finally, he prays that for no reason [E vij] might they either do or say anything out of accord with the word of our Lord. Then he sends the people off in peace.

---

224   Jer. 23:5–7.

225   Dan. 2:21; 4:32.

226   Titus 3:1; 1 Pet. 2:17; Gal. 5:13.

227   Matt. 17:24–7.

228   Deut. 17:14–20; Jer. 22:1–5; Eph. 6:4–9; Col. 3:20–25.

229   1 Tim. 2:1.

230   Acts 12:9–11.

Concerning the Visitation of the Sick

The one who bears the word of our Lord[231] must work with all diligence
to draw all to our Lord, providing the people with a good example in life
and doctrine. It is not enough that he teach the assembled church, for he
must also teach from house to house and everywhere,[232] as Jesus did and
his apostles did, comforting the afflicted[233] and above all those who are
sick. To them he must announce the very great goodness and mercy of
God, demonstrating that nothing but good can come from him who is
the fountain of all good, and that he who is almighty is our ever-merciful
Father. He must show that our Father is more attentive to us than any
father or mother was to his or her son, reminding them that although a
mother may forget her child – and a mother nurtures the very one that
nurses at the breast, that she carried in her womb! – yet our Father will not
forget us,[234] turning everything to our benefit, sending everything for our
advantage. In fact, if it could be better than it is, we would need to believe
firmly [E viiij] that God would send it and do it.

Therefore, we must submit our spirit to him and believe firmly that he
loves us, and loving us, he chastens us.[235] We must not pay attention to
the pain and poverty that we are enduring, nor think that therefore God
hates us or rejects us.[236] Rather, we are to think that we are all the more
in his grace, looking not to those who flourish in this world with their
comforts,[237] but to Jesus, more loved by the Father than all, a true Son
of God,[238] who was more afflicted than all, more tormented than all, and
altogether more poorly treated.

For not only was his extremely bitter suffering so cruel that in his
torments – when all were crying out against him like enraged dogs,
mocking him greatly, doing the worst they could – he, compelled by these
bitter torments, cried out, 'My God, my God, why have you forsaken
me?'[239] but also, sensing that the hour of his passion was near, he was
sorrowful unto death. Then, praying the Father that death might pass, he
sweat blood and water from distress and anguish.[240] Let us take note in

---

[231]   1 Cor. 9:1–2; 1 Pet. 5:1–4.
[232]   Acts 2:1–4; 10:21–7.
[233]   Luke 5:12–15; 6:13–19.
[234]   Isa. 49:14–17.
[235]   Prov. 3:11–12; Heb. 12:5–9.
[236]   Heb. 12:9–11.
[237]   Ps. 36; Luke 16:25.
[238]   Isa. 53:10.
[239]   Matt. 27:46.
[240]   Matt. 26:38; Luke 22:44.

what kind of bed this holy body of Jesus was! Was it not hung on a cruel cross? The holy head – what kind of pillow did it have to rest upon? There were only thorns with which it was crowned. The arms? The hands? The legs? The feet? [F I] How did they serve to ease the pain of that body full of torment? Did they permit him to move from one place to another? Were they not all fastened down, even cruelly nailed with large nails? What did they provide to this very good and great Saviour to eat or to drink when he was so weary from all these great torments and sorrows – his mouth all dried out and he dying from thirst? There was nothing but gall, vinegar and myrrh! What consolation, what comfort did this good Saviour have? Nothing at all but pain, sorrow, great torment and anguish!

The sick must look to him because he is not being treated as harshly as this good Saviour was for us. This should move him to give thanks to God, since it pleased him to deliver this good Saviour to death for us. This should make him ask for mercy and grace in the name of this good Jesus[241] and have perfect confidence and assurance that in his goodness our Father forgives him, for he is entirely full of all kindness, slow to anger and quick to show mercy.[242] Let the sick person commit and give himself over entirely into the hand of the Lord who, according to his good will, does his good pleasure with our body and soul. Let the minister admonish the sick to do to his neighbour as he would like done to him, without wronging anyone.[243] Let the sick person also give such orders to his relatives that he leaves them in peace after his death and they have no complaint or strife,[244] [F ii] if God calls him from this world, so that he disposes everything as a true believer should.

Let him never forget our Lord nor despair of his great mercy,[245] but in all his afflictions and agonies let him continually have recourse to the great sea of all good – to our Father in whom alone he has all his trust.

The true servant of God will make these and like admonitions, looking to what is helpful for the ailing person. If he has his trust in the good works he has done, God's servant will show him that by these he cannot evade the judgement, that he can only be condemned before God, and that all is for nothing if God does not show mercy and grace.[246] In these alone must he hope for salvation in Jesus Christ – not in any other person nor by

---

241 John 15:1–4.

242 Exo. 34:6–7; Ps. 30.

243 Matt. 7:12.

244 Gen. 25:5–6.

245 Ps. 49.

246 Isa. 64:6–7; Luke 17:10; Eph. 2:8–10.

any other thing.[247] Let him ask mercy from God, acknowledging himself to be a poor sinner and liable to eternal death.

If he fears the judgement, the wrath and the fury of God, let the minister declare the holy promises that our Lord made to all those who come to him and call upon him from the heart, namely, how through our Saviour Jesus the Father promises us forgiveness when we ask of him.[248] The true evangelist must work faithfully in this to draw and carry the poor sick one to our Lord, exhorting the servants who are near the ailing patient to comfort him and exhort him in our Lord. [F iij] And if the minister has something with which he can offer comfort – also bodily – such as bread, wine, fruits, or anything else, he shall spare nothing, showing to all a true example of love. He shall frequently visit the sick to comfort and strengthen him as much as possible by the word of our Lord and, wherever possible, also help the poor afflicted body.

After the death, he must, by holy exhortations, give courage to those left behind,[249] that they praise God and conform themselves to his holy will. In place of former times when the poor desolate widow who had lost her husband was made responsible for the whole cost of singing and eating while she wept and fasted (as also for the orphans), we must, as our Lord gives us the ability, have pity on them and help them with advice and goods so as not to add insult to injury.

Let the minister labour towards having the children well-instructed in the doctrine of God so that they will grow up to live as Christians, follow the commandments of God, and work for their living as God ordained.

> May the Father of all mercy lead all into the perfect understanding of the truth. May he give one and the same heart and spirit to all. May he grant that each one serve him alone in spirit and in truth, love him [F iiij] above all, and love his neighbour as the Lord God desires and commands. Amen.

Mark 1:15

Repent and believe the gospel.

Matthew 11:28

Come to me all who are burdened, and I will give you rest.

Romans 1:16

---

247   Acts 4:12; Phil. 3:7–9.
248   Matt. 11:28–30; 25:20–23; 2 Tim. 1:14–17; Rom. 10:10–13; John 16:23–7.
249   1 Thess. 4:13–18.

I am not ashamed of the gospel, for it is the power of God for the salvation of all who believe.

Printed by Pierre de Vingle at Neuchatel, August 29, 1533.

Bibliography

1. Primary sources

Augustijn, Cornelis and Van Stam, Frans Pieter. eds. *Ioannis Calvini Epistolae Vol. 1 (1530–Sep. 1538)*. Geneva: Droz, 2005.

Baum, G., Cunitz, E. and Reuss, E. eds. Brunswick. *Ioannis Calvinis Opera Quae Supersunt Omnia*. : C. A. Schwetschke, 1863–1900. 58 vols.

Beza, Theodore. *The Life of John Calvin*. trans. Henry Beveridge. Carlisle, PA: Banner of Truth Trust, 1982.

Borelli, Anne and Pastore Passaro, Maria. trans. and ed. *Selected Writings of Girolamo Savonarola*, New Haven, CT: Yale University Press, 2006.

Calvin, Jean. *Theological Treatises*. trans. and ed. J.K.S. Reid. Philadelphia: The Westminster Press, 1954.

——. *Institutes of the Christian Religion*, 1536 Edition. trans. and ed. Ford Lewis Battles. Grand Rapids: Eerdmans, 1975.

——. *Commentary on the Book of Psalms*. Pt. I. trans. James Anderson. *Calvin's Commentaries Vol. IV*. Grand Rapids: Baker, 1979.

——. *Calvin-Studienausgabe Vol. 1*. eds. Eberhard Busch *et al.* Neukirchen-Vluyn: Neukirchener, 1994.

——. *Writings on Pastoral Piety*, ed. and trans. Elsie Anne McKee. New York: Paulist Press, 2001.

——. *Contre les libertins spirituelz, epistre contre un Cordelier, response a un certain holandois, Series IV. Scripta didacta et polemica*. ed. Mirjam Van Veen. Geneva: Droz, 2005.

——. *De la tressaincte cene de nostre seigneur Jesus et de la messe qu'on chante communement*. ed. Francis Higman. In his *Lire et Découvrir: La Circulation des idées au temps de la Réforme*. Geneva: Droz, 1998, pp. 233–88.

Dentière, Marie. *Epistle to Marguerite de Navarre and Preface to a Sermon by John Calvin*. trans. and ed. Mary B. McKinley. Chicago: University of Chicago Press, 2004.

Farel, Guillaume. *Determinatio Facultatis Theologiae Parisiensis*. Basel, 1524.

——. *Le Pater Noster, et le Credo en francoys*. Basel: Andreas Cratander, 1524.

——. *La Maniere et fasson qu'on tient en baillant le sainct baptesme*. Neuchâtel, Pierre de Vingle, 1533.

——. *Letres certaines daucuns grandz troubles et tumultes advenuz a Geneve. lan. 1534.* [Pagination added in IDC Microfiche PFA – 152.]

——. *Summaire et briefue declaration daucuns lieux fort necessaires a ung chascun Chrestien pour mettre sa confiance en Dieu et ayder son prochain.* [Neuchâtel]: [Pierre de Vingle], 1534.

——. *Le Pater noster [et] le Credo en francoys.* Geneva: Wigand Koeln, 1536.

——. *La Tres Saincte Oraison que Nostre Seigneur Iesus a bailée à ses Apostres, les enseignant comme ilz et tous vrays crestiens doivent prier,* 1541.

——. *Summaire et briefve declaration daucuns lieux fort necessaires a ung chascun Chrestien pour mettre sa confiance en Dieu et ayder son prochain,* 1542.

——. *Oraison Tresdevote en laqulle [sic] est faicte la confession des pechez, des fidelles qui ainsi crient apres Dieu.* [Strasbourg: J. Knobloch, 1542].

——. *Epistre Envoyee au Duc de Lorraine.* Geneva: Jehan Girard, 1543.

——. *Epistre Envoyee aux Reliques de la dissipation horrible de l'Antechrist, par Guillaume Farel prescheur de l'Evangile de Iesus Christ.* 1544.

——. *Epistre exhortatoire à tous ceux qui ont congnoissance de l'Evangile, les admonestant de cheminer purement et vivre selon iceluy, glorifiant Dieu, et edifiant le prochain par parolles, et par œuvres, et saincte conversation.* 1544.

——. *Forme d'oraison pour demander a Dieu la saincte predication de l'Evangile.* Geneva: Jehan Girard, 1545.

——. *Le glaive de la parole véritable, tiré contre le Bouclier de defense: duquel un Cordelier Libertin s'est voulu servir, pour approuver ses fausses et damnables opinions.* Geneva: Jean Girard, 1550.

——. *Du Vray Usage de la Croix de Iesus-Christ suivi de divers écrits du même auteur.* Geneva: Imprimerie de Jules-Guillaume Fick, 1865.

——. *Sommaire et briefve declaration.* Fac-similé de l'edition originale publié sous le patronage de la Société des textes français modernes. ed. Arthur Piaget. Paris: Droz, 1935.

——. *Du Vrai usage de la croix et autres traités.* ed. Edouard Urech. La Chaux-de-Fonds: Editions G. Saint-Clair, 1980.

——. *Sommaire et Brève déclaration. 1525.* ed. Arthur L. Hofer. Neuchâtel: Editions 'Belle Rivière', 1980.

——. *Le Pater Noster et le Credo en Françoys.* ed. Francis Higman. Geneva: Droz, 1982.

——. 'William Farel's Summary (1529)', In *Reformed Confessions of the 16th and 17th Centuries in English Translation Vol. 1.* trans. and ed.

James T. Dennison, Jr. Grand Rapids: Reformation Heritage Books, 2008, pp. 51–111.

———. *Oeuvres imprimées. Vol. 1: Traités messins*. eds. Reinhard Bodenmann and Françoise Breigel with Olivier Labarthe. Geneva: Droz, 2009.

[———.] 'Confession de la Foy laquelle tous bourgeois et habitans de Genève et subjectz du pays doyvent jurer de garder et tenir, extraicte de l'Instruction dont on use en l'Eglise de la dicte ville'. In *La Vraie Piété: Divers Traités de Jean Calvin et Confession de foi de Guillaume Farel*. eds. Irena Backus et Claire Chimelli. Geneva: Labor et Fides, 1986, pp. 39–53.

[———] 'L'Epistre Chrestienne Tresutile'. eds. Isabelle C. Denommé and William Kemp. In *Le Livre Evangélique en français avant Calvin*. eds. Jean-François Gilmont and William Kemp. Turnhout, Belgium: Brepols, 2004, pp. 54–70.

Herminjard, A. J. *Correspondance des réformateurs dans les pays de langue française*. 7 vols. Geneva et Paris: Georg/Fischbacher, 1866–86.

Hochuli-Dubuis, Paule and Coram-Mekkey, Sandra. eds. *Registres du Conseil de Genève à l'Epoque de Calvin Vol. 2, Pt I*. Geneva: Droz, 2003.

Jussie, Jeanne de. *The Short Chronicle: A Poor Clare's Account of the Reformation of Geneva*. Chicago: University of Chicago Press, 2006.

La manyere de faire prieres. Geneva, 1542.

Luther, Martin. *Devotional Writings II* in *Luther's Works Vol. 43*. ed. Helmut T. Lehmann. Philadelphia: Fortress Press, 1968.

———. *D. Martin Luthers Werke Vol. 7*. Weimar: Nachfolger, 1897.

[Marcourt, Antoine]. *Articles veritables sur les horribles, grandz et insupportables abuz de la Messe papalle, inventee directement contre la saincte Cene de Jesus Christ*. [Neuchâtel: Pierre de Vingle, 1534].

Olivétan, Pierre Robert. *Instrvction des enfans*. Geneva: 1533.

La Saincte Bible en francoys, translatée selon la ... traduction de Saint Hierome, trans. Jacques Lefèvre d'Etaples. Anvers: Martin Lempereur, 1534.

Le Synode de Berne de 1532. Lausanne, 1936.

Schuler, Melchior and Schulthess, Johanness. eds. *Huldrici Zuinglii Opera*. Zurich: Friedrich Schulthes, 1830.

Viret, Pierre. *L'Exposition familière de l'oraison de nostre Seigneur Jesus Christ*. Geneva: Jean Girard, 1548.

Zwingli, Huldrych. *Huldrych Zwingli Schriften IV*. ed. H.U. Bächtold. Zurich: Theologischer Verlag, 1995.

2. Secondary sources

Agbasiere, Joseph Therese. 'The Rosary: its history and relevance'. *African Ecclesial Review* Vol 30. No. 4 (August 1988), pp. 242–54.

Aston, Margaret E. 'The Northern Renaissance'. In *The Meaning of Renaissance and Reform*. ed. Richard L. DeMolen, Boston: Houghton Mifflin, 1974, pp. 71–129.

Aubert, Louis. 'Un Opuscule de Farel'. *Musée Neuchatelois* (1930), pp. 167–79.

Audisio, Gabriel. *Preachers by Night: The Waldensian Barbes (15th–16th Centuries)*. trans. Claire Davison. Leiden: Brill, 2007.

Augustijn, Cornelis. 'Farel und Calvin in Bern 1537–1538'. In *Calvin im Kontext der Schweizer Reformation*. ed. Peter Opitz. Zurich: Theologischer Verlag, 2003, pp. 9–23.

Backus, Irena. *The Disputations of Baden, 1526 and Berne, 1528: Neutralizing the Early Church*. Princeton: Princeton Theological Seminary, 1993.

———. 'The Apocalypse and Prayers of the Saints', In *Oratio: das Gebet in patristischer und reformatorischer Sicht*. eds. Emidio Campi, Leif Grane, and Adolf Martin Ritter. Göttingen: Vandenhoek & Ruprecht, 1999.

———. 'Prière en latin au 16e siècle et son rôle dans les Eglises issues de la Réforme', *Archiv für Reformationsgeschichte* Vol. 93 (2002), pp. 43–71.

———. *Life Writing in Reformation Europe: Lives of Reformers by Friends, Disciples and Foes*. Aldershot: Ashgate, 2008.

Bagchi, David N. 'Sic et Non: Luther and Scholasticism'. In *Protestant Scholasticism*. eds. Carl R. Trueman and R. Scott Clark. Carlisle, Cumbria: Paternoster, 1999, pp. 3–15.

Barthel, Pierre, Scheurer, Rémy and Stauffer, Richard. eds. *Actes du Colloque Guillaume Farel*, 2 vols. Cahiers de la Revue de Théologie et de Philosophie 9. Geneva: Droz, 1983.

Bedouelle, Guy. 'La lecture christologique du psautier dans le *Quincuplex Psalterium* de Lefèvre d'Etaples'. In *Histoire de l'exégèse au XIVe siècle*. eds. Olivier Fatio and Pierre Fraenkel. Geneva: Droz, 1978, pp. 133–43.

Benedict, Philip. *Christ's Churches Purely Reformed: A Social History of Calvinism*. New Haven: Yale, 2002.

———. 'Propaganda, Print and Persuasion in the French Reformation: A Review Article'. *Bibliothèque d'Humanisme et Renaissance* Vol. 69. No. 2 (2007), pp. 447–72.

Berthoud, Gabrielle. 'Farel, Auteur du Traité de Purgatoire'. In *Actes du Colloque Guillaume Farel*, Vol. 1, eds. P. Barthel, R. Scheurer, and R. Stauffer. Geneva: Droz, 1983, pp. 241 – 52.

Bietenholz, Peter G. *Basle and France in the Sixteenth Century.* Toronto: University of Toronto Press, 1971.

Blakeley, James J. 'Popular Responses to the "Reformation from Without" in The Pays de Vaud'. Ph. D. diss., University of Arizona, 2006.

Bodenmann, Reinhard. 'Farel et le Livre Réformé Français'. In *Le Livre Evangélique en français avant Calvin.* eds. William Kemp and Jean-François Gilmont, pp. 13–40. Turnhout, Belgium: Brepols, 2004.

———. 'Les Vaudois et la production du livre évangélique français (1525–1550)'. In *Libri, biblioteche e cultura nelle valli valdesi in età moderna.* ed. Marco Fratini, pp. 21–59. Turin: Claudiana, 2006.

Brobinskoy, Boris, ed. *Communio Sanctorum. Mélanges offerts à Jean-Jacques von Allmen.* Geneva: Labor et Fides, 1982.

Bruening, Michael. *Calvinism's First Battleground: Conflict and Reform in the Pays de Vaud, 1528–1559.* Dordrecht: Springer, 2005.

Burger, Christoph. 'Farels Frömmigkeit'. *Actes du Colloque Guillaume Farel.* Geneva: Revue de theologie et de philosophie, 1983, Vol. 1, pp. 149–60.

Burger, Jean-Daniel. 'Le pasteur Guillaume Farel'. *Theologische Zeitschrift* 21 (1965), pp. 410–26.

Bürki, Bruno. 'La Saincte Cène selon l'ordre de Guillaume Farel 1533'. *Coena Domini I: die Abendmahlsliturgie der Reformationskirchen im 16./17. Jahrhundert*, ed. Irmgared Pahl. Schweiz: Universitätsverlag Freiburg, 1983.

Burnett, Amy Nelson. *Teaching the Reformation: Ministers and Their Message in Basel, 1529–1629.* Oxford: Oxford University Press, 2006.

Cameron, Euan. *Waldenses: Rejections of Holy Church in Medieval Europe* (Oxford: Blackwell, 200), Ch. 9.

Campi, Emidio, Grane, Leif and Ritter, Adolf Martin. eds. *Oratio: das Gebet in patristischer und reformatorischer Sicht.* Göttingen: Vandenhoek & Ruprecht, 1999.

Carbonnier-Burkard, Marianne. 'Jours de fêtes dans les églises réformées de France au XVIIe siècle'. *Études théologiques et religieuses* Vol. 68. No. 3 (1993), pp. 347–58.

Cooper, Catherine Fales and Gregory, Jeremy. *Elite and Popular Religion: Papers Read at the 2004 Summer Meeting and the 2005 Winter Meeting of the Ecclesiastical History Society.* Woodbridge, England: Boydell Press, 2006.

Cottier, Jean-François. ed. *La prière en latin, de l'Antiquité au XVIe siècle: formes, évolutions, significations.* Turnhout: Brepols, 2006.

Cottret, Bernard. *Calvin: A Biography*. trans. M. Wallace McDonald. Grand Rapids: Eerdmans, 2000.

Courouau, Jean-François. 'La Réforme et les langues de France'. *Bulletin de la Société de l'Histoire du Protestantisme Français* 154 (October–December 2008), pp. 509–29.

Courvoisier, Jacques. 'Farel and Geneva'. *McCormick Quarterly* Vol. 21 (1967–68), pp. 123–35.

Denommé, Isabelle C. and Kemp, William. 'L'Epistre Chrestienne Tresutile (c. 1524), Un Ecrit de Guillaume Farel? Présentation et Edition'. In *Le Livre Evangélique en français avant Calvin*. eds. William Kemp and Jean-François Gilmont, pp. 41–70. Turnhout, Belgium: Brepols, 2004.

Despland, Michel. *Le recul du sacrifice*. Quebec: PUL, 2009.

Doumergue, Émile. *Jean Calvin*. 5 vols. Lausanne: G. Bridel et Cie., 1899–1910.

Eire, Carlos, M.N. *War Against the Idols: The Reformation of Worship from Erasmus to Calvin*. Cambridge: Cambridge University Press, 1986.

Elwood, Christopher. *The Body Broken: The Calvinist Doctrine of the Eucharist and the Symbolization of Power in Sixteenth-Century France*. Oxford: Oxford University Press, 1999.

Esser, Hans Helmut. 'Die Stellung des 'Summaire' von Guillaume Farel innerhalb der frühen reformierten Bekenntnisschriften'. In *Reformiertes Erbe: Festschrift für Gottfried W. Locher zu seinem 80 Geburtstag. Vol. 1*. eds. Heiko A. Oberman, Ernst Saxer, Alfred Schindler, and Heinzpeter Stucki. [*Zwingliana* 19.1 (1992)], pp. 93–114. Zurich: Theologischer Verlag Zürich, 1992.

Faber, Jelle. 'The Saving Work of the Holy Spirit in Calvin'. *Essays in Reformed Doctrine*. Neerlandia, AB: Inheritance Publications, 1990.

Farge, James K. *Orthodoxy and Reform in Early Reformation France: The Faculty of Theology of Paris, 1500–1543*. Leiden: Brill, 1985.

Garnier-Mathez, Isabelle. *L'épithète et la connivence: écriture concertée chez les évangéliques français (1523–1534)*. Geneva: Droz, 2005.

Gilmont, Jean-François. *The Reformation and the Book*. trans. Karin Maag. Aldershot: Ashgate, 1998.

——. *John Calvin and the Printed Book*, trans. Karin Maag. Kirksville, MO: Truman State University Press, 2005.

——. *Le livre réformé au XVIe siècle*. Paris: Bibliothèque nationale de France, 2005.

——, and Kemp, William. eds, *Le livre évangélique en français avant Calvin*. Turnhout: Brepols, 2004.

——. 'Wigand Koeln Libraire a Genève (1516–1545), Éditeur du *Pater Noster* De Guillaume Farel'. *Bibliothèque d'Humanisme et Renaissance* Vol. 70. No. 1 (2008), pp. 131–46.

Gordon, Bruce. *The Swiss Reformation*. Manchester: Manchester University Press, 2002.

——. *Calvin*. New Haven, CT: Yale, 2009.

Grunewald, Eckhard, Jürgens, Henning P. and Luth, Jan R. eds. *Der Genfer Psalter und seine Rezeption in Deutschland, der Schweiz und den Niederlanden*. Tübingen: Max Niemeyer Verlag, 2004.

Guillaume Farel, 1489–1565. *Biographie nouvelle écrite...par un groupe d'historiens, professeurs et pasteurs de Suisse, France et d'Italie*. Neuchâtel et Paris, 1930.

Hagenbach, K.R. *History of the Reformation in Germany and Switzerland Chiefly*, trans. Evelina Moore. Edinburgh: T&T Clark, 1878.

Hammerling, Roy, ed. *A History of Prayer: The First to the Fifteenth Century*. Leiden: Brill, 2008.

Heller, Henry. *The Conquest of Poverty: The Calvinist Revolt in Sixteenth Century France*. Leiden: Brill, 1986.

——. 'Reform and Reformers at Meaux: 1518–1525'. Ph.D. diss., Cornell University, 1969.

Heyer, Henri. *Guillaume Farel: An Introduction to his Theology*. trans. Blair Reynolds. Lewiston: Edwin Mellen Press, 1990.

Higman, Francis M. *The Style of John Calvin in his French Polemical Treatises*. Oxford: Oxford University Press, 1967.

——. *Censorship and the Sorbonne: A Bibliographical Study of Books in French Censured by the Faculty of Theology of the University of Paris, 1520–1551*. Geneva: Droz, 1979.

——. 'Farel, Calvin, et Olivétan, sources de la spiritualité gallicane'. *Actes du Colloque Guillaume Farel*. Geneva: Revue de théologie et de philosophie, 1983, pp. 45–61.

——. 'Luther et la Piété de l'Église Gallicane: Le Livre de Vraye et Parfaicte Oraison'. *Revue d'Histoire et de Philosophie Religieuses* Vol. 63 (1983), pp. 91–111.

——. 'Theology for the Layman in the French Reformation 1520–1550'. *The Library*, Sixth series, Vol. 9. No. 2 (Jun 1987), pp. 105–27.

——. *La Diffusion de la Réforme en France 1520–1565*. Geneva: Labor et Fides, 1992.

——. 'Calvin and Farel'. In *Calvinus Sacrae Scripturae Professor: Calvin as Confessor of Holy Scripture*. ed. Wilhelm H. Neuser, pp. 214–23. Grand Rapids: Eerdmans, 1994.

——. *Piety and the People: Religious Printing in French, 1511–1551*. Aldershot: Scolar Press, 1996.

——. 'French-speaking regions, 1520–62'. In *The Reformation and the Book*. ed. Jean-François Gilmont. English ed. and trans. Karin Maag, pp. 104–53. Aldershot: Ashgate, 1998.

———. *Lire et Découvrir: La Circulation des idées au temps de la Réforme.* Geneva: Droz, 1998.

———. 'Viret en anglais'. *Bulletin de la Société de l'histoire du protestantisme français* 144.4 (1998), pp. 881–93.

———. 'Histoire du livre et histoire de la Réforme'. *Bulletin de la Société de l'histoire du protestantisme français* 148 (2002), pp. 837–50.

———. 'Farel's *Summaire*: The Interplay of Theology and Polemics'. In *Le Livre Evangélique en français avant Calvin*. eds. William Kemp and Jean-François Gilmont, pp. 71–86. Turnhout, Belgium: Brepols, 2004.

Hobbins, Daniel B. 'Gerson on Lay Devotion'. In *A Companion to Jean Gerson*. ed. Brian Patrick McGuire, Leiden: Brill, 2006, pp. 41–78.

———. *Authorship and Publicity before Print: Jean Gerson and the Transformation of Late Medieval Learning.* Philadelphia: University of Pennsylvania Press, 2009.

Holder, Arthur G. ed. *The Blackwell Companion to Christian Spirituality.* Malden, MA: Blackwell, 2005.

Holmes, Urban T. III. *A History of Christian Spirituality: An Analytical Introduction.* New York: Seabury Press, 1980 [2nd ed. Morehouse Publishing, 2002].

Hörcsik, Richard. 'John Calvin in Geneva, 1536–38 – Some Questions about Calvin's First Stay at Geneva'. In *Calvinus Sacrae Scripturae Professor: Calvin as Confessor of Holy Scripture*. ed. Wilhelm H. Neuser, Grand Rapids: Eerdmans, 1994, pp. 155–65.

Hower, Robert G. 'William Farel: Theologian of the Common Man, and the Genesis of Protestant Prayer'. Th. D. diss., Westminster Theological Seminary, 1983.

Hughes, Philip Edgcumbe. 'Jacques Lefèvre d'Etaples (c. 1455–1536), Calvin's Forerunner in France'. In *Calvin's Early Writings and Ministry*. ed. Richard C. Gamble, pp. 1–17. New York: Garland Publishing, 1992. Originally in *Calvinus Reformator*, 1982, pp. 93–108.

———. *Lefèvre: Pioneer of Ecclesiastical Renewal in France.* Grand Rapids, Mich.: Eerdmans, 1984.

Jacobs, Elfriede. *Die Sakramentslehre Wilhelm Farels.* Zürich: Theologischer Verlag, 1978.

———. 'Die Abendmahlslehre Wilhelm Farels'. In *Actes du Colloque Guillaume Farel*, Vol. 1, eds. P. Barthel, R. Scheurer, and R. Stauffer, Geneva: Droz, 1983, pp. 161–71.

Jungmann, Joseph-André. *Missarum Sollemnia: Explication Génétique de la Messe Romaine.* 3 vols. Paris: Aubier, 1954.

Junod, Eric, ed. *La Dispute de Lausanne (1536), La théologie réformée après Zwingli et avant Calvin.* Bibliothèque Historique Vaudoise, No. 90. Lausanne, 1988.

Kaltenrieder, Andre Emile. 'The Liturgies of Guillaume Farel, Their Meaning and Relevance'. Ph. D. diss., Rhodes University, 1980.

Kemp, William and Gilmont, Jean-François. eds. *Le Livre Evangélique en français avant Calvin*. Turnhout, Belgium: Brepols, 2004.

Kingdon, Robert. 'Worship in Geneva Before and After the Reformation'. In *Worship in Medieval and Early Modern Europe*. eds. Karin Maag and John D. Witvliet, pp. 41–62. Notre Dame, IN: University of Notre Dame Press, 2004.

Kirchhofer, Melchior. *Das Leben Wilhelm Farels*. 2 vols. Zurich: Drell, 1831–33.

————. *Life of William Farel: The Swiss Reformer*. London: Religious Tract Society, 1837.

Krey, Philip D.W. and Peter, D.S. eds. and trans. *Luther's Spirituality*. New York: Paulist Press, 2007.

Labarthe, Olivier. 'La relation entre le premier catéchisme de Calvin et la première confession de foi de Geneve: Recherche historique à partir d'une comparaison de textes catéchétiques et de particularités typographiques'. *Thesis for Licence en théologie*. University of Geneva, 1967.

Lambert, Thomas. 'Preaching, Praying and Policing the Reform in Sixteenth-Century Geneva'. Ph.D. diss., University of Wisconsin-Madison, 1998.

Léchot, Pierre-Olivier. 'L'impact de la prédication Évangélique à Neuchâtel (1529–1530)'. In *Annoncer l'Évangile (XVe–XVIIe siècles): Permanences et mutations de la prédication*. ed. Matthieu Arnold. Paris: Le Cerf, 2006, pp. 329–50.

LeClercq, Jean, Vandenbroucke, François and Bouyer, Louis eds. *The Spirituality of the Middle Ages*. London: Burn & Oates, 1968.

Les Imprimes Reformes de Pierre de Vingle: (Neuchatel, 1533–1535). Revue Littératures. Montreal: McGill, 2007.

Liechty, Daniel. ed. and trans. *Early Anabaptist Spirituality: Selected Writings*. New York: Paulist Press, 1998.

Lienhard, Marc. 'Prier au 16e siècle: regards sur le Biblisch Bettbüchlin du Strasbourgeois Othon Brunfels'. *Revue d'histoire et de philosophie religieuses* Vol. 66. No. 1 (Jan–Mar 1986), pp. 43–55.

Littré, Émile M.P. *Dictionnaire de la langue française*. Paris: Hachette, 1863–73.

Lovy, René-Jacques. *Les Origines de la Réforme Française: Meaux, 1518–1546*. 2nd ed. Paris: Concordia/Les Presses du Village, 1983.

Lutton, Robert and Salter, Elisabeth eds. *Pieties in Transition: Religious Practices and Experiences, c. 1400–1640*. Aldershot: Ashgate, 2007.

Maag, Karin. 'Education and works of religious instruction in French'. In *The Sixteenth-Century French Religious Book*. eds. Andrew Pettegree,

Paul Nelles, and Philip Conner, pp. 96–109. Aldershot: Ashgate, 2001.

Manetsch, Scott M. 'A Mystery Solved? Maister Beza's Household Prayers'. *Bibliothèque d'Humanisme et Renaissance* Vol. 65. No. 2 (2003), pp. 275–88.

Martines, Lauro. *Fire in the City*. Oxford: Oxford University Press, 2006.

Massaut, J.P. 'Erasme et Farel'. *Actes du Colloque Guillaume Farel*, Vol. 1, eds. P. Barthel, R. Scheurer, and R. Stauffer, pp. 11–30. Geneva: Droz, 1983.

McGrath, Alister. *Iustitia Dei: A History of the Christian Doctrine of Justification*. 3rd ed. Cambridge: Cambridge University Press, 1998.

McGuire, Brian Patrick. ed. and trans. *Jean Gerson's Early Works*. New York: Paulist Press, 1998.

McKee, Elsie A. *Reforming Popular Piety in Sixteenth-Century Strasbourg: Katharina Schütz Zell and Her Hymnbook*. Princeton, NJ: Princeton Theological Seminary, 1994.

———. 'Katharina Schütz Zell and the "Our Father"'. In *Oratio: das Gebet in patristischer und reformatorischer Sicht*. eds. Emidio Campi, Leif Grane and Adolf Martin Ritter, pp. 239–47. Göttingen: Vandenhoek & Ruprecht, 1999.

Meyhoffer, J. 'Une édition du Sommaire de Farel (1525)'. *Bulletin de la Société de l'Histoire du Protestantisme français* Vol. 78 (1929), pp. 361–70.

Meylan, Henri. 'Les étapes de la conversion de Farel'. In *L'humanisme français au début de la Renaissance. Colloque International de Tours*, pp. 253–9. Paris: Librarie Philosophique J. Vrin, 1973.

Millet, Olivier. Calvin et la dynamique de la parole. Étude de rhétorique réformée. Paris: Librairie Honoré Champion, 1992.

Monter, E. William. *Calvin's Geneva*. New York: John Wiley & Sons, 1967.

Moore, W. G. *La Réforme Allemande et la Littérature Française: Recherches sur la Noteriété de Luther en France*. Strasbourg: Publications de la Faculté des Lettres, 1930.

Muller, Richard A. *Christ and the Decree: Christology and Predestination in Reformed Theology from Calvin to Perkins*. Grand Rapids: Baker, 1988.

———. 'Reformed Confessions and Catechisms'. In *The Dictionary of Historical Theology*, ed. Trevor A. Hart, pp. 466–85. Grand Rapids: Eerdmans, 2000.

———. *Post-Reformation Reformed Dogmatics*. 4 vols. Grand Rapids: Baker, 2003.

Naef, Henri. *Les Origines de la Réforme à Genève*. 2 vols. Geneva: Droz, 1968.

Nauta, Doede. *Guillaume Farel. In leven en werken geschetst*. Amsterdam: Bolland, 1978.

Nicholls, David J. 'The Nature of Popular Heresy in France, 1520–1542'. *The Historical Journal* Vol. 26. No. 2 (1983), pp. 261–75.

———. 'Heresy and Protestantism, 1520–1542: Questions of perception and communication'. *French History* Vol. 10. No. 2 (1996), pp. 182–205.

Oberman, Heiko A. '*Initia Calvini*: The Matrix of Calvin's Reformation'. In *Calvinus Sacrae Scripturae Professor: Calvin as Confessor of Holy Scripture*. ed. Wilhelm H. Neuser, pp. 113–54. Grand Rapids: Eerdmans, 1994.

———. 'Calvin and Farel: The Dynamics of Legitimation in Early Calvinism'. *Reformation and Renaissance Review* Vol 1. No. 1 (1999), pp. 7–40.

Old, Hughes Oliphant. 'Daily Prayer in the Reformed Church of Strasbourg, 1525–1530'. *Worship* Vol. 52. No. 2 (Mar 1978), pp. 121–38.

Olson, Jeannine. 'Calvin as pastor – administrator during the Reformation in Geneva'. *Pacific Theological Review* Vol. 14 (1981), pp. 10–7.

O'Malley, John W. and Perraud, Louis A. eds. *Collected Works of Erasmus, Vol. 69*. Toronto: University of Toronto Press, 1992.

Overfield, James H. 'Scholastic Opposition to Humanism in Pre-Reformation Germany'. *Viator* Vol. 7 (1976), pp. 391–420.

———. *Humanism and Scholasticism in Late Medieval Germany*. Princeton: Princeton University Press, 1985.

Ozment, Steven E. *The Reformation in the Cities: The Appeal of Protestantism to Sixteenth-Century Germany and Switzerland*. New Haven: Yale, 1975.

———. *The Age of Reform 1250–1550: An Intellectual and Religious History of Late Medieval and Reformation Europe*. New Haven: Yale, 1980.

Parker, T.H.L. *Calvin: A Biography*. Philadelphia: Westminster Press, 1975.

Partee, Charles. 'L'Influence de Farel sur Calvin'. In *Actes du Colloque Guillaume Farel*, Vol. 1, eds. P. Barthel, R. Scheurer, and R. Stauffer, Geneva: Droz, 1983, pp. 173–86.

Peronnet, Michel. 'Images de Guillaume Farel pendant la Dispute de Lausanne (1536)'. In *La Dispute de Lausanne (1536), La théologie réformée après Zwingli et avant Calvin*. ed. Eric Junod, Bibliothèque Historique Vaudoise, No. 90. Lausanne, 1988, pp. 133–41.

Peter, Rodolphe. 'Recherches sur l'imprimeur de la *Determinatio* attribué à Guillaume Farel'. In *Actes du Colloque Guillaume Farel*, Vol. 1, eds.

P. Barthel, R. Scheurer, and R. Stauffer, pp. 221–30. Geneva: Droz, 1983.

Petey–Girard, Bruno. 'Bible et tradition liturgique dans les prières Françaises de la fin du XVIᵉ siècle'. *Bibliothèque d'Humanisme et Renaissance* 64.2 (2002), pp. 353–68.

Pettegree, Andrew. *Reformation and the Culture of Persuasion.* Cambridge: Cambridge University Press, 2005.

———. *The French Book and the European Book World.* Leiden: Brill, 2007.

———, Walsby, Malcolm and Wilkinson, Alexander eds. *French Vernacular Books: Books Published in the French Language Before 1601.* Leiden: Brill, 2007.

Pidoux, Pierre. *Le Psautier Huguenot.* Basel: Baerenreiter, 1962.

Po-Chia Hsia, R. ed. *The Cambridge History of Christianity, Vol. 6, Reformation and Expansion 1500–1600.* Cambridge: Cambridge University Press, 2007.

Porrer, Sheila M. *Jacques Lefèvre d'Etaples and the Three Maries Debates.* Geneva: Droz, 2009.

Raitt, Jill, ed. *Christian Spirituality: High Middle Ages and Reformation.* New York: Crossroad, 1987.

Reid, Jonathan A. 'France'. In *The Reformation World.* ed. Andrew Pettegree, pp. 211–24. London: Routledge, 2000.

———. 'King's sister – Queen of dissent. Marguerite de Navarre (1492–1549) and her evangelical network'. Ph.D. diss., University of Arizona, 2001.

Rice, Eugene F., Jr. *The Prefatory Epistles of Jacques Lefèvre d'Etaples and Related Texts.* New York and London: Columbia University Press, 1972.

Rioux-Couillard, Benoît. 'Volontés de respect et respect accordé dans la réforme française pré calviniste: l'articulation des arguments de tolérance dans le *Summaire* de Guillaume Farel (1534)', M.A. diss., Université du Québec à Montréal, 2008.

Roulet, Louis-Ed. 'Farel, agent bernois? (1528 – 1536)'. *Actes du Colloque Guillaume Farel*, Geneva: Revue de theologie et de philosophie, 1983, pp. 99–106.

Rummel, Erika. '*Et cum theologo bella poeta gerit*: The Conflict between Humanists and Scholastics Revisited'. *Sixteenth Century Journal* Vol. 23. No. 4 (1992), pp. 713–26.

Russell, William, R. 'Luther, Prayer and the Reformation'. *Word and World* Vol. 22. No. 1 (Winter 2002), pp. 49–54.

Salter, Elisabeth. '"The Dayes Moralised': Reconstructing Devotional Reading, *c.* 1450–1560'. In *Pieties in Transition: Religious Practices and Experiences, c. 1400–1640.* eds. Robert Lutton and Elisabeth Salter, Aldershot: Ashgate, 2007, pp. 145–62.

Savonarola, Girolamo. *Prison Meditations on Psalms 51 and 31.* ed. and trans. John Patrick Donnelly. Milwaukee: Marquette University Press, 1994.

Sayous, André, *Études Littéraires sur Les Écrivains Français de la Réformation.* Paris: Gratiot, 1854.

Schaff, Philip. *The Creeds of Christendom*, 3 vols. Grand Rapids, MI: Baker, 1993.

Schmitt, Charles B. 'Aristotle as a Cuttlefish: The Origin and Development of a Renaissance Image'. In *The Aristotelian Tradition and Renaissance Universities*, London: Variorum, 1984, pp. 60–72.

Selderhuis, Herman J. *John Calvin: A Pilgrim's Life* (Downers Grove, IL: InterVarsity Press, 2009), p. 55.

Sheldrake, Philip. 'Spiritualities in the Age of Reformations: 1450–1700'. In his *A Brief History of Spirituality* Malden, MA: Blackwell Publishing, 2007., pp. 106–38, 223–6.

Smolenski, Stanley. 'Rosary or chaplet?' *Homiletic and Pastoral Review* Vol. 86. No. 1 (Oct. 1985), pp. 9–15.

Spruyt, B.J. 'Wessel Gansfort and Cornelis Hoen's *Epistola Christiana*: The Ring as a Pledge of my Love'. In *Wessel Gansfort (1419–1489) and Northern Humanism.* eds. F. Akkerman, G. C. Huisman and A. J. Vanderjagt, Leiden: Brill, 1993, pp. 122–41.

Stam, Frans P. van. 'Le Livre de Pierre Caroli de 1545 et son conflit avec Calvin'. In *Calvin et ses contemporains.* ed. Olivier Millet. Geneva: Droz, 1998, pp. 21–41

——. 'Farels und Calvins Ausweisung aus Genf am 23. April 1538'. *Zeitschrift für Kirchengeschichte* Vol. 110 (1999), pp. 209–28.

——. 'Die Genfer Artikel vom Januar 1537: aus Calvins oder Farels Feder?' *Zwingliana* Vol. 27 (2000), pp. 87–101.

——. 'The Group of Meaux as First Target of Farel and Calvin's Anti-Nicodemism'. *Bibliothèque d'Humanisme et Renaissance* Vol. 68. No. 2 (2006), pp. 253–75.

Steinmetz, David. Reformers in the Wings: From Geiler von Kaysersberg to Theodore Beza. 2nd ed. Oxford: Oxford University Press, 2001.

Stucki, Alfred. *Guillaume Farel: Evangelist, Kämpfer, Reformator.* St. Gallen: Buchhandlung der Evangelischen Gesellschaft, 1942.

Strand, Kenneth A. 'John Calvin and the Brethren of the Common Life'. *Andrews University Seminary Studies* Vol. 13 (1975), pp. 67–78. Reprinted in *Calvin's Opponents.* ed. Richard C. Gamble, pp. 133–44. New York: Garland Publishing, 1992.

Swanson, R.N. *Religion and Devotion in Europe, c.1215–c.1515.* Cambridge: Cambridge University Press, 1995.

Tentler, Thomas N. *Sin and Confession on the Eve of the Reformation.* Princeton: Princeton University Press, 1977.

Thompson, James Westfall. *The Literacy of the Laity in the Middle Ages.* New York: Burt Franklin, 1960.

Tinsley, Sister Lucy. *The French Expressions for Spirituality and Devotion: A Semantic Study.* Washington, D.C.: The Catholic University of America Press, 1953.

Van Engen, John, ed. *Devotio Moderna: Basic Writings.* New York: Paulist Press, 1988.

———. *Sisters and Brothers of the Common Life.* Philadelphia: University of Pennsylvania Press, 2008.

Van Raalte, Theodore G. 'Guillaume Farel's Spirituality: Leading in Prayer'. *Westminster Theological Journal* Vol. 70. No. 2 (Fall 2008), pp. 277–301.

Veissière, Michel. *L'évêque Guillaume Briçonnet (1470–1534) contribution à la croissance de la Réforme catholique à la veille du Concile de Trente.* Provins: Société d'histoire de d'archéologie, 1986.

Volz, Carl A. *The Medieval Church: From the Dawn of the Middle Ages to the Eve of the Reformation.* Nashville, TN: Abingdon Press, 1997.

Warfield, Benjamin B. *Calvin as a Theologian and Calvinism Today.* Philadelphia: Presbyterian Board, 1909.

Wendel, François. *Calvin: sources et évolution de sa pensée religieuse.* Paris: Presses Universitaires de France, 1950.

Wiley, David N. 'Toward a Critical Edition of Farel's *Sommaire*: The Dating of the Editions of 1525 and 1542'. In *Actes du Colloque Guillaume Farel*, Vol. 1, eds. P. Barthel, R. Scheurer, and R. Stauffer, Geneva: Droz, 1983, pp. 203–18.

———. 'The Dispute of Lausanne and the Theology of William Farel: The Doctrine of Justification and its Sources'. In *La Dispute de Lausanne (1536): La théologie réformée après Zwingli et avant Calvin.* ed. Eric Junod, pp. 142–8. Bibliothèque Historique Vaudoise, No. 90. Lausanne: Presses Centrales Lausanne, 1988.

White, Robert. 'An Early Doctrinal Handbook: Farel's *Summaire et Briefve Declaration*'. *Westminster Theological Journal* Vol. 69 (2007), pp. 21–38.

Wieck, Roger S. 'Prayer for the People: The Book of Hours'. In *A History of Prayer: The First to the Fifteenth Century.* ed. Roy Hammerling, pp. 389–416. Leiden: Brill, 2008.

———. *Time Sanctified: The Book of Hours in Medieval Art and Life.* New York: Braziller, 1988.

Winston-Allen, Anne. *Stories of the Rose: The Making of the Rosary in the Middle Ages.* Pennsylvania: Pennsylvania State University Press, 1997.

Wyrell, Hubert. *Réforme et Contre-Réforme en Savoie, 1536–1679: de Guillaume Farel à François de Sales.* Lyon: Réveil Publications, 2001.

Yarnell, Malcolm. 'The First Evangelical Sinner's Prayer Published in English: William Tyndale's "Here foloweth a treates of the pater noster"'. *Southwestern Journal of Theology* Vol. 47. No. 1 (Fall 2004), pp. 27–43.

Zuidema, Jason. '"Levez vos coeurs en hault" : Le fondement théologique de la réflexion de Guillaume Farel sur l'Eucharistie'. In *Les Imprimés Réformés de Pierre de Vingle: (Neuchatel, 1533–1535)*, Montreal: McGill, 2007, pp. 103–25. In the series *Littératures* Vol. 24. No. 1 (2007).

———. *Peter Martyr Vermigli (1499–1562) and the Outward Instruments of Divine Grace.* Göttingen: Vandenhoeck & Ruprecht, 2008.

———. 'The Doctrine of Justification in the Early French Reformation'. *Revue Farel* Vol. 4 (2009): pp. 27–35.

Index

St Andrews Studies in Reformation History

Commonwealth and the English Reformation
Protestantism and the Politics of Religious Change in the Gloucester Vale,
1483–1560
Ben Lowe